The
Nystrom
UNITED STATES
HISTORY
Series

Teacher's Guide

NYSTROM
HERFF JONES EDUCATION DIVISION

Using The Nystrom United States History Series

Wall Maps and Transparencies

The map reproductions in this Teacher's Guide are for your reference convenience, but please remember that referring to them at this reduced size cannot replace viewing them as wall maps or projections.

If you're using the History Series wall maps:

These wall maps are markable.

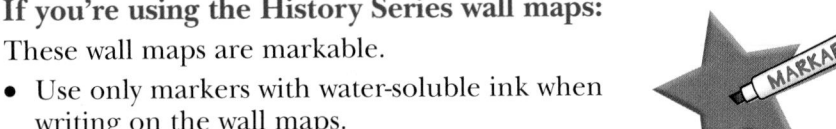

- Use only markers with water-soluble ink when writing on the wall maps.
- For fast and easy clean-up, use a spray bottle of water to dampen a paper towel.
- For best results, clean the maps shortly after using them.

If you're using the History Series transparencies:

These transparencies are also markable.

- Use very fine point markers with water-soluble ink specially designed for transparencies.
- When using the lessons in this guide, you may need to use abbreviations or initials as you write on the transparencies.
- For fast and easy clean-up, use a spray bottle of water to dampen a paper towel.
- For best results, clean the transparencies shortly after using them.

2004 Edition
Copyright © 2001 NYSTROM Herff Jones Education Division
3333 N. Elston Avenue, Chicago, Illinois 60618

10 9 8 7 6 5 4 3   10 09 08 07 06 05 04

ISBN 0-7825-0799-9   Product Code Number 1USH60
Printed in U.S.A

For ordering information call toll free 800-621-8086.

Teacher's Guide

There are many ways you can use these maps—to introduce topics; to focus on events or patterns; to highlight movement and change; to provide chronology; to show cause and effect; to summarize or review. To help you recognize their usage potential, this Teacher's Guide includes **overview questions** and three **lessons** for each map.

Overview Questions

- Each map includes several layers of information. The "Getting Started" questions provide a basic overview of the map.

Lessons

- The lessons focus on underlying layers of information.
- Choose the lessons that match your curriculum.
- Expand the use of the maps beyond the lessons in this Teacher's Guide. You and your students can use these lessons as models for further discussions and presentations.
- Each lesson includes the following:

Teaching Notes
- ~ Background teaching notes are part of each lesson.
- ~ Use them as an outline for a lecture or a class discussion.

Mapping Activity
- ~ Each lesson includes suggestions for marking on the map. Marking focuses student attention.
- ~ Involve students: have them name places; point to locations; add labels; or trace rivers, routes, and boundaries with a marker.

Starred Activities
- ☆ Questions are provided for further discussion.
- ☆ Activity suggestions can be used for individual, small group, and extra credit assignments.

Correlation

Lessons are correlated to two other key Nystrom products:

- *The Nystrom Atlas of United States History*
- *Mapping United States History*

Teacher's Guide Contents

The Nystrom United States History Series

 NYSTROM
HERFF JONES EDUCATION DIVISION

NATIVE AMERICANS
1500

Key Elements

★ *Native Americans* map

★ *Trade Routes* map

★ *Main Sources of Food* map

★ *People in Three Worlds* graph

Getting Started

To give students an overview of *Native Americans,* ask them:

- What is the title of the main map?

- What part of the world does this map show?

- What year does the map cover?

- What do the colors represent?

- On the *Trade Routes* map, what do the green symbols represent?

- On the *Main Sources of Food* map, what do the colors represent?

- Look at the bar graph. In 1500 which continent had the most people?

Teaching Notes and Mapping Activities

~ The Gatherers

~ The Farmers

~ Trade Centers

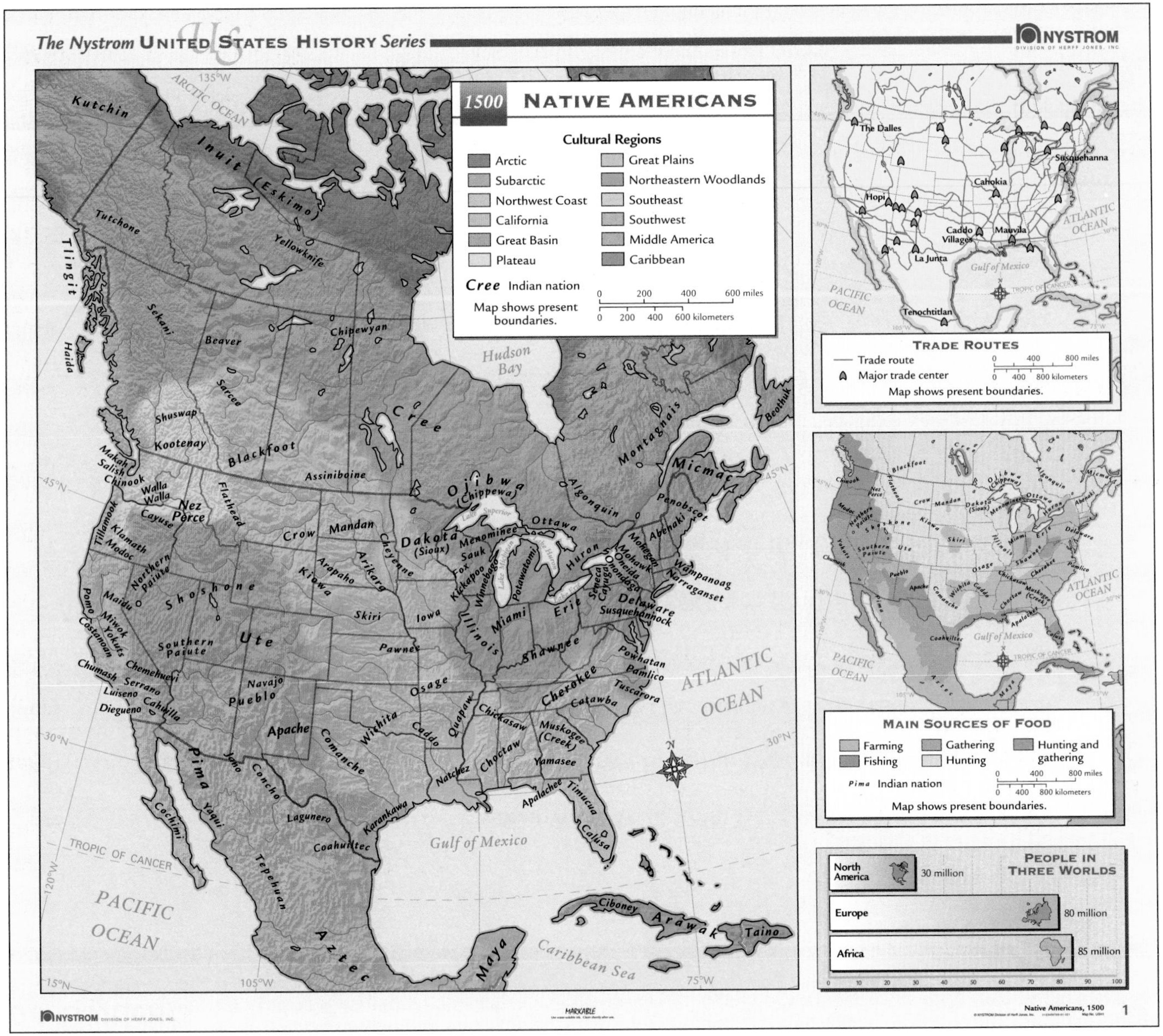

The Nystrom UNITED STATES HISTORY Series

NYSTROM
DIVISION OF HERFF JONES, INC.

1500 NATIVE AMERICANS

Cultural Regions

Arctic	Great Plains
Subarctic	Northeastern Woodlands
Northwest Coast	Southeast
California	Southwest
Great Basin	Middle America
Plateau	Caribbean

Cree Indian nation

Map shows present boundaries.

0 200 400 600 miles

0 200 400 600 kilometers

TRADE ROUTES

— Trade route

▲ Major trade center

0 400 800 miles

0 400 800 kilometers

Map shows present boundaries.

MAIN SOURCES OF FOOD

Farming	Gathering	Hunting and gathering
Fishing	Hunting	

Pima Indian nation

0 400 800 miles

0 400 800 kilometers

Map shows present boundaries.

PEOPLE IN THREE WORLDS

North America	30 million
Europe	80 million
Africa	85 million

0 10 20 30 40 50 60 70 80 90 100

NYSTROM DIVISION OF HERFF JONES, INC.

HARKABLE

The Gatherers

Objective: *To compare four Native American cultural regions and their food sources.*

Teaching Notes and Mapping Activity

You or your students can mark the following on the *Native Americans* map.

1. In the Northwest Coast, California, Plateau, and Great Basin regions of North America, Native American cultural groups relied completely on their natural environment for food. Indians in these regions did not farm. They **fished**, **hunted**, and **gathered** all their food.

   a. Outline each of the four cultural regions mentioned above.

   b. Near each of these regions, write and underline its name. Then draw an arrow to each appropriate region.

2. The **Northwest Coast** region was richer in natural resources than any other cultural region. Food was plentiful.

   a. Have students identify several Indian nations in the region.

   b. Northwest Coast Indians fished for salmon. They also hunted whales, seals, bears, caribou, elk, and moose. They gathered bulbs and berries too. Below the region name, write Ѱ Ѱ Ѱ Ѱ Ѱ = **ABUNDANT FOOD**.

   c. In this region, there were a moderate number of Indians. Below the region name, write ⚲ ⚲ = **SOME PEOPLE**.

3. The **California** region was also rich in natural resources.

   a. Have students identify several Indian nations in the region.

   b. California Indians gathered acorns, seeds, and nuts. They caught fish and shellfish. They also hunted deer and wild game. Below the region name, write Ѱ Ѱ Ѱ Ѱ = **PLENTIFUL FOOD**.

   c. This region had a denser population than the Northwest Coast. Below the region name, write ⚲ ⚲ ⚲ = **MANY PEOPLE**.

4. The Indians of the **Plateau** region relied on rivers for their food.

   a. Have students identify several Indian nations in the region.

   b. Fish, especially salmon, were the main source of food for Indians living in the Plateau region. They also gathered wild roots, bulbs, and berries. Below the region name, write Ѱ Ѱ Ѱ = **ADEQUATE FOOD**.

   c. This region was sparsely populated compared to California and the Northwest Coast. Below the region name, write ⚲ = **ALMOST NO PEOPLE**.

5. The **Great Basin** region had a dry, harsh climate. There were few edible natural resources.

   a. Have students identify several Indian nations in the region.

   b. Indians in this region gathered snakes, lizards, insects, rodents, nuts, seeds, and berries. They were called "diggers" because they dug for most of their food. Below the region name, write Ѱ = **LITTLE FOOD**.

   c. The population of Great Basin was sparse. Below the region name, write ⚲ = **ALMOST NO PEOPLE**.

 For further discussion:
   - How did the availability of food affect the population of a region?
   - How did the availability of food affect the culture of a region?

 Have students compare hunting and gathering in the sparsely populated Arctic and Subarctic regions with regions further south.

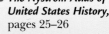

Correlates with:

- *The Nystrom Atlas of United States History,* pages 25–26
- *Mapping United States History* To the Present, Lesson 8 To the Early 1900s, Lesson 10

The Farmers

Objective: *To compare four Native American cultural regions and their food sources.*

Teaching Notes and Mapping Activity

You or your students can mark the following on the *Native Americans* map.

1. In the Northeast Woodlands, Southeast, Great Plains, and Southwest regions of North America, Native American cultural groups did not rely completely on their natural environment for food. Indians in these regions **farmed**, as well as **fished**, **hunted**, and **gathered** food.

   a. Outline each of the four cultural regions mentioned above.

   b. Near each of these regions, write and underline its name. Then draw an arrow to each appropriate region.

2. In the **Northeastern Woodlands** region, the forests, arable land, and surrounding lakes were the most valued natural resources. Indians there rarely went hungry.

   a. Have students identify several Indian nations in the region.

   b. Indians in the region grew corn, beans, and squash. They also gathered nuts and berries. In addition, those living near the Great Lakes gathered wild rice. Below the region name, write Ｗ Ｗ Ｗ Ｗ = **PLENTIFUL FOOD**.

   c. There were a moderate number of Indians in the Northeastern Woodlands. Below the region name, write ♀ ♂ = **SOME PEOPLE**.

3. Like the Northeastern Woodlands, the **Southeast** region was heavily forested and had land suitable for productive farming.

   a. Have students identify several Indian nations in the region.

   b. Indians in this region relied mainly on farming. They grew corn, beans, squash, and sweet potatoes. Below the region name, write Ｗ Ｗ Ｗ Ｗ = **PLENTIFUL FOOD**.

   c. The Southeast was as populated as the Northeastern Woodlands. Below the region name, write ♂ ♂ = **SOME PEOPLE**.

4. The **Great Plains** region was largely treeless grassland.

   a. Have students identify several Indian nations in the region.

   b. The sod of the Great Plains was difficult to plow. So most Native Americans lived along rivers where the land was easier to cultivate. They grew beans, corn, squash, and sunflowers. They also hunted deer, elk, and buffalo—which was difficult to do on foot. (European horses hadn't arrived on the plains yet.) Below the region name, write Ｗ Ｗ Ｗ = **ADEQUATE FOOD**.

   c. Before the arrival of horses, few people lived on the plains. Below the region name, write ♀ = **ALMOST NO PEOPLE**.

5. The **Southwest** region was dry. Most of the rain it did get arrived in just a few weeks of the summer.

   a. Have students identify several Indian nations in the region.

   b. Indians in this region were either farmers or gatherers. The farmers irrigated the land to grow corn, beans, and squash. The gatherers hunted deer and rabbits and gathered cactus fruit and piñon nuts. Depending on the rain, food could be plentiful or sparse. Below the region name, write Ｗ Ｗ Ｗ Ｗ – Ｗ = **FOOD VARIES**.

   c. This region was as populated as the Northeastern Woodlands and Southeast. Below the region name, write ♀ ♂ = **SOME PEOPLE**.

☆ Have students make a chart that compares the population density of Indian cultural regions with the availability of food.

☆ Have students compare farming in the densely populated Middle America region with farming in regions further north.

Correlates with:

- *The Nystrom Atlas of United States History,* pages 25–26
- *Mapping United States History* To the Present, Lesson 8 To the Early 1900s, Lesson 10

Trade Centers

Objective: *To identify key trade centers and the goods traded at these centers.*

Teaching Notes and Mapping Activity

You or your students can mark the following on the *Native Americans* map.

1. Native American **trade centers** were not permanent stores or markets. Many were trade gatherings held at special times of the year.

    a. On the *Trade Routes* map, point out several trade centers.

    b. One trade center in the northwest was **The Dalles**. Circle the label for The Dalles.

    c. On the *Native Americans* map, near the Walla Walla nation, write **TC** for trade center.

2. Many trade routes to these centers existed for thousands of years. Before Europeans arrived, Native Americans had no horses. So they traveled to trade centers **by water** or **on foot**.

    a. The Dalles was on the Columbia River. On the main map, use a marker to trace the Columbia from the Pacific Ocean to The Dalles.

    b. Trace two other waterways that lead to The Dalles.

    c. From southern California to The Dalles, along the western boundary of the Great Basin cultural region, draw a footpath with a dotted line.

3. Indians from **many nations** traded at these trade centers. Name several Indian nations who may have come to trade at The Dalles.

4. Both **goods and ideas** were exchanged at trade centers. At The Dalles, Native Americans traded a variety of goods, including fish, whale oil, salt, fur pelts, sheep horns, canoes, and human slaves. Near The Dalles, draw two of the items sold at this trade center.

5. There were other Native American trade centers in the Americas.

    a. One trade center in the southwest was **Hopi**. On the *Trade Routes* map, circle the Hopi center.

    b. On the *Native Americans* map, west of the Pueblo nation, write **TC**.

6. Indians from a variety of nations came to exchange goods at southwest trade centers.

    a. Indians in the southwest had turquoise and blue opals to trade. Near the Hopi trade center, draw a precious stone.

    b. Indians from Middle America brought exotic birds and feathers to trade. In Mexico, draw a bird. Then draw an arrow from the bird to the Hopi center.

    c. Indians from Pacific coast brought seal skins and shells to trade. Along the Pacific coast, draw a shell. Then draw an arrow from the shell to the Hopi center.

    d. Indians from the Great Plains brought buffalo robes, deer skin, and jerky to trade. In the Great Plains cultural region, draw a buffalo. Draw an arrow from the buffalo to the Hopi center.

 There were dozens of other major trade centers in North America. Assign pairs of students to a trade center. Have them use the maps on this wall map or transparency to determine which Indian nations traded there and which trade routes they used. Compile the information on a class chart.

For further discussion:
- How do you think conflicts between Indian nations might have affected trade?
- Some feel trade encouraged Indian nations to become more alike. How?

Correlates with:
- ***The Nystrom Atlas of United States History,*** page 26

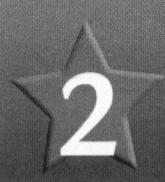

2

Spanish Explorers 1492–1543

Key Elements

★ *Spanish Explorers* map
★ Locator map
★ *Spanish Explorers* timeline

Getting Started

To give students an overview of *Spanish Explorers*, ask them:

- What is the title of this map?
- What part of the world is shown on this map?
- What years does the map cover?
- What do the colored arrows represent?
- What years does the timeline cover?
- What events are listed on the timeline?

Teaching Notes and Mapping Activities

~ Columbus' Other Voyages to the Indies
~ De Soto Searches for Gold in the Southeast
~ Coronado Searches for Gold in the Southwest

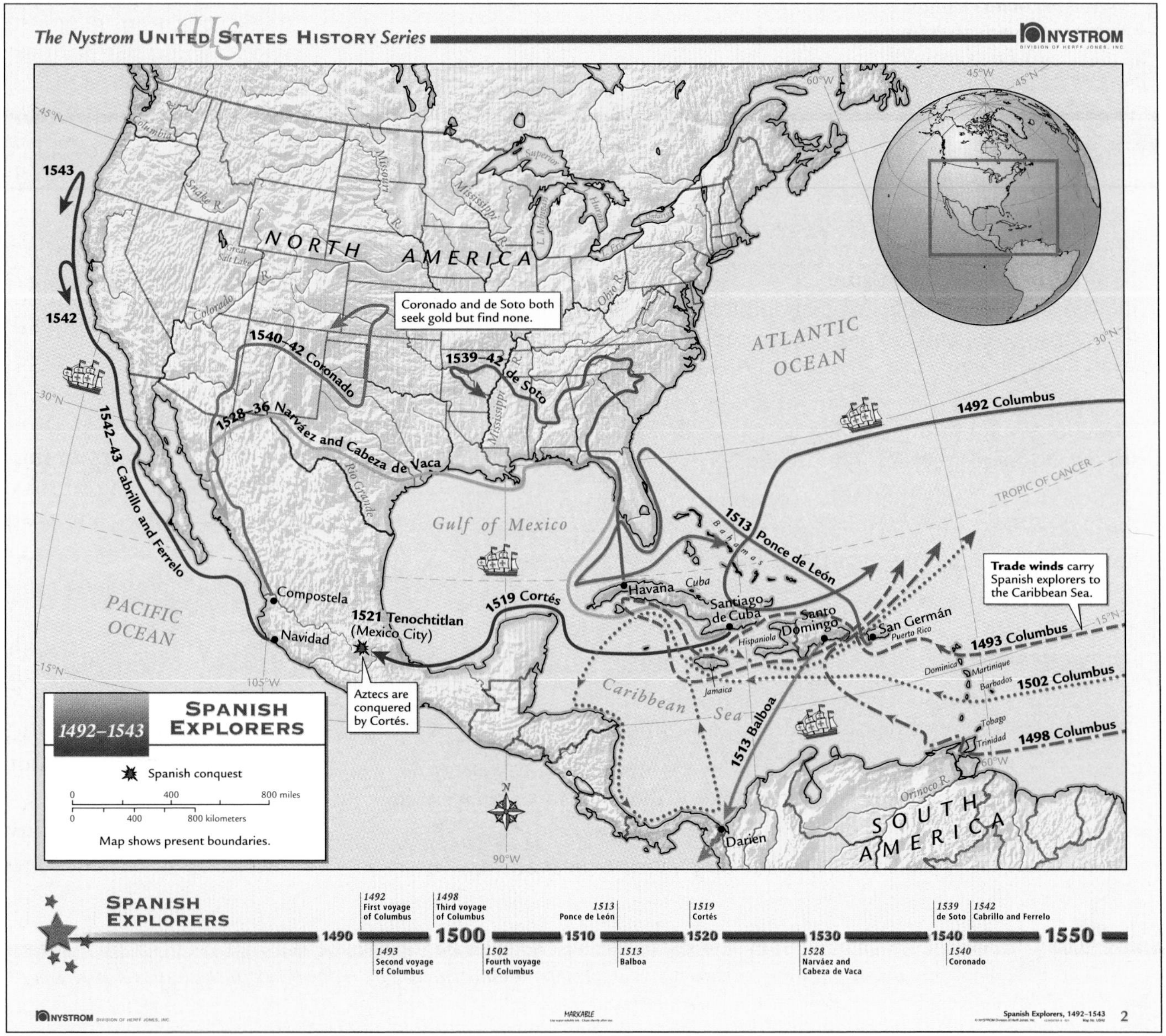
The Nystrom United States History Series
NYSTROM
DIVISION OF HERFF JONES, INC.
NORTH AMERICA
SOUTH AMERICA
ATLANTIC OCEAN
PACIFIC OCEAN
Gulf of Mexico
Caribbean Sea
Coronado and de Soto both seek gold but find none.
Trade winds carry Spanish explorers to the Caribbean Sea.
Aztecs are conquered by Cortés.
1543
1542
1542–43 Cabrillo and Ferrelo
1540–42 Coronado
1539–42 de Soto
1528–36 Narváez and Cabeza de Vaca
1521 Tenochtitlan (Mexico City)
1519 Cortés
1513 Ponce de León
1513 Balboa
1492 Columbus
1493 Columbus
1502 Columbus
1498 Columbus
Compostela
Navidad
Havana
Cuba
Santiago de Cuba
Santo Domingo
Hispaniola
San Germán
Puerto Rico
Jamaica
Bahamas
Dominica
Martinique
Barbados
Tobago
Trinidad
Darien
Orinoco R.
Columbia
Snake R.
Missouri R.
Mississippi R.
Colorado R.
Rio Grande
Ohio R.
Great Salt Lake
Superior
Huron
L. Michigan
TROPIC OF CANCER
45°N
30°N
15°N
45°W
60°W
90°W
105°W
N
1492–1543
SPANISH EXPLORERS
Spanish conquest
0 400 800 miles
0 400 800 kilometers
Map shows present boundaries.
SPANISH EXPLORERS
1490
1500
1510
1520
1530
1540
1550
1492 First voyage of Columbus
1493 Second voyage of Columbus
1498 Third voyage of Columbus
1502 Fourth voyage of Columbus
1513 Ponce de León
1513 Balboa
1519 Cortés
1528 Narváez and Cabeza de Vaca
1539 de Soto
1540 Coronado
1542 Cabrillo and Ferrelo
NYSTROM DIVISION OF HERFF JONES, INC.
MARKABLE
Spanish Explorers, 1492–1543
2

Columbus' Other Voyages to the Indies

Objective: *To trace Columbus' routes on his second, third, and fourth voyages and identify places he sighted.*

Teaching Notes and Mapping Activity

You or your students can mark the following on the *Spanish Explorers* map. Introduce this lesson by tracing Columbus' 1492 voyage.

1. In 1493 Christopher Columbus set off on his **second voyage** to what he assumed were the Indies. This voyage and his other three were sponsored by King Ferdinand and Queen Isabella of Spain. On this voyage, Columbus commanded 17 ships and 1,200 men, including fortune hunters, colonists, and missionaries.

   a. Above the map label *1493 Columbus*, write **2ND VOYAGE**.

   b. With your finger, trace his route.

   c. After just 21 days at sea, Columbus spotted **Dominica**. Circle the word *Dominica*. Point out to students that the island and country names used in this lesson are modern-day names.

   d. He spotted several other islands, including **Puerto Rico**. Circle the words *Puerto Rico*.

   e. On his 1492 voyage, Columbus had built a fort on **Hispaniola**, and left behind 40 men. In 1493, he returned to the island and found that the fort had been destroyed and the men were all killed. Columbus established a new colony on the island and became its governor. Circle the word *Hispaniola*.

   f. Colonists on Hispaniola criticized Columbus for mistreating the Indians and governing poorly. Many returned to Spain.

   g. Intending to sail to China and find gold, Columbus sailed to **Cuba** and **Jamaica** instead. Circle the words *Cuba* and *Jamaica*.
   - In the upper left corner of the map, write and underline **2ND VOYAGE—1493–1496**.
   - Below that, list the islands circled on your map.

2. On Columbus' **third voyage**, few men wanted to join him. Ferdinand and Isabella had to pardon prisoners in order to get a crew for Columbus' six ships.

   a. Above the map label *1498 Columbus*, write **3RD VOYAGE**.

   b. With your finger, trace this route.

   c. This time, Columbus sailed further south. The first island he reached was **Trinidad**. Circle the word *Trinidad*.

   d. Columbus also spotted the coast of Venezuela. On South America, near Trinidad, write **VENEZUELA**.

   e. When he arrived in **Hispaniola**, the colonists on this island arrested Columbus and sent him back to Spain in chains.
   - On the left side of the map, write and underline **3RD VOYAGE—1498–1500**.
   - Below that, list any new places that you circled or labeled.

3. Columbus' **fourth voyage** was perhaps his most exciting.

   a. Above the map label *1502 Columbus*, write **4TH VOYAGE**.

   b. With your finger, trace this route.

   c. Columbus was forbidden to return to Hispaniola. He weathered out a storm nearby. South of Santo Domingo, draw a **hurricane**.

   d. Columbus went on to explore **Middle America**. Label **HONDURAS**, **NICARAGUA**, **COSTA RICA**, and **PANAMA**.

   e. Hit by another storm, Columbus beached his sinking ships in Jamaica. He was **marooned** for a year.
   - On the left side of the map, write and underline **4TH VOYAGE—1502–1504**.
   - Below that, list the last four places you labeled on your map.

 Columbus has been called a great explorer, a fool, a brutal enslaver, and a fortune hunter. Have students choose one descriptor and write a paragraph supporting their choice.

Correlates with:
- *The Nystrom Atlas of United States History,* page 21
- *Mapping United States History* To the Present, Lesson 5 To the Early 1900s, Lesson 6

Objective: *To trace de Soto's route and identify major natural features along it.*

Teaching Notes and Mapping Activity

You or your students can mark the following on the *Spanish Explorers* map.

1. **Hernando de Soto** was a conquistador. *Conquistador* is a Spanish word meaning conqueror. He had served under Balboa in Middle America and Pizarro in South America. Later, de Soto was given the right to explore and conquer Florida for Spain. At that time, no one knew exactly how large Florida was. Some thought it was an island. Along Florida's eastern coast, write **FLORIDA**. (Point out to students that the place names used in this lesson are modern-day names.)

2. De Soto read the accounts of earlier explorers of Florida and tried to learn from their mistakes.

   a. With your finger, trace **Ponce de León's** and **Narváez and Cabeza de Vaca's** routes.

   b. Then use the *Spanish Explorers* timeline to compare the dates of their explorations with de Soto's.

3. In May of 1539, de Soto, nine ships, over 600 men, and hundreds of horses began their expedition. The ships sailed from Cuba to Tampa Bay on Florida's west coast. With your finger, trace this route.

4. Soon after the expedition landed, they met Juan Ortiz, a survivor of the Narváez expedition. He had lived among the Indians for years. Ortiz became the expedition's interpreter. On Florida, write **+ ORTIZ.**

5. De Soto brought along armor, weapons, tools, seeds, food, and clothing. He relied on Indians to carry them. To force the Indians into service, de Soto's troops would hold a chief for ransom. The chief was released once the tribe supplied men to carry baggage. Some tribes resisted. Near de Soto's landing, draw a conflict symbol ✹ .

6. The expedition marched across the countryside in a specific order: first conquistadores on horseback; then foot soldiers; then African slaves, Indian guides, and Indians slaves hauling supplies; then pigs; and finally more conquistadores. Across the top of the map, draw stick figures showing this procession.

7. De Soto and his men often tortured Indians to find out where **gold** deposits were located. Because there was no gold in Florida, Indians lied and sent the expedition in a different direction.

   a. With your finger, from Tampa Bay to western North Carolina, trace de Soto's route.

   b. De Soto and his expedition were the first Europeans to cross the **Appalachian Mountains**. Mark the Appalachians with mountain symbols ∧∧∧ .

8. Near central Alabama, the expedition fought a bloody battle. A village was destroyed, thousands of Indians were killed, and almost every Spaniard was wounded. With your finger, trace de Soto's route to Alabama. There, draw a conflict symbol ✹ .

9. De Soto learned that his fleet was anchored nearby on the gulf. Having no gold to take home, de Soto lead his men in the opposite direction.

   a. With your finger, trace de Soto's route northwest.

   b. DeSoto and his men were the first Europeans to cross the Mississippi River. Trace the Mississippi from source to mouth.

   c. The expedition never found gold. De Soto died near the Mississippi in May of 1542. At the end of his route, draw a cross † to mark his death.

☆ For further discussion:
   - How many future states did de Soto travel through?
   - What Indian nations did he meet?
   - How were de Soto's and Cabeza de Vaca's journeys alike?

Correlates with:
- *The Nystrom Atlas of United States History,* pages 23
- *Mapping United States History* To the Early 1900s, Lesson 8

Coronado Searches for Gold in the Southwest

Objective: *To trace Coronado's route and identify major natural features along it.*

Teaching Notes and Mapping Activity

You or your students can mark the following on the *Spanish Explorers* map.

1. **Cabeza de Vaca**, returning to Spanish territory after a long expedition, reported rumors of cities of gold—the seven cities of **Cibola**. With your finger, trace **Cabeza de Vaca's** route.

2. The Viceroy of New Spain (Mexico) asked **Francisco Vásquez de Coronado** to lead an expedition to find these cities. Coronado sent an **advance party** to locate Cibola. The party included Esteban, a survivor of the Cabeza de Vaca expedition, and several friars. Esteban was killed in one of the seven cities. But Friar Marcos, who never reached the city himself, reported that the city was beautiful and larger than Mexico City.

   a. Use the *Spanish Explorers* timeline to compare the date of Cabeza de Vaca's exploration with Coronado's.

   b. Draw a dotted line from Compostela north to the sharp bend in Coronado's route.

   c. At the bend, draw a city symbol ● for one of the seven cities.

3. For the actual **expedition**, Coronado pulled together 300 Spanish soldiers and over 1,000 Indians.

   a. Several ships sailed up the Gulf of California with supplies for the expedition. From Compostela, draw a dotted line up the gulf. Also draw a ship along the line.

   b. Coronado marched toward the seven cities. With your finger, trace Coronado's route to the city symbol.

4. When Coronado reached the first city of Cibola, he was extremely disappointed. The city turned out to be a small, crowded pueblo village. There was no gold.

   a. Label the city symbol **CIBOLA**.

   b. Coronado discovered that the other cities of Cibola were also small pueblos. In the same area, draw six more city symbols ●.

5. Disappointed, Coronado sent troops in several directions.

   a. López de Cárdenas searched for a water route to the Pacific. Instead, he found the Grand Canyon. From Cibola west to the Colorado River, trace the unnamed river with a dotted line. Label the junction of the two rivers **GRAND CANYON**.

   b. Hernando de Alvarado headed east. From Cibola east to the Texas panhandle, draw a dotted line. Label the land east of the panhandle **GREAT PLAINS**.

6. Alvarado returned with a Plains Indian who had been made a slave. Coronado called the Indian **Turk**. Turk told Coronado of Quivira, a wealthy city where bowls were made of gold.

   a. On route to Quivira, Coronado and his expedition got lost on the Plains. With your finger, from Cibola trace their route to the point furthest northeast.

   b. Coronado and his men were the first Europeans to see **buffalo**. Draw a buffalo along the route.

7. **Quivira**, in modern-day Kansas, was a village of mud huts.

   a. On the northeast tip of the route, write ● **QUIVIRA**.

   b. Coronado returned to New Spain disappointed. With your finger, retrace his route to Compostela.

 Have students research the other explorations labeled on the map.

Correlates with:
- ● *The Nystrom Atlas of United States History,* pages 23
- ● *Mapping United States History* To the Early 1900s, Lesson 8

3

ENGLISH, FRENCH, AND DUTCH EXPLORERS
1497–1682

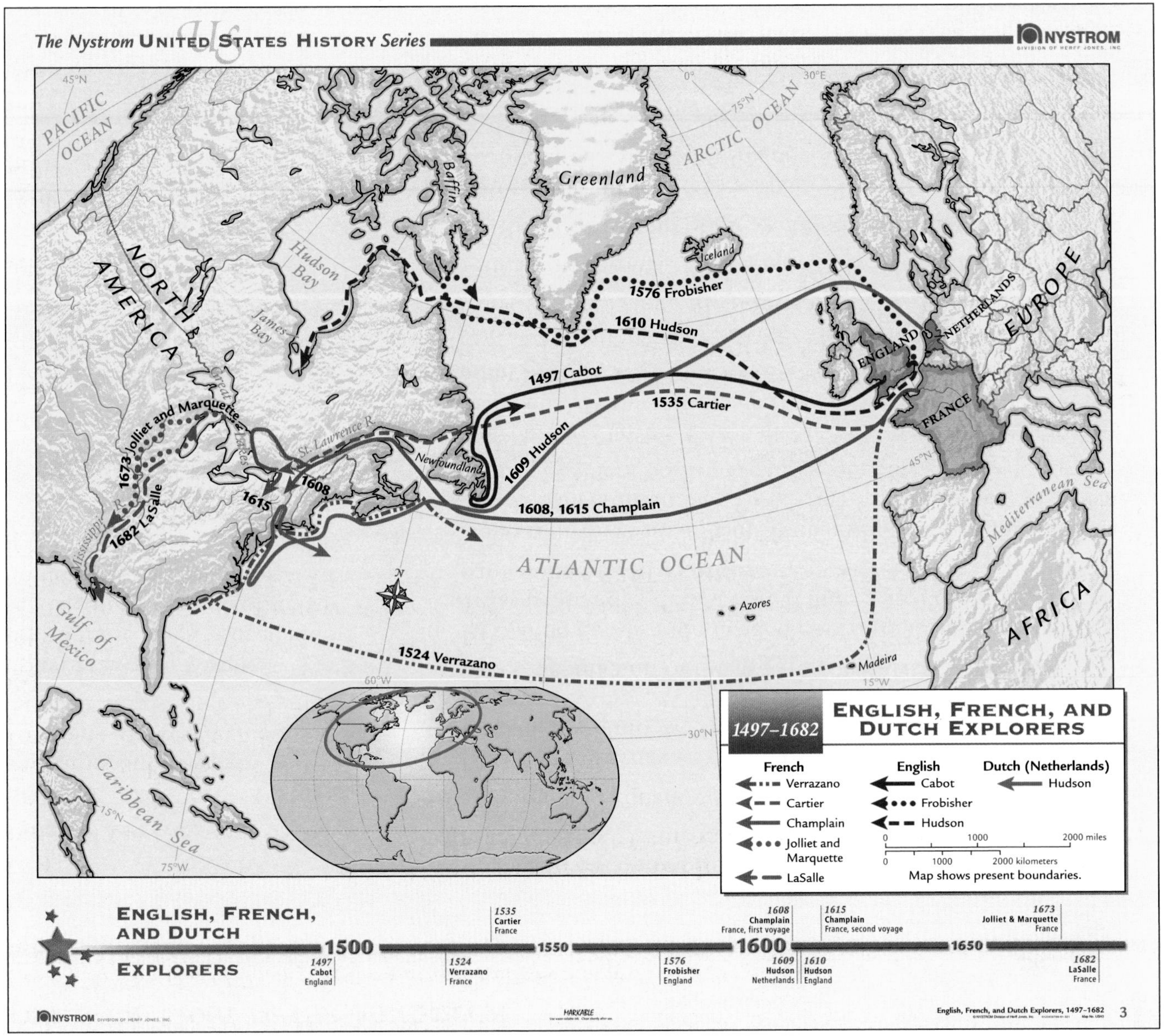

Key Elements

★ *English, French, and Dutch Explorers* map

★ Locator map

★ *English, French, and Dutch Explorers* timeline

Getting Started

To give students an overview of *English, French, and Dutch Explorers,* ask them:

• What is the title of the map?

• What part of the world is shown on this map?

• What years does the map cover?

• What do the colored arrows represent?

• There are two ways to tell when each expedition took place. What are they?

• Which explorer sailed for two different countries?

Teaching Notes and Mapping Activities

~ Searching for the Northwest Passage

~ French Explorers, French Claims

~ English and Dutch Explorers and Claims

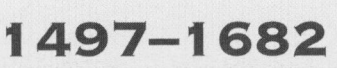

The Nystrom UNITED STATES HISTORY Series

NYSTROM
DIVISION OF HERFF JONES, INC.

PACIFIC OCEAN

NORTH AMERICA

Baffin I.

Hudson Bay

James Bay

Greenland

Iceland

ARCTIC OCEAN

NETHERLANDS

EUROPE

ENGLAND

FRANCE

1576 Frobisher

1610 Hudson

1497 Cabot

1535 Cartier

1609 Hudson

Newfoundland

1673 Jolliet and Marquette

St. Lawrence R.

1608

1615

1682 LaSalle

Mississippi R.

1608, 1615 Champlain

ATLANTIC OCEAN

Azores

Mediterranean Sea

AFRICA

Gulf of Mexico

1524 Verrazano

Madeira

Caribbean Sea

ENGLISH, FRENCH, AND DUTCH EXPLORERS
1497–1682

French	English	Dutch (Netherlands)
Verrazano	Cabot	Hudson
Cartier	Frobisher	
Champlain	Hudson	
Jolliet and Marquette		
LaSalle		

0   1000   2000 miles
0   1000   2000 kilometers
Map shows present boundaries.

ENGLISH, FRENCH, AND DUTCH EXPLORERS

	1535 Cartier France	**1608** Champlain France, first voyage
1500	**1550**	**1600**

1497 Cabot England

1524 Verrazano France

1576 Frobisher England

1609 Hudson Netherlands

1610 Hudson England

1615 Champlain France, second voyage

1650

1673 Jolliet & Marquette France

1682 LaSalle France

NYSTROM DIVISION OF HERFF JONES, INC.

HARKABLE

English, French, and Dutch Explorers, 1497–1682

3

Searching for the Northwest Passage

Objective: To explain that the search for the Northwest Passage motivated English, French, and Dutch exploration.

Teaching Notes and Mapping Activity

You or your students can mark the following on the *English, French, and Dutch Explorers* map, the locator map, and the timeline.

1. For nearly 10 years after Columbus' first voyage, Europeans still believed that he had reached Asia. Explorers such as **John Cabot** searched the coasts of North and South America for China, India, and other destinations of Eurasian trade. On the *English, French, and Dutch Explorers* timeline, to the right of the entry for Cabot, write **ASIA?**

2. By the 1520s, Europeans realized that the Americas were not Asia, but previously unexplored continents. Ferdinand Magellan's voyage provided a route around these new continents to Asia. But Magellan's route was so long and dangerous that later explorers sought **a different route to Asia**.

   a. Magellan's route required going around South America. On the locator map, draw an arrow from Europe around South America to the Pacific Ocean. Label the arrow **MAGELLAN**.

   b. Most explorers hoped to find a northern route that was shorter and safer than Magellan's. On the locator map, draw an arrow from Europe pointing slightly northwest. Label the arrow **NORTHWEST PASSAGE?**

3. In 1524 **Giovanni da Verrazano's** search for the Northwest Passage covered over 1,500 miles of North America's coastline. He did not find a route to the Pacific, but his maps and descriptions of North America's east coast were used by generations of future explorers.

   a. On the timeline, to the right of the entry for Verrazano, write **ATLANTIC COASTLINE**.

   b. On the *English, French, and Dutch Explorers* map, label the arrow that represents Verrazano's journey **MAPS HELP FUTURE EXPLORERS**.

4. In 1535 **Jacques Cartier** became the first European to sail up what is today called the St. Lawrence River. When his journey was halted by rapids, he realized that he had not found a route to the Pacific. However, he did note that the land surrounding the river was worth settling.

   a. On the timeline, to the right of the entry for Cartier, write **ST. LAWRENCE RIVER**.

   b. On the map, label the arrow that represents Cartier's journey **FINDS LAND WORTH SETTLING**.

5. In 1609 **Henry Hudson** became the first European to sail up the river that would eventually be named for him. He realized that this river did not lead to the Pacific, but, like Cartier, he noted that the land surrounding the river was worth settling.

   a. On the timeline, below the 1609 entry for Hudson, write **HUDSON RIVER**.

   b. On the map, label the arrow that represents Hudson's 1609 journey **FINDS LAND WORTH SETTLING**.

6. A year later Hudson, still looking for **a northern route to the Pacific Ocean**, became the first European to explore the enormous bay that would eventually be named for him. His journey spurred further exploration of the region.

   a. On the timeline, below the 1610 entry for Hudson, write **HUDSON BAY**.

   b. On the map, label the arrow that represents Hudson's 1610 journey **SPURS FURTHER EXPLORATION**.

 Ask your students to evaluate the accomplishments of the explorers above and rank them in their order of importance. Then, have students write a paragraph explaining their choices.

Correlates with:
- *The Nystrom Atlas of United States History,* page 22
- *Mapping United States History,* To the Present, Lesson 6 To the Early 1900s, Lesson 7

Objective: *To show early French exploration of North America and later settlement patterns.*

Teaching Notes and Mapping Activity

You or your students can mark the following on the *English, French, and Dutch Explorers* map and timeline.

1. The search for the Northwest Passage eventually led to European settlements in North America. French explorer **Jacques Cartier** explored the St. Lawrence River and claimed the land surrounding the river for France. He later brought the first French settlers to mainland North America.

   a. On the *English, French, and Dutch Explorers* map, below the arrow marking Cartier's journey, write **1541 FIRST FRENCH SETTLERS**. [Note: These first settlements were unsuccessful and were abandoned in 1543.]

   b. Cartier brought these settlers to the region he had named New France. Along the St. Lawrence River, write **NEW FRANCE**.

   c. Like most Europeans, Cartier gave names to the places he explored. Many of these names are still in use today, including a name Cartier borrowed from the Indians—Canada. On the timeline, to the right of the entry for Cartier, write **CANADA**.

   d. You might want to tell your students that Cartier used the Huron-Iroquois word *kanata*, meaning a town or a village, to describe *all* the land west of the St. Lawrence River. (The Indians were just using it to describe a *village* located west of the St. Lawrence.)

2. From 1608 to 1616, another French explorer, **Samuel de Champlain**, continued the explorations begun by Cartier. He founded many French settlements, extending the borders of New France. He also became the first European to see the Great Lakes.

   a. On the map, below the arrow marking Champlain's journeys, write **FOUNDS FRENCH SETTLEMENTS**.

   b. Just north of the Great Lakes, write **NEW FRANCE**.

   c. On the timeline, to the right of the 1615 entry for Champlain, write **GREAT LAKES**.

3. In 1673 fur trader **Louis Jolliet** and **Father Jacques Marquette**, a Catholic missionary, traveled partway down the Mississippi River. They realized that the river and the land along it had great potential for settlers.

   a. On the timeline, to the right of the entry for Jolliet and Marquette, write **MISSISSIPPI RIVER**.

   b. Jolliet and Marquette did not travel all the way to the mouth of the Mississippi because Spaniards had settled the southern region, and France and Spain were at odds. Across the Gulf of Mexico and the Florida peninsula, write **SPANISH**.

4. In 1682 **Rene-Robert de La Salle** completed the journey to the mouth of the Mississippi. La Salle claimed the Mississippi River and "all the rivers that enter it and of all the country watered by them" for France.

   a. On the map, show the extent of the French claim by pointing out all the rivers that flow into the Mississippi River.

   b. Draw one line around all the rivers that flow into the Mississippi from the west.

   c. Draw another line around all the rivers that flow into the Mississippi from the east.

   d. La Salle named this territory after the French ruler, King Louis XIV. Across the territory bounded by the two lines, write **LOUISIANA (FRANCE)**.

☆ Turn to the Native Americans, 1500 map (USH1). Have your students compile a list of Indian nations already living in the regions claimed by French explorers.

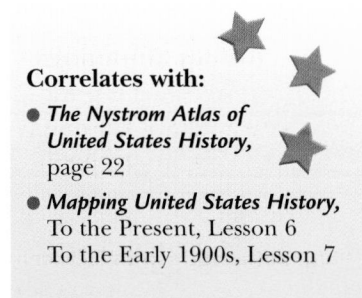

Correlates with:
- *The Nystrom Atlas of United States History,* page 22
- *Mapping United States History,* To the Present, Lesson 6 To the Early 1900s, Lesson 7

English and Dutch Explorers and Claims

Objective: *To show early English and Dutch exploration of North America and later settlement patterns.*

Teaching Notes and Mapping Activity

You or your students can mark the following on the *English, French, and Dutch Explorers* map and timeline.

1. Like the French, English and Dutch explorations often led to English and Dutch settlements. In 1497 **John Cabot** found seas off the coast of Newfoundland teeming with fish. Ships from all over Europe arrived to cash in on these fishing grounds, but English fishermen were the first to settle the island in 1610.

    a. On the *English, French, and Dutch Explorers* map, in the ocean east of Newfoundland, draw a fish ⊂⋈ .

    b. Across the island of Newfoundland, write **1610 - ENGLISH SETTLERS**.

    c. On the *English, French, and Dutch Explorers* timeline, to the right of the entry for Cabot, write **FINDS N.F. FISHERIES**.

2. In 1609 **Henry Hudson** became the first European to sail up what later became known as the Hudson River. Though English, Hudson was sailing for the Netherlands, and his explorations led to the first **Dutch settlement** in North America in 1614.

    a. On the timeline, below the 1609 entry for Hudson, write **HUDSON RIVER**.

    b. On the map, label the area along the Hudson River **1614 - NEW NETHERLANDS**.

3. In 1610 **Hudson**, still searching for the Northwest Passage, discovered a huge inland sea. England based its claim to the Hudson Bay region on this voyage. However, **English settlement** of the area did not begin until the 1660s, more than 50 years after Hudson explored the region.

    a. On the timeline to the right of the 1610 entry for Hudson, write **HUDSON BAY**.

    b. French fur traders had been trapping in the region south of Hudson Bay for years. On the map, write **FUR TRADE** between the Great Lakes and Hudson Bay.

    c. Traders realized that furs could be shipped to Europe quickly and easily from Hudson Bay, so a group of English businessmen decided to finance fur trading settlements along the shores of Hudson Bay and James Bay. Along the shore of Hudson Bay, write **1668 - HUDSON BAY COMPANY (ENGLAND)**.

4. You might want to provide your students with the following information about Cabot and Hudson:

    a. Though John Cabot sailed for England, he was actually an Italian whose real name was Giovanni Caboto.

    b. In 1498 Cabot made a second journey to the Americas from which he never returned.

    c. Cabot's son, Sebastian, was also an explorer. He made several journeys in search of the Northwest Passage in the early 1500s.

    d. During his 1610 journey, Hudson's crew mutinied and set him adrift in Hudson Bay. Hudson is presumed to have died in the bay that bears his name.

    e. You may also want to remind your students that neither the Hudson River nor Hudson Bay were called by those names prior to Henry Hudson's discovery of them.

 Have your students compare the locations of English, French, and Dutch settlements in North America. Then have them identify regions where settlers from the different nations of Europe might come into conflict.

Correlates with:
- *The Nystrom Atlas of United States History,* page 22
- *Mapping United States History,* To the Present, Lesson 6
  To the Early 1900s, Lesson 7

THE GREAT EXCHANGE
1492–1640s

Key Elements

★ *The Great Exchange* map
★ *Big Arrivals* timeline

Getting Started

To give students an overview of *The Great Exchange*, ask them:

- What is the title of the map?
- What parts of the world does this map show?
- What do the different symbols on this map represent?
- What do the arrows on this map represent?
- What events are shown on the timeline?
- Did more diseases come from Europe, Africa, and Asia or from the Americas?
- What was the first American animal to arrive in Europe? What year did it arrive?

Teaching Notes and Mapping Activities

~ From Old World to New
~ From New World to Old
~ The Culinary Columbus

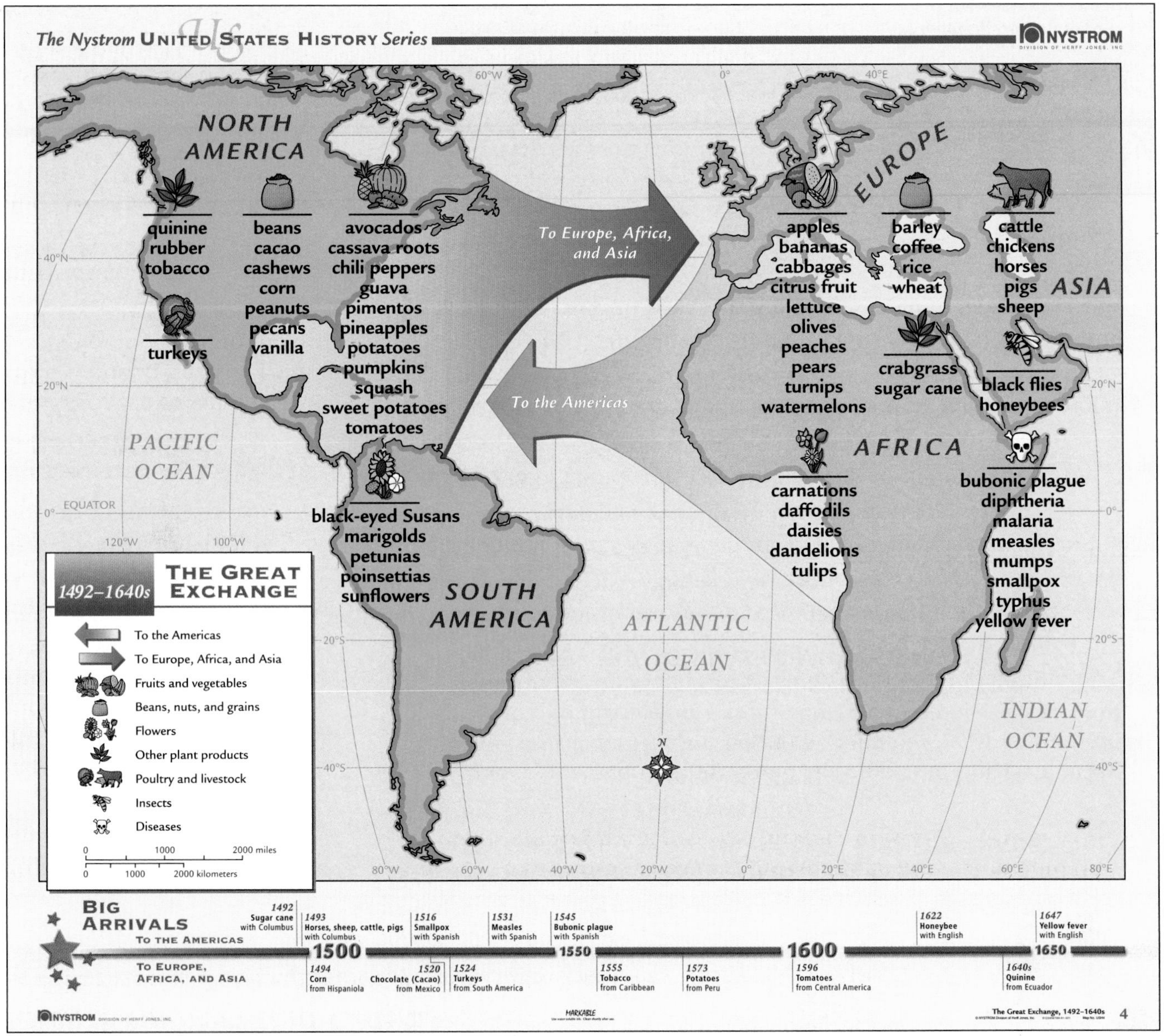

The Nystrom **UNITED STATES HISTORY** *Series*

NYSTROM
DIVISION OF HERFF JONES, INC.

NORTH AMERICA

quinine
rubber
tobacco

beans
cacao
cashews
corn
peanuts
pecans
vanilla

avocados
cassava roots
chili peppers
guava
pimentos
pineapples
potatoes
pumpkins
squash
sweet potatoes
tomatoes

turkeys

To Europe, Africa, and Asia

To the Americas

EUROPE

apples
bananas
cabbages
citrus fruit
lettuce
olives
peaches
pears
turnips
watermelons

barley
coffee
rice
wheat

crabgrass
sugar cane

ASIA

cattle
chickens
horses
pigs
sheep

black flies
honeybees

AFRICA

carnations
daffodils
daisies
dandelions
tulips

bubonic plague
diphtheria
malaria
measles
mumps
smallpox
typhus
yellow fever

SOUTH AMERICA

black-eyed Susans
marigolds
petunias
poinsettias
sunflowers

PACIFIC OCEAN

ATLANTIC OCEAN

INDIAN OCEAN

EQUATOR

THE GREAT EXCHANGE
1492–1640s

- To the Americas
- To Europe, Africa, and Asia
- Fruits and vegetables
- Beans, nuts, and grains
- Flowers
- Other plant products
- Poultry and livestock
- Insects
- Diseases

0   1000   2000 miles
0   1000   2000 kilometers

BIG ARRIVALS

TO THE AMERICAS

1492 Sugar cane with Columbus
1493 Horses, sheep, cattle, pigs with Columbus
1516 Smallpox with Spanish
1531 Measles with Spanish
1545 Bubonic plague with Spanish
1622 Honeybee with English
1647 Yellow fever with English

1500   **1550**   **1600**   **1650**

TO EUROPE, AFRICA, AND ASIA

1494 Corn from Hispaniola
1520 Chocolate (Cacao) from Mexico
1524 Turkeys from South America
1555 Tobacco from Caribbean
1573 Potatoes from Peru
1596 Tomatoes from Central America
1640s Quinine from Ecuador

NYSTROM DIVISION OF HERFF JONES, INC.

The Great Exchange, 1492–1640s   **4**

From Old World to New

Objective: *To map the movement of select items from the Old World to the New.*

Teaching Notes and Mapping Activity

You or your students can mark the following on *The Great Exchange* map.

1. Most Europeans referred to the Americas as the New World. Europe, Africa, and Asia were called the Old World. Many items taken to this New World by Europeans originated in Asia and Africa. Draw arrows from the labels for Asia and Africa to the label for Europe.

2. The cultivation of **sugar cane** began in Asia and spread to Europe in the 600s. Columbus brought the first sugar cane to North America in 1493. It quickly became the main crop in the Caribbean.

   a. Circle the words *sugar cane* on the map, and draw an arrow from it to the islands of the Caribbean.

   b. Making sugar from sugar cane was back-breaking work. Europeans enslaved Native Americans and Africans to perform the hard labor necessary for the production of sugar. Label the arrow **REQUIRED SLAVE LABOR**.

3. The **coffee** plant originated in Ethiopia, and people there soon learned that it could be made into a stimulating drink. Coffee became popular in Europe in the 1600s and was brought to the Americas by Spanish and Portuguese explorers. By the 1700s there were large coffee plantations in Brazil.

   a. Circle the word *coffee* and draw an arrow from it to the label for South America.

   b. Today Brazil and Columbia are the top two coffee-growing countries in the world. Label the arrow **BRAZIL #1, COLOMBIA #2**.

4. **Citrus fruits**, such as oranges, were first cultivated in Asia more than 4,000 years ago. Portuguese traders took orange trees back to Europe in the 1400s. By the 1500s, European explorers had planted citrus trees in Brazil and Florida.

   a. Circle the words *citrus fruit* and draw one arrow from it to the label for South America and another to North America.

   b. Today Brazil and the United States are the top two orange-growing countries in the world. Label the arrow pointing to South America **BRAZIL #1 (ORANGES)**. Label the arrow pointing to North America **U. S. #2 (ORANGES)**.

5. Spanish explorers brought **horses** with them when they came to the New World. At first, Native Americans were terrified of the animals. Later they learned how useful horses could be, particularly for hunting on the Great Plains of North America.

   a. Circle the word *horses* and draw an arrow from it to the label for North America.

   b. Label the arrow **CHANGED NAT. AM. LIFESTYLE**.

6. In addition to beneficial plants and animals, Europeans also brought **diseases** to the New World. Over the centuries, Europeans had developed immunities to these diseases, but Native Americans had not.

   a. Circle the symbol for diseases and draw an arrow from it to the Americas.

   b. These diseases are believed to have killed more than 90 percent of the original Native American population. Label the arrow **KILLED 90% OF NAT. AM.**

 Ask your students to choose and research an item introduced to the Americas by Europeans.
  - How did this item affect the lives of Europeans, Native Americans, Asians, and/or Africans living then?
  - Does it have any affect on your life or theirs today? If so, how?

Correlates with:
- *The Nystrom Atlas of United States History,* pages 26–27

Objective: *To map the movement of select items from the New World to the Old.*

Teaching Notes and Mapping Activity

You or your students can mark the following on
The Great Exchange map.

1. The **potato** originated in South America. Spanish explorers took it to Europe in the mid-1500s. Today potatoes are the most widely grown vegetable in the world.

   a. Circle the word *potatoes* on the map, and draw an arrow from it to the label for Europe.

   b. Label the arrow **MOST WIDELY GROWN VEGETABLE**.

2. In 1492, Native Americans were growing **corn** as far south as Chile and as far north as Canada. Columbus took corn back to Europe after his first voyage. By the late 1500s, corn was being grown throughout Europe.

   a. Circle the word *corn* and then draw an arrow from it to the label for Europe.

   b. Today, corn ranks second in world grain production, after wheat. It supplies more than 20% of the world's food calories. Label the arrow **20% OF WORLD'S CALORIES**.

3. **Tobacco** was unknown to Europeans in 1492, but people in the Americas had been smoking it for centuries. By the 1700s, it was the most valuable export from mainland North America.

   a. Circle the word *tobacco* and draw an arrow from it to the label for Europe.

   b. Label the arrow **MOST VALUABLE N.A. EXPORT**.

4. Native Americans cultivated **cacao** trees for centuries before Europeans arrived. The beans of the trees were used to make chocolate. In the 1520s a European explorer took cacao beans back to Spain. By the 1700s cocoa—a drink made from the beans—had become popular in Europe.

   a. Circle the word *cacao* and then draw an arrow from it to the label for Europe.

   b. Label the arrow **FOR CHOCOLATE**.

5. **Quinine** is made from the bark of cinchona trees, which originated in South America. It is used to treat malaria and other diseases that cause fevers.

   a. Circle the word *quinine* and draw an arrow from it to the label for Europe.

   b. Quinine helped combat malaria, which made it easier for Europeans to colonize tropical areas where the disease was a common ailment. Label the arrow **FIGHTS MALARIA**.

6. New World items taken to Europe quickly made their way to Africa and Asia. Today, many plants that originated in the Americas have become extremely important crops in Europe, Africa, and Asia. In some cases, more of these crops are being grown in the Old World than in the New!

   a. Draw arrows from the label for Europe to the labels for Africa and Asia.

   b. Today seven of the top ten potato-growing countries are in Europe. Below the label for Europe, write **POTATOES**.

   c. Three of the top five tobacco-growing countries are in Asia. Below the label for Asia, write **TOBACCO**.

   d. Three of the top five cacao-growing countries are in Africa. Below the label for Africa, write **CACAO**.

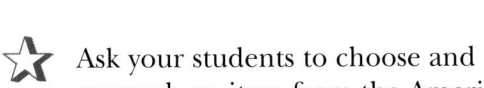 Ask your students to choose and research an item from the Americas that was introduced to Europe.

- How did this item affect the lives of Europeans, Native Americans, Asians, and/or Africans living then?
- Does the item have any affect on your life or theirs today? If so, how?

Correlates with:
- *The Nystrom Atlas of United States History,* pages 26–27

The Culinary Columbus

Objective: *To show how the Great Exchange influenced diets throughout the world.*

Teaching Notes and Mapping Activity

You or your students can mark the following on *The Great Exchange* map.

1. Have your students look at the *Big Arrivals* timeline. On the *Great Exchange* map, label the items shown on the timeline from 1 to 14, according to the chronological order of their arrival in either the New World or the Old. For example, sugar cane, the first item on the timeline, will be labeled ①.

2. Below is a list of the dates of arrival for other items shown on the *Great Exchange* map. You might have your students:

   a. Use the map to identify which items originated in the Americas, and which originated in Europe, Africa, or Asia.

   b. Add the new items to the *Big Arrivals* timeline.

   c. Create a timeline of their own incorporating the items from both the *Big Arrivals* timeline and the list below.

   - apples   1620s
   - avocado   1526
   - bananas   1510s
   - cheese*   1490s
   - chickens   1494
   - chili peppers   1493
   - citrus fruits   1493
   - coffee   1660s
   - olives   1560s
   - pears   1630
   - pineapples   1493
   - pumpkins   1490s
   - rice   1490s
   - wheat   1493

*Not included on *The Great Exchange* map. It was first made in Asia 4,000 years ago.

 Have students use *The Great Exchange* timeline and their own timelines to create **Pre-Columbus menus**.
- New World menus should include only foods made from items indigenous to the Americas prior to 1492.
- Old World menus should include only only foods made from items indigenous to Europe, Africa, and Asia prior to 1492.

 Have your students research **Post-Columbus recipes**. Below is a list of foods from different cultures around the world. Have your students research one of the foods listed below, or provide them with a recipe for the dish. Then have them estimate at what point in history the main ingredients would have been available for that food to be made. You or your students may want to add your own dishes to the list.
- Arroz con pollo
- Carne asada
- Chocolate chip cookies
- Enchiladas
- Guacamole
- Huevos rancheros
- Indian curry
- Irish stew
- Jamaican jerk beef
- Kung pao chicken
- Milk chocolate candy bars
- Pizza with Canadian bacon and pineapple
- Potatoes au gratin
- Pumpkin pie
- Quesadillas
- Spaghetti with marinara sauce
- Szechuan pork
- Turkey with stuffing

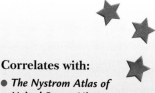

Correlates with:
- *The Nystrom Atlas of United States History,* pages 26–27

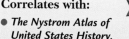

EUROPEAN SETTLEMENTS
1640

Key Elements

★ *European Settlements* map
★ *Northeastern Settlements* map
★ *Newcomers to the Americas* graph

Getting Started

To give students an overview of
European Settlements, ask them:

- What is the title of the main map?
- What part of the world is shown on this map?
- What do the colors on this map mean?
- What do the dates on the map represent?
- What is the title of the smaller map?
- How is it related to the main map?
- What do the words in all capital letters show on this map?
- Look at the graph. What does it show? How?

Teaching Notes and Mapping Activities

~ Who Settled Where?
~ Spanish Settlements
~ Northeastern Settlements

The Nystrom UNITED STATES HISTORY Series

NYSTROM
DIVISION OF HERFF JONES, INC.

1494 Treaty Line of Tordesillas

See detail at right.

1609 Santa Fe

1565 St. Augustine

1531 Guadalajara

1519 Havana

1325 Tenochtitlan (Mexico City)

1521 Aztecs conquered.

1533 Cartagena

1567 Caracas

1591 San Juan

1496 Santo Domingo

1630 Dutch seize control of Portuguese territory.

1534 Quito

1538 Santa Fe de Bogota

1532 Incas conquered.

1535 Recife

1535 Lima

1300 Cuzco

1549 Salvador

1532 Sao Vicente

NORTH AMERICA

SOUTH AMERICA

ASIA

ARCTIC OCEAN

North Pole

EUROPE

ATLANTIC OCEAN

PACIFIC OCEAN

EQUATOR

Gulf of Mexico

Hispaniola

Puerto Rico

Cuba

Jamaica

WEST INDIES

Caribbean Sea

Spain

Portugal

TROPIC OF CANCER

TROPIC OF CAPRICORN

1640 EUROPEAN SETTLEMENTS

Settlement Regions

- English
- French
- Dutch
- Portuguese
- Swedish
- Spanish

1565 Date founded
• Settlement

| 0 | 1000 | 2000 miles |
| 0 | 1000 | 2000 kilometers |

Map shows present boundaries.

See map at left for key to regions.

1608 Quebec

1642 Montreal

1614 Fort Nassau

1633 Windsor

PEQUOT

1626 Salem

1630 Boston

1620 Plymouth

1636 Providence

1638 New Haven

1624 New Amsterdam (Manhattan Island)

1638 Fort Christina

1634 St. Mary's

1607 Jamestown

"Lost Colony" is abandoned by 1590.

1585 Roanoke Island

IROQUOIS

WAMPANOAG

POWHATAN

ATLANTIC OCEAN

Lake Ontario

Lake Erie

Lake Huron

Lake Champlain

St. Lawrence R.

Connecticut R.

Delaware R.

James R.

Chesapeake Bay

NORTHEASTERN SETTLEMENTS

PEQUOT Indian nation

| 0 | 100 | 200 miles |
| 0 | 100 | 200 kilometers |

Map shows present boundaries.

NEWCOMERS TO THE AMERICAS

Dutch 200

French 360

English 7,600

Portuguese 45,000

1640 Almost all Africans in the Americas are slaves.

African 107,000

Spanish 450,000

| 0 | 100,000 | 200,000 | 300,000 | 400,000 | 500,000 |

NYSTROM DIVISION OF HERFF JONES, INC.

MARKABLE

European Settlements, 1640 **5**

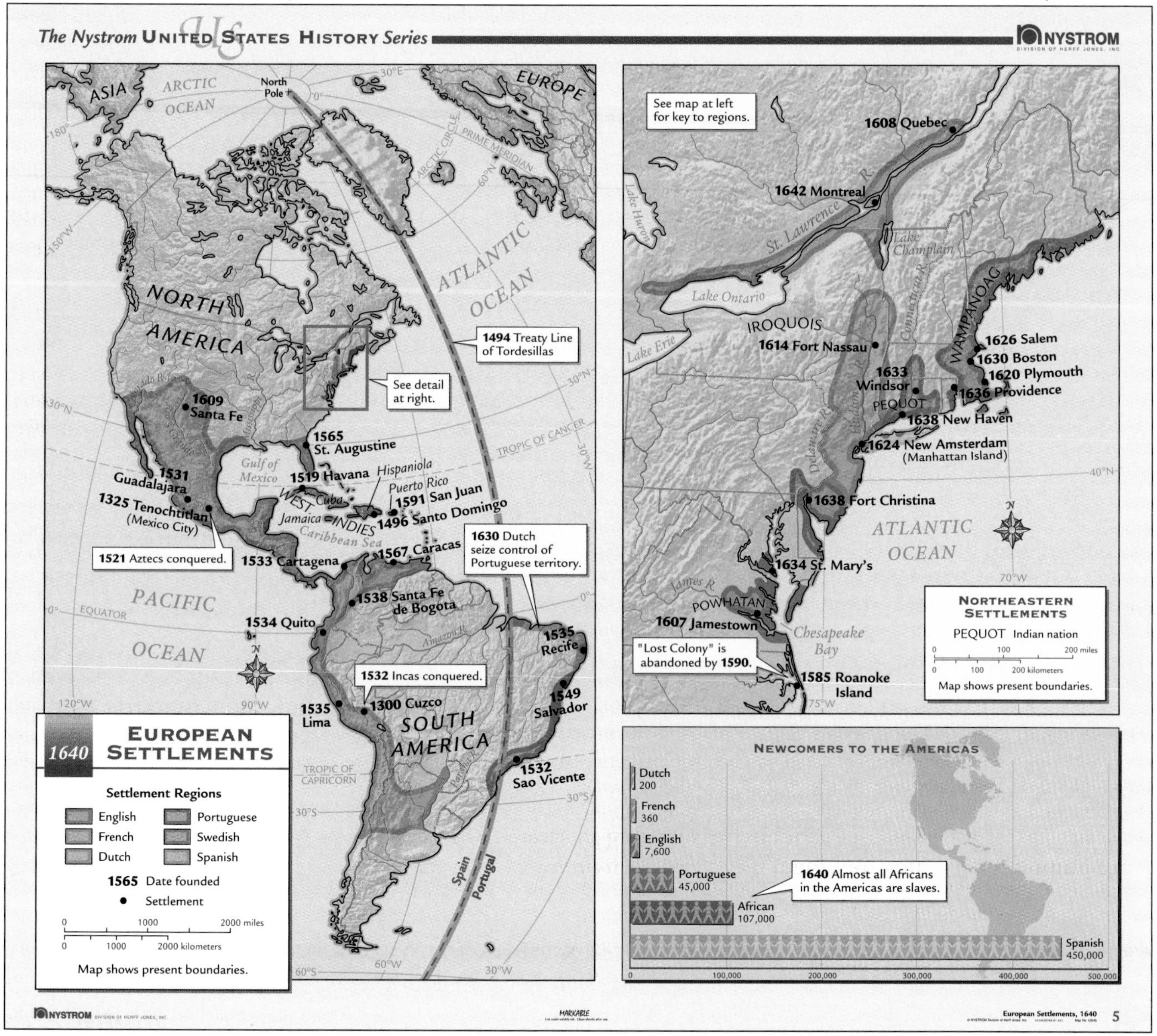

Who Settled Where?

Objective: *To identify regions in which people from various European countries established settlements.*

Teaching Notes and Mapping Activity

You or your students can mark the following on the *European Settlements* map.

1. Long before Europeans arrived, North and South America were settled by **Native Americans**. With your finger, outline the continents.

2. Vikings had settled in North America 500 years before the Spanish arrived. However, by 1640, their settlements in **Greenland** and **Newfoundland** had been abandoned. Across Greenland, write **VIKINGS**. Then draw a slash **/** through it.

3. The Spanish settlements in the Americas were more widespread and permanent than the Viking settlements.

   a. Trade winds carried Spanish ships to the Caribbean region. By 1640, the Spanish settlement region was spread between 35°N and 35°S. With your finger, outline areas of Spanish settlement.

   b. Label one of the large orange areas **SPANISH**.

4. The Portuguese were the next Europeans to begin settling in the Americas. The **Treaty of Tordesillas** limited the area the Portuguese could settle.

   a. The treaty line was set before most of the Americas were explored. The treaty gave Spain land west of the line and Portugal land east of the line. With your finger, outline the area east of the treaty line that Portugal could settle.

   b. By 1640, Portugal had already lost some territory in South America to the Dutch. With your finger, outline the remaining areas of Portuguese settlement.

   c. Label the largest brown area **PORTUGUESE**.

5. The English were the next Europeans to settle in the Americas. Their first settlement on **Roanoke Island** was abandoned. Their second settlement at **Jamestown** struggled, but survived.

   a. On the *Northeastern Settlements* map, with your finger, outline the three areas of English settlement.

   b. On the *European Settlements* map, at the top of the area outlined in red, write **ENGLISH**.

6. The French also began settling in the Americas. Their first settlements in **Florida** were destroyed by the Spanish or abandoned. Their later settlements along the **St. Lawrence River** survived.

   a. On the *Northeastern Settlements* map, with your finger, outline the area of French settlement.

   b. On the *European Settlements* map, in the area outlined in red, add **FRENCH**.

7. The Dutch began settling in North America along the **Hudson River**.

   a. On the *Northeastern Settlements* map, with your finger, outline the area of Dutch settlement.

   b. On the *European Settlements* map, in the area outlined in red, add **DUTCH**.

8. Swedish settlers clustered in **Delaware** and **New Jersey**.

   a. On the *Northeastern Settlements* map, with your finger, outline the area of Swedish settlement.

   b. On the *European Settlements* map, in the area outlined in red, add **SWEDISH**.

 On the *Newcomers to the Americas* graph, have students add the date of each group's first settlement to the bar. (African Americans were brought to the Americas starting around 1510.) Then ask students to compare date of arrival with size of population in 1640.

Correlates with:
● *The Nystrom Atlas of United States History,* pages 28, 30–31

Objective: *To identify areas claimed by Spanish explorers and their later settlements.*

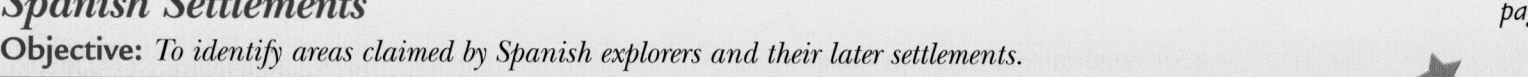

Teaching Notes and Mapping Activity

You or your students can mark the following on the *European Settlements* map.

1. Between 1492 and 1504, Christopher Columbus made four voyages to the Americas. On each voyage he claimed more land in the **Caribbean** for Spain. (Point out to students that the place names used in this lesson are modern-day names.)

   a. Optional: Use *The Nystrom United States History Series 2* wall map or transparency to trace Columbus' four voyages.

   b. On the *European Settlements* map, mark each of the following places with a dot.
   - The Bahamas, north of Cuba
   - Trinidad, the island along the north coast of South America (below the word *Caracas*)
   - The boundary between South America and Panama
   - The boundary between Mexico and the rest of Middle America

   c. In the same order, draw a circle to connect the dots.

   d. To the right of the circle, write **COLUMBUS**.

2. In 1496, Columbus established **Santo Domingo** on the island of Hispaniola. This was the first Spanish settlement in the Americas. Label Santo Domingo **#1**.

3. In 1513, Ponce de León claimed **Florida** for Spain.

   a. Optional: Use the *U.S. History Series 2* wall map or transparency to trace Ponce de León's route.

   b. On the *European Settlements* map, outline Florida.

   c. North of Florida, write **PONCE DE LEÓN**.

   d. St. Augustine is the oldest permanent settlement in what is now the United States. Label it **#1 U.S.**

4. In 1521, Cortés conquered the **Aztec** empire in Mexico. He claimed the land for Spain.

   a. Optional: Use *U.S. History Series 2* wall map or transparency to trace Cortés' route.

   b. On the *European Settlements* map, outline Mexico, going only as far north as the Tropic of Cancer.

   c. To the left of Mexico, write **CORTÉS**.

   d. Have students identify any settlements in this region.

5. In 1532, Pizarro conquered the **Inca** empire in South America. He claimed the land for Spain.

   a. Pizarro marched along western South America. From Quito to Cuzco, with your finger, draw a line.

   b. To the left of South America, write **PIZARRO**.

   c. Have students identify settlements along western South America.

6. Between 1528 and 1543, Cabeza de Vaca, Coronado, and Cabrillo explored the North American **southwest**. Each claimed land for Spain.

   a. Optional: Use *U.S. History Series 2* wall map or transparency to trace each of their routes across the southwest.

   b. On the *European Settlements* map, outline the remaining Spanish settlement region north of Aztec Mexico.

   c. Above the region, write **CABEZA DE VACA**, **CORONADO**, and **CABRILLO**.

   d. Have students identify any settlements in this region.

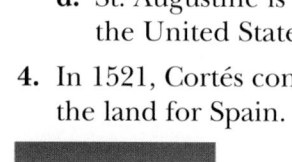 For further discussion:
   - Which cities were established before the Spanish arrived?
   - Do you think Spain was right to claim land in the Americas? Why?

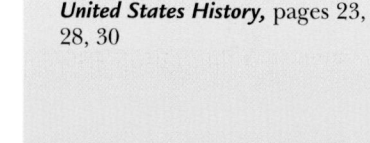

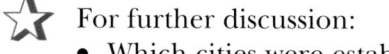

Correlates with:
- *The Nystrom Atlas of United States History,* pages 23, 28, 30

Northeastern Settlements

Objective: *To identify areas in northeast North America claimed by European explorers and their later settlements.*

Teaching Notes and Mapping Activity

You or your students can mark the following on the *Northeastern Settlements* map.

1. Between 1524 and 1615, France sent three explorers to the Americas. **Verrazano** explored the east coast of North America. **Cartier** and **Champlain** both explored the St. Lawrence River. Cartier and Champlain claimed the land along this river for France.

    a. Optional: Use *The Nystrom United States History Series 3* wall map or transparency to trace each of their routes to North America.

    b. On the *Northeastern Settlements* map, outline the French settlement region.

    c. North of the region, write and underline **FRANCE**.

    d. Below FRANCE, write **CARTIER** and **CHAMPLAIN**.

    e. Have students identify any settlements that the French established in the region.

2. In 1609 the Dutch sent one explorer to the Americas. **Hudson** explored the east coast and the river that now bears his name. Hudson claimed the Hudson River Valley for the Netherlands.

    a. Optional: Use the *U.S. History Series 3* wall map or transparency to trace Hudson's route to the Hudson River.

    b. On the *Northeastern Settlements* map, outline Dutch settlements.

    c. To the left of the region, write and underline **NETHERLANDS**.

    d. Below that, write **HUDSON**.

    e. Have students identify any Dutch settlements in the region.

3. Between 1497 and 1610, England sent three explorers to the Americas. **Cabot** explored Newfoundland, **Frobisher** explored Greenland, and **Hudson** (who also sailed for the Dutch), explored the bay that now bears his name. They each claimed land for England.

    a. Optional: Use the *U.S. History Series 3* wall map or transparency to trace Cabot's, Frobisher's, and Hudson's routes.

    b. On the *European Settlements* map, locate their land claims.
       - On Newfoundland, write **ENGLAND-CABOT**.
       - On Greenland, write **ENGLAND-FROBISHER**.
       - On Hudson Bay, write **ENGLAND-HUDSON**.

    c. The English also settled in regions of the modern-day United States unclaimed by the French and Dutch. On the *Northeastern Settlements* map, outline three English settlement regions.

    d. To the right of each region, write **ENGLAND**.

    e. Have students identify the settlements in each region.

4. Around the year 1000, Vikings from Scandinavia explored and claimed land in the Americas. **Bjarni Herjolfsson** claimed Greenland and **Leif Ericson** claimed Newfoundland for the Vikings. These land claims were long forgotten by 1640. So the Swedish could not claim these regions and had to settle in regions unclaimed by the French, Dutch, and English.

    a. On the *European Settlements* map, write **HERJOLFSSON** on Greenland and **ERICSON** on Newfoundland.

    b. Now put an **X** through their names.

    c. On the *Northeastern Settlements* map, outline the Swedish settlement.

    d. To the left of the region, write **SWEDEN**.

 Have students compare Spanish settlements with other European settlements. In terms of size and location, how do they correlate with the *Newcomers to the Americas* graph?

Correlates with:
- *The Nystrom Atlas of United States History,* pages 22, 31

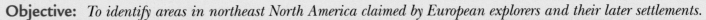

THIRTEEN COLONIES
1750

Key Elements

★ *Thirteen Colonies* map

★ *Religion in the Colonies* map

★ *Colonial Region Today* map

★ Locator map

Getting Started

To give students an overview of *Thirteen Colonies*, ask them:

- What is the title of the main map?

- What year does it represent?

- What part of the United States does this map show? (Point out the locator map.)

- What part of the United States is shown on the two smaller maps?

- What does the map in the upper right show?

- What does the map in the lower right show?

- On the *Thirteen Colonies* and *Colonial Region Today* maps, what do the colors represent?

Teaching Notes and Mapping Activities

~ Establishing Colonies

~ Religion in the Colonies

~ Colonial Region Then and Now

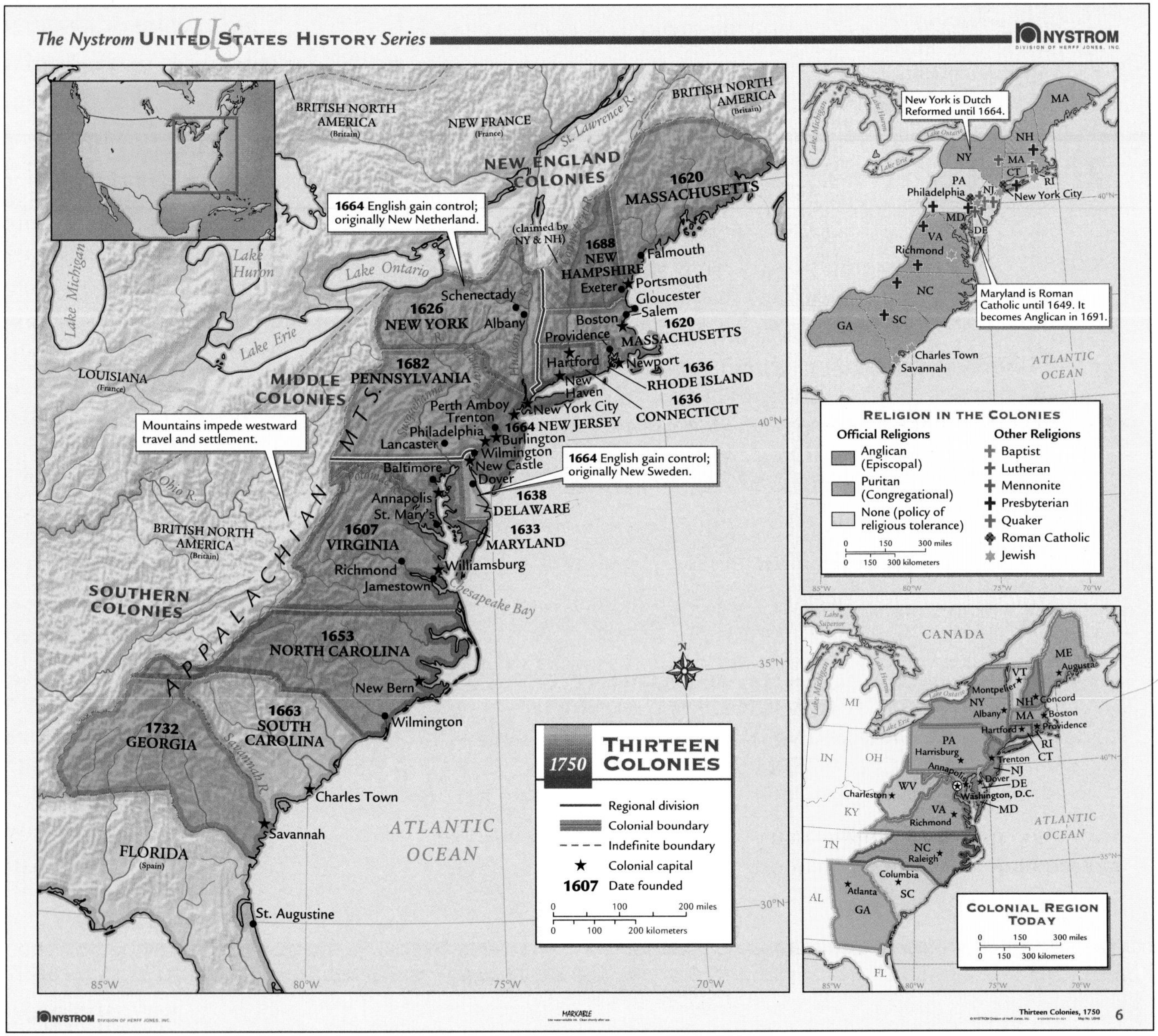

The Nystrom UNITED STATES HISTORY Series

NYSTROM
DIVISION OF HERFF JONES, INC.

BRITISH NORTH AMERICA (Britain)

NEW FRANCE (France)

NEW ENGLAND COLONIES

1620 MASSACHUSETTS

1664 English gain control; originally New Netherland.

(claimed by NY & NH)

1688 NEW HAMPSHIRE
Falmouth
Exeter
Portsmouth
Gloucester
Salem

Schenectady

1626 NEW YORK
Albany

Boston
Providence
1620 MASSACHUSETTS

Lake Michigan
Lake Huron
Lake Ontario
Lake Erie

LOUISIANA (France)

1682 MIDDLE PENNSYLVANIA COLONIES

Hartford
New Haven
Newport
1636 RHODE ISLAND
1636 CONNECTICUT

Mountains impede westward travel and settlement.

Perth Amboy
Trenton
Philadelphia
Lancaster
Burlington
1664 NEW JERSEY
New York City

Ohio R.

Baltimore
Wilmington
New Castle
Dover

1664 English gain control; originally New Sweden.

BRITISH NORTH AMERICA (Britain)

Annapolis
St. Mary's
1638 DELAWARE
1633 MARYLAND

1607 VIRGINIA

Richmond
Jamestown
Williamsburg
Chesapeake Bay

SOUTHERN COLONIES

1653 NORTH CAROLINA
New Bern

1663 SOUTH CAROLINA
1732 GEORGIA
Wilmington

Charles Town

FLORIDA (Spain)

Savannah

ATLANTIC OCEAN

St. Augustine

THIRTEEN COLONIES
1750

— Regional division
▨ Colonial boundary
--- Indefinite boundary
★ Colonial capital
1607 Date founded

0   100   200 miles
0   100   200 kilometers

85°W   80°W   75°W   70°W

RELIGION IN THE COLONIES

New York is Dutch Reformed until 1664.

MA
NH
NY
MA CT
PA
Philadelphia
NJ
New York City
MD
DE
VA
Richmond

Maryland is Roman Catholic until 1649. It becomes Anglican in 1691.

NC
GA SC
Charles Town
Savannah

ATLANTIC OCEAN

Official Religions
▨ Anglican (Episcopal)
▨ Puritan (Congregational)
□ None (policy of religious tolerance)

Other Religions
✝ Baptist
✝ Lutheran
✝ Mennonite
✝ Presbyterian
✝ Quaker
✝ Roman Catholic
✡ Jewish

0   150   300 miles
0   150   300 kilometers

85°W   80°W   75°W   70°W

COLONIAL REGION TODAY

CANADA

Lake Superior
Lake Michigan
Lake Huron
Lake Erie
Lake Ontario

MI

ME
Augusta
VT
Montpelier
NH Concord
NY
Albany
MA Boston
Hartford Providence
RI
CT
PA
Harrisburg
Trenton NJ
Annapolis Dover DE
Washington, D.C.
MD
WV
Charleston
VA
Richmond

IN
OH

KY

TN

NC
Raleigh

SC
Columbia

AL
Atlanta
GA

FL

ATLANTIC OCEAN

0   150   300 miles
0   150   300 kilometers

85°W   80°W   75°W   70°W

NYSTROM DIVISION OF HERFF JONES, INC.

MARKABLE

Thirteen Colonies, 1750   **6**

Establishing Colonies

Objective: *To describe the country of origin of the first settlers in each colony.*

Teaching Notes and Mapping Activity

You or your students can mark the following on the *Thirteen Colonies* map. Before introducing a colony, ask students to identify the colony that was founded next.

1. The first *permanent* **English** colony was established in 1607 in **Virginia** and was named Jamestown. Its first settlers were men and boys looking for gold. Outline Virginia and label it **E** for English.

2. Thirteen years later, the English settled a second colony in Plymouth, **Massachusetts**. Many of its first settlers were Pilgrim families looking for religious freedom. Label Massachusetts **E**.

3. **Dutch** settlers founded the third colony, New Netherland, in 1626. In 1664, the Dutch surrendered their territory to the English. New Netherland became **New York**. Label New York **D** for its original Dutch settlers.

4. **Maryland**, the fourth colony, was given to the first Lord Baltimore, George Calvert, by the king. However, Calvert died before the charter was signed. His son received the land. Maryland was settled by the English, but neither Calvert ever saw the colony. Label Maryland **E**.

5. The fifth and sixth colonies were settled by English colonists who left or who were driven out of Massachusetts. Many of these colonists moved to **Connecticut** and **Rhode Island** looking for religious freedom. Label both colonies **E**.

6. The seventh colony, **Delaware**, was first settled by the **Swedish**. In 1654, New Sweden (as it was called) was captured by the Dutch and became part of New Netherland. Ten years later, it was captured by the English. Label Delaware **S** for its original Swedish settlers.

7. The very first English colony wasn't Jamestown; it was Roanoke in what is now **North Carolina**. Arriving in 1587, the English settlers mysteriously disappeared a few years later.

Over a century later, North Carolina and **South Carolina** became part of one large land grant. These eighth and ninth colonies were settled by the English. Label both colonies **E**.

8. **New Jersey**, the tenth colony, was settled by the Dutch in the north and the Swedes in the south. Like its neighbor, Delaware, the Swedes were forced out by the Dutch and the Dutch land was captured by the English. Label New Jersey **D** in the north and **S** in the south.

9. **Pennsylvania**, the eleventh colony, was originally part of New Sweden. But, like its neighbors, New Sweden was captured by the Dutch and then by the English. In 1681, the colony was granted to William Penn in payment for a debt. Label Pennsylvania **S** for its original settlers.

10. **New Hampshire**, the twelfth colony, was settled by the English. It was part of Massachusetts from 1641 to 1680 before it became its own colony. Label New Hampshire **E**.

11. The thirteenth colony, **Georgia**, was originally part of South Carolina. English settlers arrived in 1732. Label Georgia **E**.

 Ask students to look at the groups that originally settled each colony. Have them look for patterns, comparing New England, Middle, and Southern colonies.

 Using the *Thirteen Colonies* map, have students make a timeline charting the founding of the colonies and other key events in their histories.

Correlates with:
- **The Nystrom Atlas of United States History,** pages 31–33
- **Mapping United States History** To the Present, Lesson 9 To the Early 1900s, Lesson 11

Religion in the Colonies

Objective: *To explain why different colonies had different religions.*

Teaching Notes and Mapping Activity

You or your students can mark the following on the *Religion in the Colonies* map.

1. The **New England Colonies** were settled by **Puritans** looking for freedom to practice their religion. The Pilgrims who settled in Plymouth were Puritans.

   a. Draw a line along the eastern boundary of New York. At the top of the map, east of that line, write and underline **NEW ENGLAND**.

   b. Most of the New Englanders were Puritan. Below your regional label, write **PURITAN**.

2. While Puritans found religious freedom for themselves in New England, they did not grant the same freedom to other religious groups. Some religious groups were forced out, others left voluntarily. Roger Williams, a minister who called for religious and political freedom, was driven out of Massachusetts. He and many other religious exiles settled in **Rhode Island**.

   a. Outline Rhode Island.

   b. Have students name the religious groups that settled in Rhode Island.

3. Many **Southern Colonies** were founded by English noblemen who were **Anglican**, members of the Church of England. In many of these colonies, people could not vote unless they were Anglican. Colonists were also taxed to support the Anglican Church.

   a. Draw a line along the northern boundary of Maryland. West of the colonies and south of that line, write and underline **SOUTHERN**.

   b. Most of the people in the Southern Colonies were Anglican. Below your regional label, write **ANGLICAN**.

4. However, one of the Southern Colonies was not founded by Anglicans. **Maryland** was founded by an English nobleman who was **Roman Catholic**. His colony was founded for religious freedom for all Christians. (However, non-Christians would be hanged.)

   a. Outline Maryland.

   b. Have students name the religious groups that settled in this colony.

5. The **Middle Colonies** tended to be tolerant of all religions. Delaware, originally part of New Sweden, had a policy of religious tolerance. New Jersey's charter granted freedom of religion. Men of any religion could vote. Pennsylvania was founded by William Penn, a **Quaker**. He felt all religions were equal. In New Netherlands (later New York), the Dutch West Indies Company forced the **Dutch Reformed** settlers to admit **Jewish** settlers.

   a. West of Pennsylvania and New York, write and underline **MIDDLE**.

   b. Many settlers in the Middle Colonies were tolerant of most religions. Below your regional label, write **TOLERANT**.

   c. Now have students name the religions of settlers in each of the Middle Colonies.

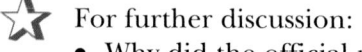 For further discussion:
   - Why did the official religion of New York change in 1664?
   - Where did Baptists settle? Lutherans? Roman Catholics? Mennonites?
   - Based on this information, why do you think Presbyterians settled so far away from the coasts?

Correlates with:
- *The Nystrom Atlas of United States History,* pages 32–33

Colonial Region Then and Now

Objective: *To compare colonial and state boundaries of 1750 and today.*

Teaching Notes and Mapping Activity

You or your students can mark the following on the *Thirteen Colonies* map.

1. Several colonies were roughly the **same size** in 1750 as they are today.

   a. Have students compare the *Thirteen Colonies* map with the *Colonial Region Today* map. Ask them to identify any colonies that were roughly the same size in 1750 as they are today. (Rhode Island, Connecticut, New Jersey, Delaware, Maryland, South Carolina)

   b. On the *Thirteen Colonies* map, label each with an *equal* sign **=**.

   c. Draw a large legend box in the Atlantic Ocean. In it, write **= SAME SIZE AS TODAY**.

2. Some colonies were **smaller** in 1750 than they are today. Many of these colonies were limited by mountains to the west.

   a. Have students again compare the two maps and identify any colonies that were smaller in size in 1750 than they are today. (New York, Pennsylvania, North Carolina, Georgia)

   b. On the *Thirteen Colonies* map, label each with a *less than* sign **<**.

   c. In the legend box, write **< SMALLER THAN TODAY**.

   d. In 1750, the Appalachian Mountains were difficult to cross. Few people settled west of them. From Georgia to New York, along their western boundaries, draw mountain symbols ∧∧∧ .

   e. When neighboring land was claimed by other countries, expansion was also limited.
   - Spain claimed Florida, which is south of Georgia. Across Florida, write **SPANISH**.
   - France claimed land north of New York. North of the 1750 New York boundary, write **FRENCH**.

   f. Extend the boundaries of all four of these smaller colonies with a dotted line to show their present-day size.

3. Two colonies were **larger** in 1750 than they are today. These colonies claimed land that is now a part of other states.

   a. Have students once again compare the two maps and identify the two colonies that were larger in size in 1750 than they are today. (Massachusetts, New Hampshire)

   b. On the *Thirteen Colonies* map, label each with a *greater than* sign **>**.

   c. In the legend box, write **> LARGER THAN TODAY**.

   d. Massachusetts included land that is now part of Maine. Label **MAINE**.

   e. New Hampshire claimed land that is now part of Vermont. (New York claimed that same land.) Label **VERMONT**.

   f. Extend the boundaries of Maine and Vermont with a dotted line

4. Virginia both gained and lost land between 1750 and today. In 1750 it included land that is now part of West Virginia. However, it did not include land in the Appalachians that is part of the present-day state.

   a. On Virginia, put a *question* mark **?**

   b. Outline West Virginia and label it **W.V.**

   c. Also extend the boundary of Virginia with a dotted line.

 Have students make a chart comparing the location of colonial capitals in 1750 with state capitals today. Ask them to indicate whether each capital was on the coast or inland and possible reasons for these locations.

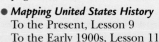

Correlates with:
- *The Nystrom Atlas of United States History,* pages 32–33, 6–7
- *Mapping United States History* To the Present, Lesson 9 To the Early 1900s, Lesson 11

SLAVERY IN THE AMERICAS
1400s–1800s

Key Elements

★ *Slavery in the British Colonies* map

★ *Triangles of Trade* map

★ *Destinations of the Slave Trade* map

★ Locator map

Getting Started

To give students an overview of *Slavery in the Americas*, ask them:

- What do the symbols in the *Slavery in the British Colonies* map mean?

- What do the arrows on this map indicate?

- What do the arrows on the *Triangles of Trade* map indicate?

- Which three continents were involved in the Triangle Trade?

- What does the width of the arrows on the *Destinations of the Slave Trade* map indicate?

- What does the text box on this map tell you?

- Which four continents were involved in the slave trade?

Teaching Notes and Mapping Activities

～ From Indentured Servants to Slaves

～ The Economics of Slavery, Part I

～ The Economics of Slavery, Part II

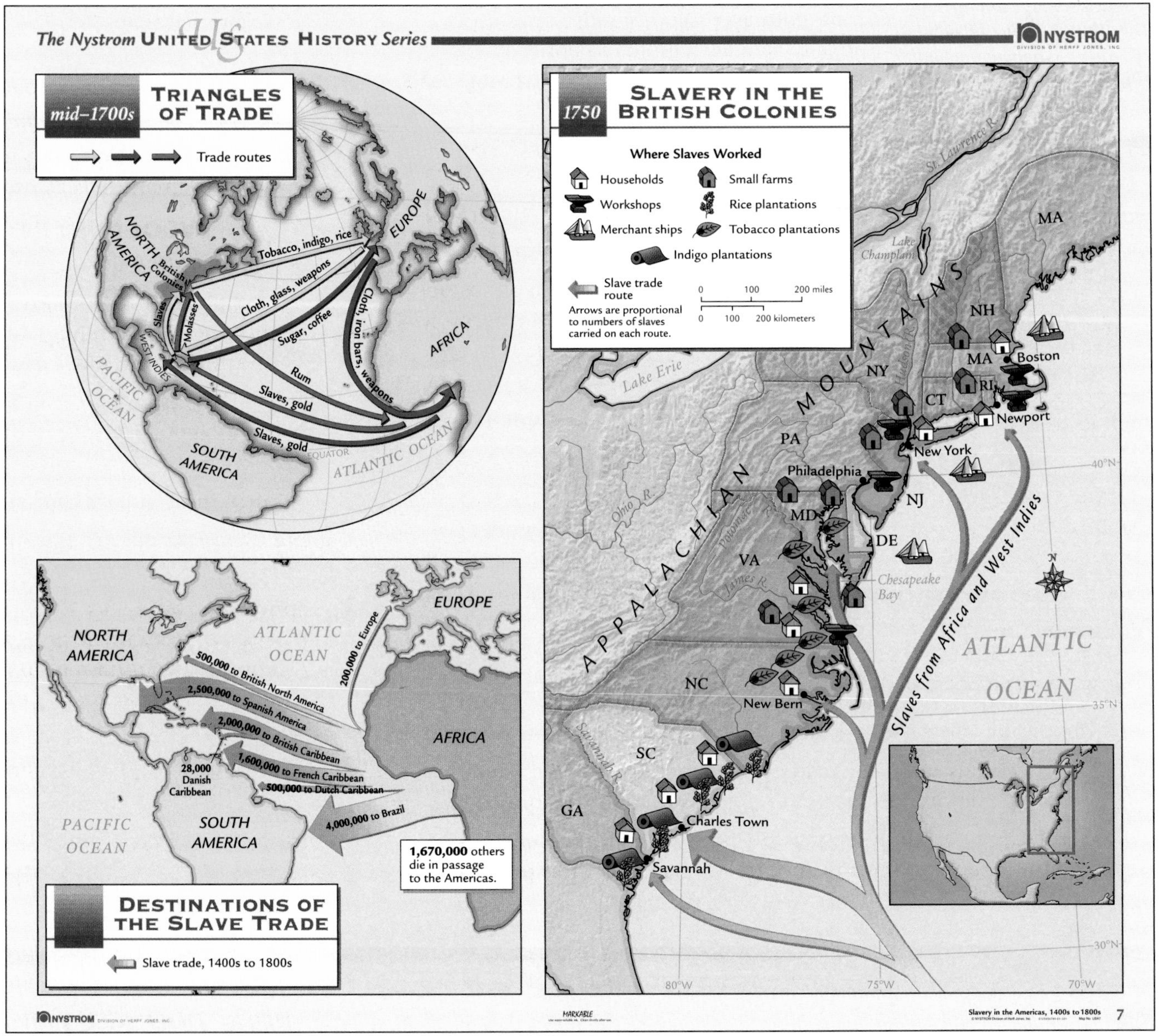

The Nystrom UNITED STATES HISTORY *Series*

NYSTROM
DIVISION OF HERFF JONES, INC.

TRIANGLES OF TRADE
mid–1700s

⇨ ⇨ ⇨ Trade routes

NORTH AMERICA
British Colonies
EUROPE
AFRICA
SOUTH AMERICA
WEST INDIES
PACIFIC OCEAN
ATLANTIC OCEAN
EQUATOR

Tobacco, indigo, rice
Cloth, glass, weapons
Cloth, iron bars, weapons
Sugar, coffee
Slaves
Molasses
Rum
Slaves, gold
Slaves, gold

DESTINATIONS OF THE SLAVE TRADE

⬅ Slave trade, 1400s to 1800s

NORTH AMERICA
ATLANTIC OCEAN
EUROPE
AFRICA
SOUTH AMERICA
PACIFIC OCEAN

200,000 to Europe
500,000 to British North America
2,500,000 to Spanish America
2,000,000 to British Caribbean
28,000 Danish Caribbean
1,600,000 to French Caribbean
500,000 to Dutch Caribbean
4,000,000 to Brazil

1,670,000 others die in passage to the Americas.

SLAVERY IN THE BRITISH COLONIES
1750

Where Slaves Worked

🏠 Households   🏚 Small farms

⚒ Workshops   🌾 Rice plantations

⛵ Merchant ships   🌿 Tobacco plantations

📜 Indigo plantations

⬅ Slave trade route

Arrows are proportional to numbers of slaves carried on each route.

| 0 | 100 | 200 miles |
| 0 | 100 | 200 kilometers |

St. Lawrence R.
Lake Champlain
Lake Erie
Ohio R.
APPALACHIAN MOUNTAINS
MA
NH
MA
Boston
NY
CT
RI
Newport
New York
PA
Philadelphia
MD
NJ
DE
Chesapeake Bay
VA
James R.
Potomac R.
NC
New Bern
SC
Savannah R.
Charles Town
GA
Savannah
ATLANTIC OCEAN
Slaves from Africa and West Indies

40°N
35°N
30°N
80°W
75°W
70°W

From Indentured Servants to Slaves

Objective: *To create a timeline that shows the gradual development of slavery in the British Colonies.*

Teaching Notes and Mapping Activity

You or your students can mark the following on the *Slavery in the British Colonies* map.

1. In the early 1600s, most Africans brought to the Colonies were not slaves, but *indentured servants*. This meant that after serving for a certain number of years, they became free.

   a. In the bottom margin of *Slavery in the Americas*, write **INDENTURED SERVANTS** in the left corner and **SLAVES** in the right corner. Create a timeline by drawing an arrow from INDENTURED SERVANTS to SLAVES.

   b. The first Africans in the British Colonies arrived in **1619**. To the right of INDENTURED SERVANTS, above the arrow, write 1619. Below the arrow, write **1ST AFRICANS**.

2. As time went on, laws limiting Africans' opportunities were passed. Each new law took away more rights, pushing black indentured servants closer to slavery.

   a. In 1639 Virginia passed the first law excluding "Negroes" from government protection. To the right of 1619, write **1639**. Below this, write **NO GOVT PROTECTION**.

   b. In 1640 three servants were caught escaping. Two white men had their indenture prolonged. A black man, John Punch, was made a servant for life—a slave. To the right of 1639, write **1640**. Below this, write **JOHN PUNCH, SLAVE**.

3. In 1641 Massachusetts became the first colony to legalize permanent, lifelong slavery based on race.

   a. Across Massachusetts, write **1641**.

   b. Eventually, each of the colonies legalized slavery. Using the following list, label each colony with the year that slavery was recognized as a legal institution.

- 1650-Connecticut
- 1661-Virginia
- 1663-Maryland
- 1664-New York
- 1664-New Jersey
- 1682-South Carolina
- 1700-Pennsylvania
- 1700-Rhode Island
- 1714-New Hampshire
- 1715-North Carolina
- 1721-Delaware
- 1750-Georgia

4. Black indentured servants did not immediately become slaves when slavery was legalized. The transformation was gradual. New laws continued to erode their rights, until finally, African Americans had no rights at all.

   a. In Europe, slaves who converted to Christianity were often freed. In 1667 Virginia passed a law that blacks who became Christians could still be enslaved. On the timeline, to the right of 1640, write **1667**. Below that, write ✝ ≠ **FREEDOM**.

   b. In 1682 Virginia passed a law establishing a racial distinction between servants and slaves. To the right of 1667, write **1682**. Below that, write **WHITE = SERVANT, BLACK = SLAVE**.

   c. In 1705 Virginia passed a law stating that all non-whites brought to the colony to work as servants were, in fact, slaves—the property of whoever bought them. As property, they had no rights. Other colonies soon followed Virginia, and slavery as a racial institution had truly begun. To the right of 1682, write **1705**. Below that, write **SLAVES = PROPERTY**.

 Tell your students to look at the Destinations of the Slave Trade map. Have them create a bar graph comparing the number of Africans transported to each region of the Americas. You may want to have them include a bar showing the number who died in passage.

Correlates with:
- *The Nystrom Atlas of United States History,* pages 34–35
- *Mapping United States History,* To the Early 1900s, Lesson 13

The Economics of Slavery, Part I

Objective: *To illustrate the economic differences between the New England, Middle, and Southern Colonies.*

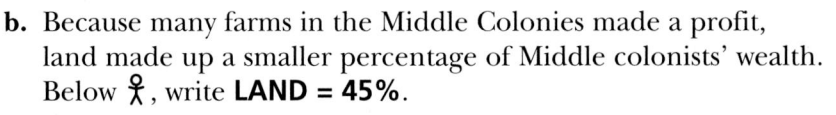

Teaching Notes and Mapping Activity

You or your students can mark the following on the *Slavery in the British Colonies* map.

1. The transformation of large areas in the British Colonies into slave societies was tied to each region's economic activity.

   a. Draw lines marking the boundaries of the New England Colonies, the Middle Colonies, and the Southern Colonies. [See USH6, *Thirteen Colonies, 1750* map.]

   b. Review the symbols on the map, their locations, and the patterns of economic activity in each region.

2. New England's climate and soil were not suited to extensive farming. Most New Englanders were *subsistence farmers*. They raised just enough to feed themselves and their families.

   a. In New England the average wealth of a free, white, male colonist was 45 British pounds. Across the New England Colonies, write ⚥ = **£45**.

   b. The farm itself was usually a New Englander's most valuable asset. Land accounted for more than 61% of his wealth. Below ⚥ write, **LAND = 61%**.

   c. About 15% of New England colonists' wealth came from financial assets, such as cash. Below LAND, write **$ ASSETS = 15%**.

   d. While slavery existed in New England, so few people could afford to own slaves that they made up less than 1% of the average colonist's wealth. Below $, write **SLAVES < 1%**.

3. Milder climates and better soil allowed farmers in the Middle Colonies to raise more crops and sell the excess for a profit. The Middle Colonies also had many *artisans*, or craftworkers.

   a. In the Middle Colonies the average wealth was about £62 per colonist. Across the Middle Colonies, write ⚥ = **£62**.

   b. Because many farms in the Middle Colonies made a profit, land made up a smaller percentage of Middle colonists' wealth. Below ⚥, write **LAND = 45%**.

   c. Trade thrived in the Middle Colonies. Financial assets made up more than one-fourth of the average colonist's wealth. Below LAND, write **$ ASSETS = 26%**.

   d. While slavery was more common than in New England, slaves accounted for only 3% of the average Middle colonist's wealth. Below $, write **SLAVES = 3%**.

4. The South's warm climate and fertile soil made it ideal for large, extremely profitable farms.

   a. In the South, the average wealth was £151 per colonist. Across the Southern Colonies, write ⚥ = **£151**.

   b. Compared farms in other regions, most Southern farms were enormous. Yet land accounted for only 37% of Southern colonists' wealth. Below ⚥, write **LAND = 37%**.

   c. Southern farms needed hundreds of workers. These workers accounted for 38% of Southern colonists' wealth. Below LAND, write **SLAVES = 38%**.

   d. Most Southern wealth consisted of land and slaves. Financial assets made up only a small portion of Southern wealth. Below SLAVES, write **$ ASSETS = 9%**.

☆ Have your students answer the questions below.
  - How would freeing slaves affect Southern plantation owners financially?
  - If a plantation owner bought more land, what else would he be likely to buy? Why?
  - Why is the "average colonist" a free white male?

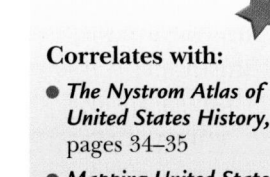

Correlates with:
- *The Nystrom Atlas of United States History,* pages 34–35
- *Mapping United States History,* To the Early 1900s, Lesson 13

The Economics of Slavery, Part II

Objective: *To show the percentage of slaves transported to the different Colonial regions at different periods of time.*

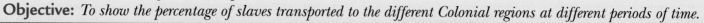

Teaching Notes and Mapping Activity

You or your students can mark the following on the *Slavery in the British Colonies* and *Triangles of Trade* maps.

1. From the time the British Colonies were founded, the South imported more slaves than the other two regions combined.

    a. On the *Slavery in the British Colonies* map, draw lines marking the boundaries of the New England Colonies, the Middle Colonies, and the Southern Colonies.

    b. Southern plantations required a huge number of workers. By 1700 more than eight out of every ten slaves brought to the Colonies were sent to the South. In the Atlantic Ocean between Charles Town and New Bern, write **1700 - 81%**. Then draw a line from it to the arrow pointing to Maryland and a line to the arrow pointing to Savannah.

    c. The smaller farms in the Middle Colonies didn't need as many agricultural laborers. In 1700 only 13% of imported slaves were sent to the Middle Colonies. Where 40°N meets the arrow pointing to New York, write **1700 - 13%**.

    d. Family farms in New England required little extra labor. Most slaves worked in households, workshops, or shipping ports. In 1700 only 6% of all imported slaves were sent to New England. Left of the arrow pointing to Newport, write **1700 - 6%**.

2. As time went on, Southern plantations grew and the number indentured servants shrank. The South imported even more slaves.

    a. In 1750 more than 9 out of every 10 imported slaves were destined for the Southern Colonies. Below 1700 - 81%, write **1750 - 91%**.

    b. The Middle Colonies were the destination of 6% of all imported slaves. Below 1700 - 13%, write **1750 - 6%**.

    c. Only 3% of slaves imported in 1750 were sent to New England.

Below 1700 - 6%, write **1750 - 3%**.

3. On the eve of American Revolution, nearly all slaves brought to the British Colonies were destined for Southern plantations. The combined number of slaves sent to the Middle Colonies and New England made up only 1% of all imported slaves.

    a. Below 1750 - 91%, write **1772 - 99%**.

    b. Below the spot where the arrows pointing to New York and Newport branch off, write **1772 - 1%**.

4. Slave labor and the plantation system made the Southern Colonies very wealthy. The three largest Southern crops were also three of the most valuable colonial exports.

    a. In 1770 the total value of indigo exports was £132,000. On the *Triangles of Trade* map, above "indigo" write **£132,000**.

    b. Rice crops were even more lucrative, with an export value of £341,000. Below "rice," write **£341,000**.

    c. Tobacco was the king of Colonial crops. The value of tobacco exports in 1770 was more than £900,000! Below "Tobacco," write **£900,000**.

    d. Few products from the Middle Colonies or New England could match the value of these Southern crops. Rum, one of New England's most profitable products, had an export value of only £22,000. Above "Rum," write **£22,000**.

 Have your students create a "slavery cycle" graphic using the phrases below.
- Make more profits
- Buy more slaves
- Grow more crops
- Sell more product

Correlates with:
- ***The Nystrom Atlas of United States History,*** pages 34–35
- ***Mapping United States History,*** To the Early 1900s, Lesson 13

REVOLUTIONARY WAR
1775–1781

Key Elements

★ *Battles in the Colonies* map
★ *Battles Near Britain* map
★ Locator map
★ *Colonists Take Sides* graph

Getting Started

To give students an overview of the *Revolutionary War*, ask them:

● What is the title of the main map?
● What years does the map cover?
● What part of the United States is shown on this map?
● What do the symbols represent?
● What part of the world is shown on the smaller map?
● What do the ship symbols represent?
● What does the graph show?
● Who were the Loyalists? the Patriots?

Teaching Notes and Mapping Activities

～ War in the North
～ War in the South
～ Battles at Sea

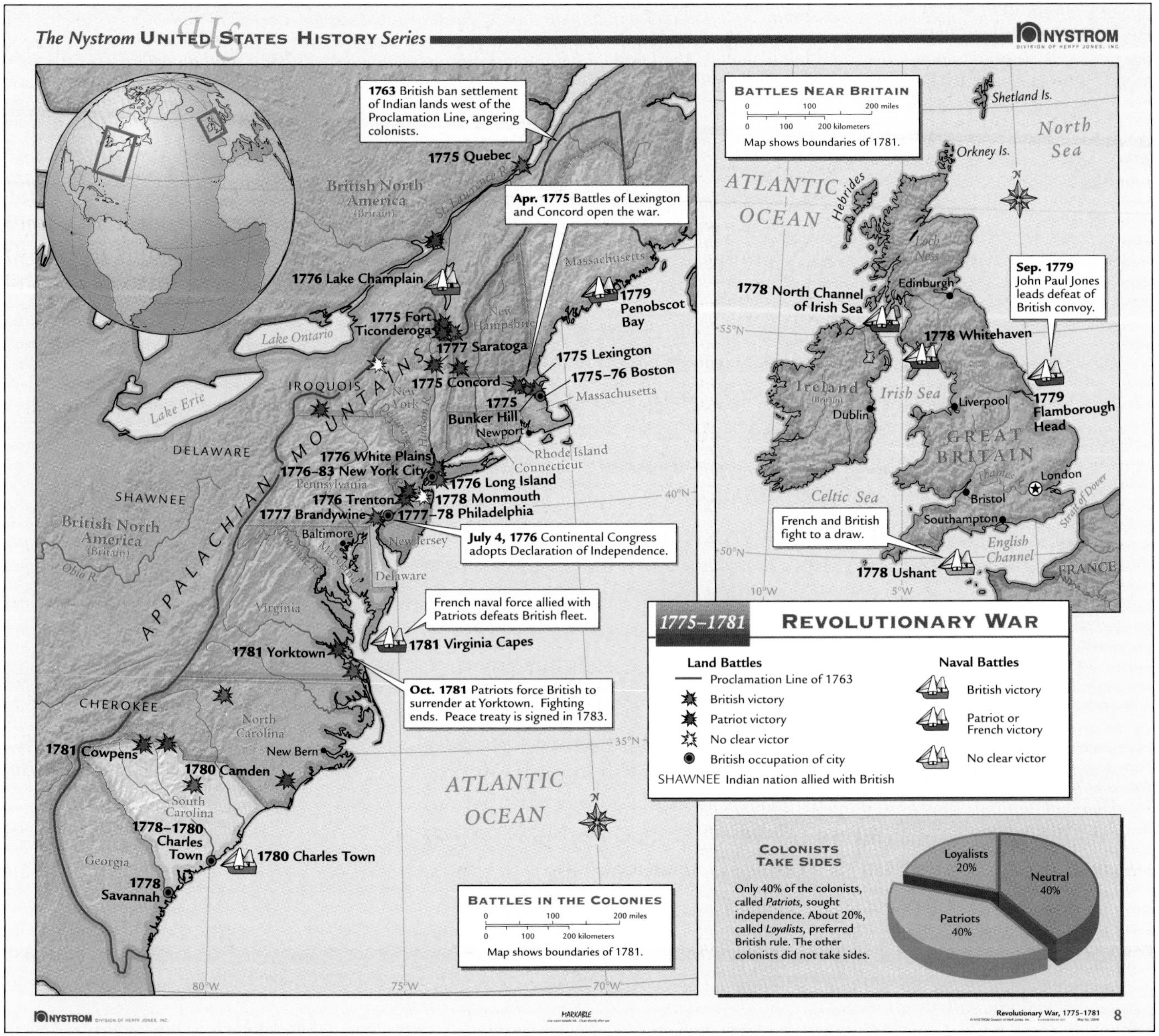

The Nystrom UNITED STATES HISTORY *Series* ◼ NYSTROM
DIVISION OF HERFF JONES, INC.

1763 British ban settlement of Indian lands west of the Proclamation Line, angering colonists.

1775 Quebec

Apr. 1775 Battles of Lexington and Concord open the war.

British North America *(Britain)*

1776 Lake Champlain

1775 Fort Ticonderoga

1777 Saratoga

1779 Penobscot Bay

1775 Lexington

1775 Concord

1775–76 Boston

IROQUOIS

1775 Bunker Hill

DELAWARE

1776 White Plains
1776–83 New York City

1776 Long Island

SHAWNEE

1776 Trenton
1777 Brandywine

1778 Monmouth
1777–78 Philadelphia

British North America *(Britain)*

July 4, 1776 Continental Congress adopts Declaration of Independence.

Baltimore

Virginia

French naval force allied with Patriots defeats British fleet.

1781 Yorktown

1781 Virginia Capes

Oct. 1781 Patriots force British to surrender at Yorktown. Fighting ends. Peace treaty is signed in 1783.

CHEROKEE

North Carolina

New Bern

1781 Cowpens

1780 Camden

South Carolina

1778–1780 Charles Town

Georgia

1780 Charles Town

1778 Savannah

ATLANTIC OCEAN

BATTLES IN THE COLONIES
0   100   200 miles
0   100   200 kilometers
Map shows boundaries of 1781.

BATTLES NEAR BRITAIN
0   100   200 miles
0   100   200 kilometers
Map shows boundaries of 1781.

Shetland Is.

North Sea

Orkney Is.

ATLANTIC OCEAN

Sep. 1779 John Paul Jones leads defeat of British convoy.

1778 North Channel of Irish Sea

Edinburgh

1778 Whitehaven

Ireland

Irish Sea

Liverpool

1779 Flamborough Head

Dublin

GREAT BRITAIN

London

Celtic Sea

Bristol

French and British fight to a draw.

Southampton

English Channel

1778 Ushant

FRANCE

1775–1781   REVOLUTIONARY WAR

Land Battles
— Proclamation Line of 1763
✸ British victory
✸ Patriot victory
✸ No clear victor
⊙ British occupation of city

Naval Battles
⛵ British victory
⛵ Patriot or French victory
⛵ No clear victor

SHAWNEE Indian nation allied with British

COLONISTS TAKE SIDES

Only 40% of the colonists, called *Patriots*, sought independence. About 20%, called *Loyalists*, preferred British rule. The other colonists did not take sides.

Loyalists 20%
Neutral 40%
Patriots 40%

◼ NYSTROM DIVISION OF HERFF JONES, INC.

MARKABLE

War in the North

Objective: *To sequence key events in the Revolutionary War from 1775 to 1777.*

Teaching Notes and Mapping Activity

You or your students can mark the following on the *Battles in the Colonies* map.

1. Colonists in **Massachusetts** were angered by new taxes and tighter British controls. They staged several protests. Concerned about this rebellion, the British decided to arrest Patriot leaders and destroy their supply of guns and gunpowder stored in Concord.

    a. On April 18, 1775, British soldiers marched toward Concord. On their way, they were confronted by colonial minutemen in **Lexington**. Shots were fired and the revolution began. The British won this first battle of the war. Near Lexington, write ①.

    b. The British continued on to **Concord**. They were stopped by minutemen at North Bridge and then retreated to Boston. This was the first Patriot victory of the war. Near Concord, write ②.

2. The Patriots needed artillery. In May, they captured **Fort Ticonderoga** and its cannons. The Patriots hauled the heavy cannons to Boston. Near Fort Ticonderoga, write ③.

3. One night in June, the Patriots dug fortifications on **Breed's Hill** near Boston. Nearby **Bunker Hill** also was occupied by Patriots. The next day British attacked both hills in the bloodiest battle of the war. Roughly 1,000 British and 440 Patriot soldiers were killed or wounded. Near Bunker Hill, write ④.

4. When the Fort Ticonderoga cannons arrived in Boston, the Patriots set them up on a hill overlooking the city. In March of 1776, the British decided to **evacuate Boston**. From Boston, draw an arrow northeast to British North America (Canada).

5. On July 4, 1776, the Continental Congress declared **independence** from Great Britain. Near the Declaration of Independence callout box, write ⑤.

6. That same summer, British troops landed on Staten Island near New York City. George Washington and his troops were on nearby **Long Island**. On August 27, the British surrounded and captured some of the Patriots. However, the rest of Washington's troops managed to escape.

    a. On Long Island, write ⑥.

    b. The British then occupied **New York City**. Circle its occupation symbol.

7. Later that year, the British set up winter quarters in New Jersey. On December 26, Washington's troops surprised Hessians in **Trenton** and took 900 prisoners. The Hessians were German soldiers hired to fight for the British. Near Trenton, write ⑦.

8. In 1777 the British took Philadelphia.

    a. The British sailed from New York City to the tip of Chesapeake Bay. Draw an arrow from New York south to the Virginia Capes. Then continue the arrow north up the bay past Baltimore.

    b. In September, the British defeated the Patriots at **Brandywine**. Near Brandywine, write ⑧.

    c. The British occupied **Philadelphia**. Circle its occupation symbol.

9. In October, the Patriots surrounded the British at **Saratoga** in northern New York. They took almost 6,000 prisoners.

    a. Near Saratoga, write ⑨.

    b. Saratoga marked the **turning point** of the revolution. This victory convinced France to help the Patriots. Near Saratoga, draw a turning point symbol .

 Have students use the information from the map, the Atlas, and their textbook to make a timeline of the events in the Revolutionary War.

Correlates with:

- ● ***The Nystrom Atlas of United States History,*** pages 38–39
- ● ***Mapping United States History*** To the Present, Lesson 12 To the Early 1900s, Lesson 16

Teaching Notes and Mapping Activity

You or your students can mark the following on the *Battles in the Colonies* map.

1. Most of the early battles of the Revolutionary War took place in the North. The British assumed that once New England was defeated, the other colonies would surrender. After years of fighting in the North, the British changed their strategy. In 1778 they focused on conquering the **Southern Colonies**.

   a. The Southern Colonies lie south of Pennsylvania. Trace the southern boundary of Pennsylvania.

   b. South of that line, along the Appalachians, write **SOUTH**.

   c. The British thought that most Southerners were **Loyalists**. On the *Colonists Take Sides* graph, compare the number of Loyalists and Patriots.

2. The British first needed a major port in the South. In late December 1778, they easily captured **Savannah**. The British soon controlled all of Georgia.

   a. Near Savannah, write ①.

   b. The British then occupied Savannah. Circle the occupation symbol on Savannah.

3. In 1780 the British invaded South Carolina. They surrounded Charles Town (now Charleston) and captured 5,500 Patriots—including most of South Carolina's Patriot leaders and almost the entire Southern army.

   a. Near Charles Town, write ②.

   b. The British also occupied **Charles Town**. Circle the occupation symbol on Charles Town.

4. Three months later, the Patriots sent a replacement army to South Carolina. They fought the British in **Camden**, South Carolina. Many of the inexperienced Patriot troops panicked and ran without firing a shot. Near Camden, write ③.

5. With several victories in the South, the British headed for North Carolina. Near the border, British troops were surrounded and captured at **Kings Mountain**. Near Kings Mountain, write ④.

6. The Patriots managed a second victory on a cow pasture along the South Carolina/North Carolina boundary. Near **Cowpens**, write ⑤.

7. The British and Patriot troops both crossed into North Carolina. In March 1781, they fought at **Guilford Court House**. Although the British won this battle, the Patriots won the campaign. Near Guilford Court House, write ⑥.

8. The British headed for Chesapeake Bay. With help from the French, George Washington and his troops defeated the British in **Yorktown**, Virginia, in October 1781. This was the last major battle of the war. Near Yorktown, write ⑦.

☆ For further discussion:
   - How many battles did the British win in the South? the Patriots?
   - Which battle would you consider to be the turning point for the Patriots in the South? Why?

☆ Have students use the information from the map, the Atlas, and their textbook to make (or add to) a timeline of the events in the war.

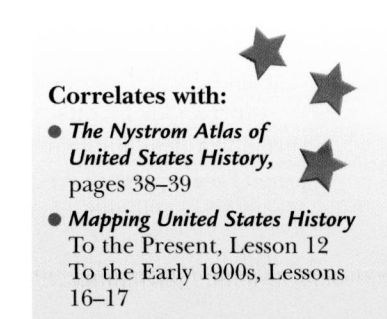

Correlates with:

- ● *The Nystrom Atlas of United States History,* pages 38–39

- ● *Mapping United States History* To the Present, Lesson 12 To the Early 1900s, Lessons 16–17

Battles at Sea

Objective: *To identify several different navies that fought in the Revolutionary War.*

Teaching Notes and Mapping Activity

You or your students can mark the following on the *Battles in the Colonies* and *Battles Near Britain* maps.

1. In 1776 Britain hoped to cut the rebellious New England Colonies off from the rest of the colonies by gaining control of the **Hudson River Valley**.

   a. On the *Battles in the Colonies* map, north of New Hampshire and northern Massachusetts (Maine), write **NEW ENGLAND**.

   b. From Fort Ticonderoga to New York City, along the Hudson River, draw a dashed line.

   c. The British sent a fleet from British North America. From Quebec, along the St. Lawrence River to **Lake Champlain**, draw an arrow.

   d. Patriots, under **Benedict Arnold**, found out the British navy was coming. Arnold had a squadron of ships built on Lake Champlain. Draw a ship symbol 🚢 and label it **BA** for Benedict Arnold.

   e. Arnold's navy fought for two days. But they were no match for the British ships. Surprisingly, the British returned to Quebec after winning the battle. From Lake Champlain back to the St. Lawrence River, draw an arrow.

2. The United States had a **Continental Navy**. However, it was very small. So privately owned ships were encouraged to capture British supply ships. These **privateers** sank or captured more than 600 British ships. Along the Atlantic coast, draw several ship symbols 🚢 and label them **P** for privateer.

3. One of the most famous privateers was helmed by **John Paul Jones**. He raided the coasts of Great Britain capturing British ships and goods.

   a. In 1778 Jones concentrated on the west coast of Britain. On the *Battles Near Britain* map, label the victories at **Whitehaven** and **North Channel of Irish Sea** with **JPJ** for John Paul Jones.

   b. In 1779, near **Flamborough Head**, Jones encountered a convoy of merchant ships escorted by a British frigate. Jones battled the frigate for three hours. Although his boat was badly damaged and leaking, Jones said "I have not yet begun to fight." Label the Flamborough Head victory symbol **JPJ**.

4. Eleven of the colonies had their own navies.

   a. In 1779 the entire **Massachusetts navy** was captured or destroyed in one battle. On the *Battles in the Colonies* map, near Penobscot Bay, draw a ship symbol 🚢 and label it **MA** for Massachusetts.

   b. In 1780 the **South Carolina navy** sank its ships across the mouth of the Cooper River, to prevent the British fleet from sailing through. The British still managed to capture Charles Town. Near Charles Town, draw a ship symbol 🚢 and label it **SC** for South Carolina.

5. In 1781, while the Patriots were defeating the British on land near Yorktown, the **French navy** helped the Patriots by defeating the British on the sea. At **Virginia Capes**, label the victory symbol **FR** for France.

 The Continental Navy sailed a variety of ships, including sloops, schooners, frigates, and brigantines. Have students research the ships, make models or draw detailed diagrams of them, and explain their advantages and disadvantages in a war.

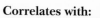
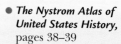

Correlates with:
- *The Nystrom Atlas of United States History,* pages 38–39
- *Mapping United States History* To the Present, Lesson 12 To the Early 1900s, Lesson 16

9

AMERICAN EXPANSION
1803–1853

Key Elements

★ *American Expansion* map

★ *New Lands, New States* timeline

Getting Started

To give students an overview of *American Expansion*, ask them:

- What is the title of this map?
- What do you think this map is about?
- What years does this map cover?
- What do the colors on the map represent?
- On the timeline, what is the title above the line?
- On the timeline, what is the title below the line?

Teaching Notes and Mapping Activities

~ Expansion to the Pacific

~ New Lands

~ New States

The Nystrom **UNITED STATES HISTORY Series** — **NYSTROM** DIVISION OF HERFF JONES, INC.

1803–1853 AMERICAN EXPANSION

0   150   300 miles
0   150   300 kilometers
Map shows present boundaries.

1846 Split by Oregon Treaty; Britain gets northern part

1818 Ceded to Britain by Convention of 1818

1818 From Britain by Convention of 1818

1842 From Britain by Webster-Ashburton Treaty

Oregon Country

Red River Basin

Louisiana Purchase

1803 From France

1819 From Spain by Adams-Onis Treaty

Mexican Cession

UNITED STATES (Before 1803)

ATLANTIC OCEAN

1848 Ceded by Treaty of Guadalupe Hidalgo

Gadsden Purchase

Texas Annexation

Florida Cession

1853 From Mexico

1819 From Spain by Adams-Onis Treaty

PACIFIC OCEAN

MEXICO

1845 Annexed by Act of U.S. Congress

Gulf of Mexico

BAHAMAS

CANADA

Hudson Bay

NEW LANDS, NEW STATES

1800	1803 Louisiana Purchase	1810	1818 Red River Basin	1819 Florida Cession	1820	1830	1840 Maine boundary agreement	1845 Texas Annexation / 1842	1846 Oregon Country / 1848 Mexican Cession

1845 Texas Annexation
1842 Maine boundary agreement
1846 Oregon Country
1848 Mexican Cession
1853 Gadsden Purchase

1803 Ohio
1812 Louisiana
1816 Indiana
1817 Mississippi
1818 Illinois
1819 Alabama
1820 Maine
1821 Missouri
1836 Arkansas
1837 Michigan
1845 Texas / Florida
1846 Iowa
1848 Wisconsin
1850 California

NYSTROM DIVISION OF HERFF JONES, INC.

American Expansion, 1803–1853 **9**

Expansion to the Pacific

Objective: *To explain how the United States expanded its borders to the Pacific Ocean.*

Teaching Notes and Mapping Activity

You or your students can mark the following on the *American Expansion* map.

1. In the early 1800s, the **United States** was about one-fourth of its size today. Its borders stretched from the Atlantic Ocean to the Mississippi River and from the Great Lakes to Florida.

   a. Show the extent of the United States in 1800. Draw an arrow from the Atlantic Ocean to the Mississippi River.

   b. Label the arrow **BEFORE 1803**.

2. The United States wasn't the only organized territory in North America. There were colonies governed by European countries.

   a. Great Britain ruled the land north of the United States. Label modern-day Canada **BRITISH**.

   b. Several countries claimed Oregon Country. Label it **BRITISH**, **SPANISH**, **RUSSIAN**, and **AMERICAN**.

   c. The Louisiana Purchase area was governed by France and then Spain. Label it **FRENCH** and **SPANISH**.

   d. Spain also governed Florida and land south of Oregon Country and the Louisiana Purchase. Label these areas **SPANISH**.

3. In the early 1800s, France persuaded Spain to return the Louisiana Purchase. When the United States asked to purchase the city of New Orleans, France offered all of the **Louisiana Territory**. For $15 million, the United States almost doubled in size.

   a. Show the growth of the United States. From the Mississippi River west to the western boundary of the Louisiana Purchase, draw an arrow.

   b. Label the arrow **1803**.

4. In 1819 Spain agreed to give **Florida** to the United States . In return, the United States surrendered its claims to Texas. From the tip of the Florida peninsula west to the Texas–Louisiana border, draw an arrow. Label it **1819**.

5. In 1821 Mexico won its independence from Spain. Change the area south of the Louisiana Purchase from SPANISH to **MEXICO**.

6. In 1836 American settlers in **Texas** won their independence from Mexico. A decade later, Texas became part of the United States. From the Texas–Louisiana border west to Texas' western boundary, draw an arrow. Label it **1845**.

7. By 1846 only Britain and the United States claimed **Oregon Country**. They divided the land along the 49°N parallel.

   a. Britain took the land north of the parallel. From your BRITISH label in Oregon Country to this area, draw an arrow.

   b. The United States took land south of the 49°N parallel. In Oregon Country, from the western boundary of the Louisiana Purchase to the Pacific Ocean, draw an arrow. Label it **1846**.

8. From 1846 to 1848, the United States and Mexico were at war. Mexico lost the war and sold the land west of Texas to the United States for $15 million. Across the **Mexican Cession**, from Texas west to the Pacific Ocean, draw an arrow. Label it **1848**.

9. In 1853 railroads wanted land for a southern route to the Pacific. The United States paid Mexico $10 million for a relatively small area. Across the **Gadsden Purchase**, write **1853**.

 For further discussion:
   • Which modern-day states were part of each purchase?
   • Which was the best buy—the Louisiana Purchase, the Mexican Cession, or the Gadsden Purchase? Why?

Correlates with:
● *The Nystrom Atlas of United States History,* pages 46, 54–55
● *Mapping United States History* To the Present, Lesson 17 To the Early 1900s, Lesson 24

New Lands

Objective: To graph the growth of the land area of the United States.

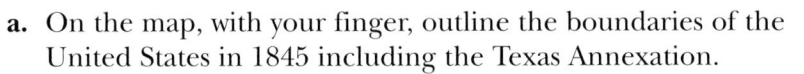

Teaching Notes and Mapping Activity

You or your students can mark the following on the *American Expansion* map. Before graphing each land acquisition, ask students to look at the timeline to determine which acquisition happened next.

1. The United States tripled in size in just 50 years.

   a. Draw a wide bar across the top of the *American Expansion* map, from the right edge of the map to the left edge.

   b. This bar represents the land area of the United States in 1853. Above the bar, write **UNITED STATES, 1853**.

   c. On the bar, mark off 10 equal sections (roughly 4 ⅝" each on the wall map or ⅞" each on the transparency). Each section represents 10 percent of the land area.

2. Before 1803, the United States was fairly small.

   a. On the map, with your finger, outline the boundaries of the United States before 1803.

   b. On the bar, at approximately 29 percent, draw a line. To the left of that line, write **1803 U.S.**

3. The Louisiana Purchase almost doubled the size of the country.

   a. On the map, with your finger, outline the boundaries of the United States in 1803 including the Louisiana Purchase.

   b. On the bar, at approximately 57 percent, draw a line. To the left of that line, write **LOUISIANA PURCHASE**.

4. The Florida Cession was small, but important. The United States gained Florida, as well as widespread access to the Gulf of Mexico.

   a. On the map, with your finger, outline the boundaries of the United States in 1819 including the Florida Cession.

   b. On the bar, at approximately 59 percent, draw a line. Below that section of the bar, write **FLORIDA CESSION**.

5. The Texas Annexation added almost 400,000 square miles to the United States.

   a. On the map, with your finger, outline the boundaries of the United States in 1845 including the Texas Annexation.

   b. On the bar, at approximately 72 percent, draw a line. To the left of that line, write **TEXAS ANNEXATION**.

6. By the 1840s, many Americans felt it was their **Manifest Destiny** to expand the borders of the United States from the Atlantic Ocean to the Pacific. Gaining the southern portion of Oregon Country, the United States finally extended from sea to shining sea.

   a. On the map, with your finger, outline the boundaries of the United States in 1846 including the Oregon Country.

   b. On the bar, at approximately 81 percent, draw a line. To the left of that line, write **OREGON COUNTRY**.

7. The Mexican Cession gave the United States more land along the Pacific coast.

   a. On the map, with your finger, outline the boundaries of the United States in 1848 including the Mexican Cession.

   b. On the bar, at approximately 99 percent, draw a line. To the left of that line, write **MEXICAN CESSION**.

8. With the Gadsden Purchase, the United States was the size of its current 48 contiguous states.

   a. On the map, with your finger, outline the boundaries of the United States in 1853 including the Gadsden Purchase.

   b. Below the remaining section of the bar, write **GADSDEN PURCHASE**.

☆ Using an outline map of the United States, have students cut apart each land acquisition and label each piece with its name and date of acquisition. Then have students put the pieces together chronologically.

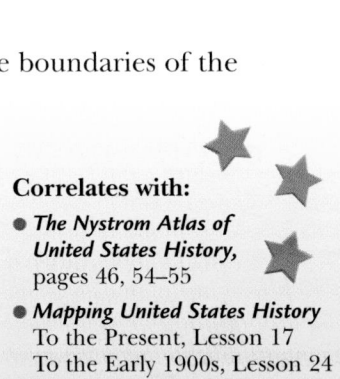

Correlates with:

● *The Nystrom Atlas of United States History,* pages 46, 54–55

● *Mapping United States History* To the Present, Lesson 17 To the Early 1900s, Lesson 24

New States

Objective: *To identify and locate the 15 states added to the Union between 1803 and 1853.*

Teaching Notes and Mapping Activity

You or your students can mark the following on the *American Expansion Map*. Before introducing each state, ask a student to point out the next state that entered the Union on the timeline.

1. In early 1803, the United States extended from the Atlantic Ocean to the Mississippi River. There were 16 states.

    a. Along the Appalachians, draw mountain symbols ∧∧∧ . (See *The Nystrom United States History Series 6* wall map or transparency if you need help locating the mountains.)

    b. Label each of the following states with a number, indicating the order it entered the Union.

• Delaware	1	• New Hampshire	9
• Pennsylvania	2	• Virginia	10
• New Jersey	3	• New York	11
• Georgia	4	• North Carolina	12
• Connecticut	5	• Rhode Island	13
• Massachusetts	6	• Vermont	14
• Maryland	7	• Kentucky	15
• South Carolina	8	• Tennessee	16

2. The Northwest Territory was north of the Ohio River and east of the Mississippi River.

    a. Above the Great Lakes, write **NORTHWEST TERRITORY**.

    b. **Ohio** was the first state in the Northwest Territory to enter the Union. Outline Ohio and number it **17**.

3. **Louisiana** was the first state west of the Mississippi River to enter the Union. Louisiana was part of the Louisiana Purchase. Outline Louisiana and number it **18**.

4. Between 1816 and 1821, six states entered the Union. Five were east of the Mississippi, one was west.

    a. **Indiana** and **Illinois** were part of the Northwest Territory. Outline each and number them **19** and **21**.

    b. **Mississippi** and **Alabama** were also east of the Mississippi. Outline each and number them **20** and **22**.

    c. The northern section of Massachusetts became an independent state. Outline **Maine** and number it **23**.

    d. **Missouri,** located west of the Mississippi River, also entered the Union. Outline Missouri and number it **24**.

5. In the 1830s, two states entered the Union.

    a. **Arkansas** was part of the Louisiana Purchase. Outline Arkansas and number it **25**.

    b. **Michigan** was part of the Northwest Territory. Outline Michigan and number it **26**.

6. Between 1845 and 1850, five states entered the Union. Four were west of the Mississippi, one was east.

    a. **Florida**, once governed by Spain, was part of the Florida Cession. Outline Florida and number it **27**.

    b. **Texas** was once part of Mexico. When Texas became a state, war with Mexico followed. Outline Texas and number it **28**.

    c. **Iowa** was part of the Louisiana Purchase. Outline Iowa and number it **29**.

    d. **Wisconsin** was part of the Northwest Territory. Outline Wisconsin and number it **30**.

    e. **California** was part of the Mexican Cession. Outline California and number it **31**.

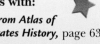

Correlates with:
● *The Nystrom Atlas of United States History,* page 63

 Have students use the *U.S. History Series 13* wall map or transparency to determine which new states entered the Union as free states and which as slave states.

EXPLORATIONS OF THE WEST
1804–1844

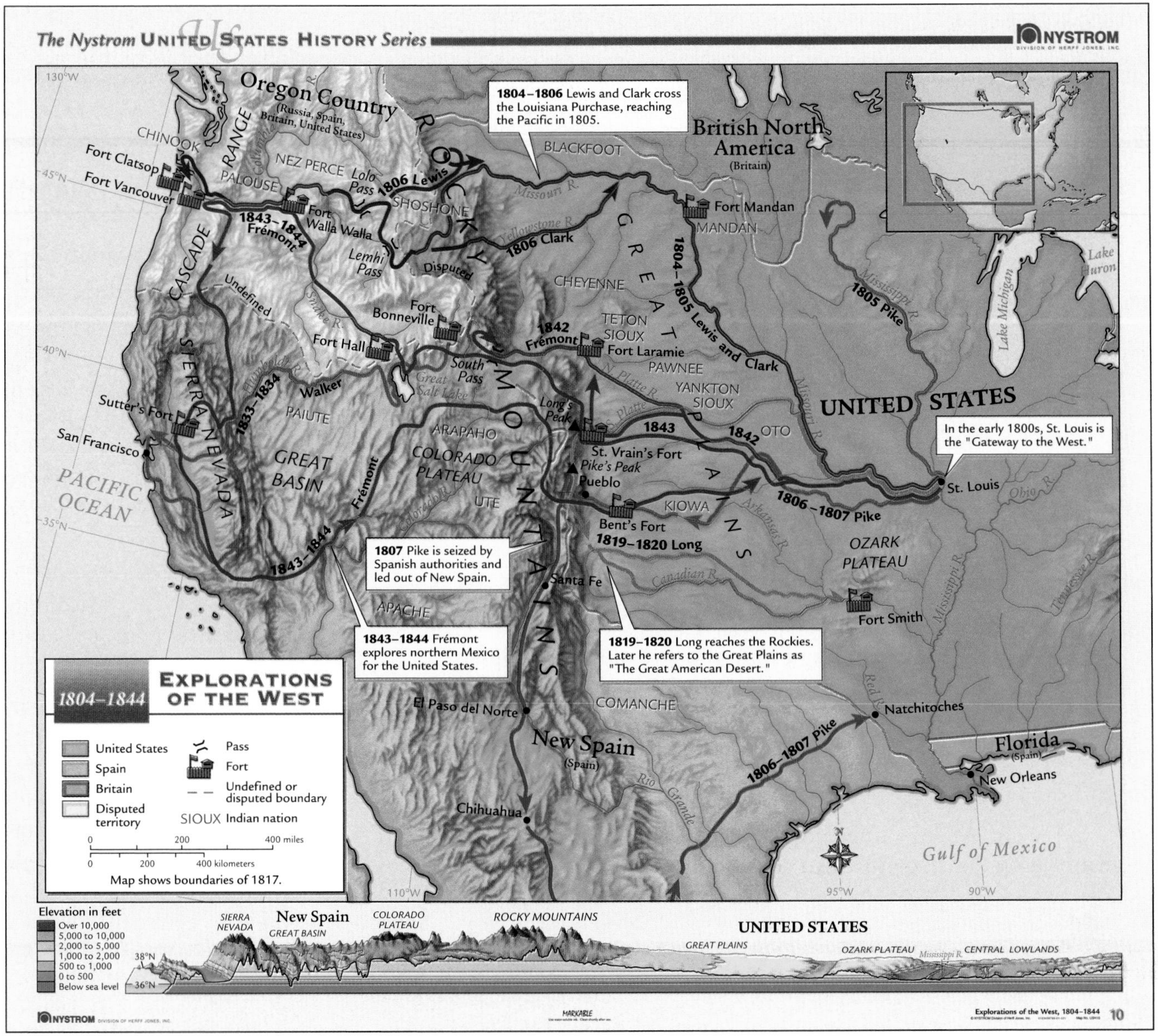

Key Elements

★ *Explorations of the West* map

★ Locator map

★ *New Spain–United States* cross section

Getting Started

To give students an overview of *Explorations of the West,* ask them:

● What is the title of this map?

● What part of North America is shown on this map?

● What years does this map cover?

● On this map, what do the colors of the land areas represent?

● What do the different colored lines represent?

● What does the gray type show?

● What does the cross section below the map show?

● On the main map, with two fingers, follow 36°N and 38°N across the map. This is the part of the map shown in the cross section. Where is the highest land?

Teaching Notes and Mapping Activities

~ The Lewis and Clark Expedition

~ Long Surveys the Plains

~ Fremont Surveys the West

The Nystrom UNITED STATES HISTORY Series

NYSTROM
DIVISION OF HERFF JONES, INC.

1804–1806 Lewis and Clark cross the Louisiana Purchase, reaching the Pacific in 1805.

Oregon Country
(Russia, Spain, Britain, United States)

British North America
(Britain)

CHINOOK

BLACKFOOT

Fort Clatsop

Fort Vancouver

NEZ PERCE

Lolo Pass

1806 Lewis

Fort Mandan

MANDAN

PALOUSE

SHOSHONE

Missouri R.

1806 Clark

1804–1805 Lewis and Clark

1843–1844 Frémont

Fort Walla Walla

Lemhi Pass

Yellowstone R.

GREAT

1805 Pike

Disputed

CHEYENNE

CASCADE RANGE

Fort Bonneville

Undefined

TETON SIOUX

1842 Frémont

Fort Laramie

PAWNEE

Fort Hall

South Pass

YANKTON SIOUX

UNITED STATES

SIERRA NEVADA

Great Salt Lake

Long's Peak

PAIUTE

1833–1834

Walker

ARAPAHO

1843

1842

OTO

In the early 1800s, St. Louis is the "Gateway to the West."

Sutter's Fort

COLORADO PLATEAU

St. Vrain's Fort

Platte R.

San Francisco

Frémont

GREAT BASIN

UTE

Pike's Peak

Pueblo

1806–1807 Pike

St. Louis

PACIFIC OCEAN

KIOWA

Arkansas R.

Ohio R.

OZARK PLATEAU

Bent's Fort

1819–1820 Long

1807 Pike is seized by Spanish authorities and led out of New Spain.

1843–1844

Canadian R.

APACHE

Santa Fe

1843–1844 Frémont explores northern Mexico for the United States.

1819–1820 Long reaches the Rockies. Later he refers to the Great Plains as "The Great American Desert."

Fort Smith

El Paso del Norte

COMANCHE

Natchitoches

Red R.

EXPLORATIONS OF THE WEST
1804–1844

New Spain
(Spain)

Florida
(Spain)

Rio Grande

1806–1807 Pike

New Orleans

Chihuahua

□ United States
□ Spain
□ Britain
□ Disputed territory

╭ Pass
▪ Fort
– – Undefined or disputed boundary
SIOUX Indian nation

0   200   400 miles
0   200   400 kilometers

Map shows boundaries of 1817.

Gulf of Mexico

Lake Huron

Lake Michigan

1805 Pike

Mississippi R.

Tennessee R.

Elevation in feet
Over 10,000
5,000 to 10,000
2,000 to 5,000
1,000 to 2,000
500 to 1,000
0 to 500
Below sea level

New Spain

SIERRA NEVADA
GREAT BASIN

COLORADO PLATEAU

ROCKY MOUNTAINS

UNITED STATES

38°N

36°N

GREAT PLAINS

OZARK PLATEAU

Mississippi R.

CENTRAL LOWLANDS

NYSTROM DIVISION OF HERFF JONES, INC.

MARKABLE

Explorations of the West, 1804–1844 **10**

The Lewis and Clark Expedition

Objective: *To trace and date Lewis and Clark's expedition to the Pacific.*

Teaching Notes and Mapping Activity

You or your students can mark the following on the *Explorations of the West* map.

1. Early in 1803, President Thomas Jefferson approached Congress about financing an expedition up the Missouri River. Later that year, the United States purchased the land surrounding the Missouri—the **Louisiana Territory**.

   a. Before 1803, the westernmost boundary of the United States was the Mississippi River. Trace the Mississippi River from its source to the Gulf of Mexico.

   b. The boundaries of the Louisiana Territory were unclear. It extended roughly from the Mississippi River to the Rocky Mountains. Along the Rocky Mountains, draw a dotted line.

   c. Between your two lines, write **LOUISIANA PURCHASE 1803**.

2. Jefferson hired **Meriwether Lewis** to lead the Corps of Discovery. Lewis hired **William Clark** to help him. On May 14, 1804, Lewis, Clark, and roughly 45 other men began the expedition. Near St. Louis, write **MAY 1804**.

3. One goal of the expedition was to establish friendly relations with **Native Americans** in the region. On August 3, the Corps of Discovery had their first council with Indians. They gave the Oto and Missouri Indians peace medals and gifts.

   a. From St. Louis west to the OTO nation, trace the Missouri.

   b. Below OTO, write **AUG 1804**.

4. On October 24, the Corps of Discovery arrived at the village of the Mandan and Hidatsas. At the time, their village was larger than the city of St. Louis. The expedition built their winter camp, **Fort Mandan**, across the river from the Indian village.

   a. Continue tracing Lewis and Clark's route to Fort Mandan.

   b. On April 7, 1805, the corps was ready to continue their journey. A French Canadian fur trader, Toussaint Charbonneau, his Shoshone wife, **Sacagawea**, and their newborn son joined them as guides. East of Fort Mandan, write **OCT 1804–APR 1805**.

5. On June 13, the expedition reached **Great Falls**. The corps had to carry their canoes 18.5 miles around the falls.

   a. From Fort Mandan to the *C* in ROCKY, trace their route.

   b. Above the C in ROCKY, write 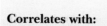 **JUNE 1805**.

6. On August 12, the corps reached the headwaters of the Missouri River and **Lemhi Pass**. On the other side of the pass, Lewis expected to see a river flowing to the Pacific Ocean. Instead, he saw more mountains. This part of the journey was especially treacherous. Mountain paths were rocky and narrow. Food was scarce.

   a. From Great Falls south to Lemhi Pass, trace their route.

   b. Trace the pass symbol and label it **AUG 1805**.

   c. On the cross section, outline the mountains between the Rockies and the Pacific Ocean.

   d. On the map, west of the Rockies, draw these symbols ∧∧∧ .

7. The corps didn't see the **Pacific Ocean** until November 7. There they spent a rainy, miserable winter at their camp, **Fort Clatsop**. On March 23, 1806, they began their 4,000-mile, six-month journey back to St. Louis.

   a. From Lemhi Pass to Fort Clatsop, trace their route.

   b. Outline the fort symbol and label it **NOV 1805–MAR 1806**.

 Using the map, have students list the Indian nations that Lewis and Clark may have encountered on their expedition.

Correlates with:
● *The Nystrom Atlas of United States History,* pages 46–47

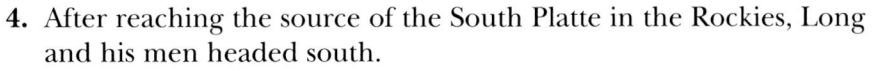

Teaching Notes and Mapping Activity

You or your students can mark the following on the *Explorations of the West* map.

1. In 1817 the Secretary of War wanted to set up a line of forts along the United States' westernmost frontier. **Major Stephen Long** of the U.S. Army's Corps of Topographical Engineers was sent to survey the land and select sites for the forts.

   a. Long selected a site on the Arkansas River as the southernmost fort on the western frontier. Outline the symbol for **Fort Smith** and label it **S** for southern.

   b. Long also selected a site on the Mississippi River for the northernmost fort. The fort was first called **Fort St. Anthony**, then Fort Snelling, and is now Minneapolis–St. Paul. West of the words *1805 Pike*, draw a fort. Label it **N** for northern.

2. The next year, Long was part of a large expedition sent to establish forts on the upper Missouri River. However, their large steamboats were only able to reach Council Bluffs. There they established **Fort Atkinson**.

   a. With your finger, trace the Missouri River upstream from St. Louis.

   b. Now, beginning in St. Louis, trace the Missouri River to the point where the Long expedition (the orange line) left the river.

   c. At that point, on the east side of the Missouri, draw a fort. This was the United States' official westernmost outpost. Label it **W** for western.

   d. Draw a line connecting your N, W, and S fort labels. Along the line, write **FRONTIER**.

3. In 1820 Long was asked to find the sources of the Platte, Arkansas, and Red Rivers. His small expedition followed the **Platte River** across the Great Plains. On the map, trace the South Platte River from Fort Atkinson to the Rocky Mountains.

4. After reaching the source of the South Platte in the Rockies, Long and his men headed south.

   a. Along the Rocky Mountains, draw mountain symbols ∧∧∧ .

   b. Long's men discovered a new mountain. Outline the mountain symbol ▲ for **Long's Peak**.

   c. Members of the expedition were also the first to climb and measure **Pike's Peak**. Outline its mountain symbol ▲.

5. South of Pike's Peak, the expedition split into two groups

   a. One group headed southeast to Fort Smith. Trace the route labeled *1819–1820 Long* to Fort Smith.

   b. Another group headed further south looking for the Red River. They mistook the Canadian River for the Red River. From Pike's Peak to Fort Smith, trace the Canadian River route.

6. On the plains, Long and his men suffered from the heat. They had difficulty finding food and drinking water. In his report, Long referred to the Great Plains as "*The Great American Desert.*"

   a. On the cross section of the United States, draw a line from the eastern Rockies to the west side of the Ozark Plateau.

   b. On the map, south of Bent's Fort, write **GREAT PLAINS = GREAT AMERICAN DESERT**.

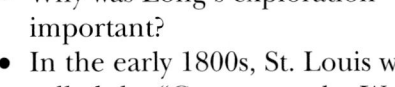 For further discussion:
   - Why was Long's exploration important?
   - In the early 1800s, St. Louis was called the "Gateway to the West." Why?
   - How do you think the label *Great American Desert* affected settlement on the plains?

Correlates with:
- *The Nystrom Atlas of United States History,* page 50
- *Mapping United States History* To the Early 1900s, Lesson 25

Fremont Surveys the West

Objective: *To trace the Oregon Trail and label the Great Basin.*

Teaching Notes and Mapping Activity

You or your students can mark the following on the *Explorations of the West* map.

1. Like Long, **John Fremont** was an officer in the U.S. Army's Corps of Topographical Engineers. In 1843 he led an expedition to map the Oregon Trail. His party included a German cartographer, several French voyageurs, mountain men, and frontiersman Kit Carson.

   a. The expedition began in St. Louis. Trace Fremont's route (the purple line) from St. Louis to St. Vrain's Fort.

   b. St. Vrain's was a supply fort. Below it, write **JULY 1843**.

2. St. Vrain's Fort is on the eastern side of the Rocky Mountains. Along the Rocky Mountains, draw mountain symbols ∧∧∧ .

3. From St. Vrain's, the expedition headed north and west across the mountains, through South Pass, to the Great Salt Lake.

   a. At South Pass, trace the pass symbol ⤙ .

   b. From St. Vrain's Fort to Fort Hall, trace Fremont's route.

   c. The expedition reached the Great Salt Lake in early September. West of the lake, write **SEPT 1843**.

4. From Fort Hall, Fremont followed the Snake and Columbia Rivers to Oregon.

   a. From Fort Hall to Fort Vancouver, trace Fremont's route.

   b. This part of his journey followed the Oregon Trail. Label the line you just traced **OREGON TRAIL**.

5. Rather than retrace his steps to return home, Fremont headed south along the eastern side of the Cascade Range and the Sierra Nevadas, into Mexican Territory.

   a. Along the Cascade Range and Sierra Nevadas, draw mountain symbols ∧∧∧ .

   b. From Fort Vancouver south to the Humboldt River, trace Fremont's route.

   c. At the time of Fremont's expedition, Mexico had won its independence. Cross out *New Spain* and write **MEXICO**.

6. In mid-winter, Fremont decided to cross the snow-packed Sierra Nevadas to Sutter's Fort. His Native American guides deserted him. The dangerous crossing took 30 days.

   a. The Sierra Nevadas are high and steep. On the cross section below the map, outline the Sierra Nevadas.

   b. On the map, from Humboldt River to Sutter's Fort, trace Fremont's route.

   c. West of Sutter's Fort, write **WINTER 1843–44**.

7. After resting and resupplying the expedition at Sutter's Fort, Fremont headed south through the San Joaquin Valley. He crossed the Sierra Nevadas into the Great Basin. He then crossed the Rockies and the Great Plains.

   a. From Sutter's Fort south to St. Louis, retrace Fremont's route.

   b. Fremont was the first to refer to the area between the Sierra Nevadas and the Rockies as the **Great Basin**. Underline the words *Great Basin*.

   c. Fremont arrived at Bent's Fort in July. Below the fort, write **JULY 1844**.

 With help from his wife Jessie, Fremont wrote a popular report about this expedition. Have students write an action-packed paragraph describing one small part of Fremont's journey.

 Have students research the other explorations labeled on the map.

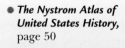

Correlates with:

- **The Nystrom Atlas of United States History,** page 50
- **Mapping United States History** To the Present, Lesson 18 To the Early 1900s, Lessons 25, 26

11

TRAILS WEST 1821–1861

Key Elements

★ *Trails West* map
★ *United States* cross section
★ Locator map

Getting Started

To give students an overview of *Trails West,* ask them:

- What part of the United States does the main map show?
- What do the green areas represent? The yellow areas?
- What do the other colored areas represent?
- What do the different colored lines represent?
- What does the cross section map show?
- What three regions have the highest elevations in the United States?

Teaching Notes and Mapping Activities

~From Trade Routes to Trailheads
~The Long Journey Overland
~Seeking a Better Life

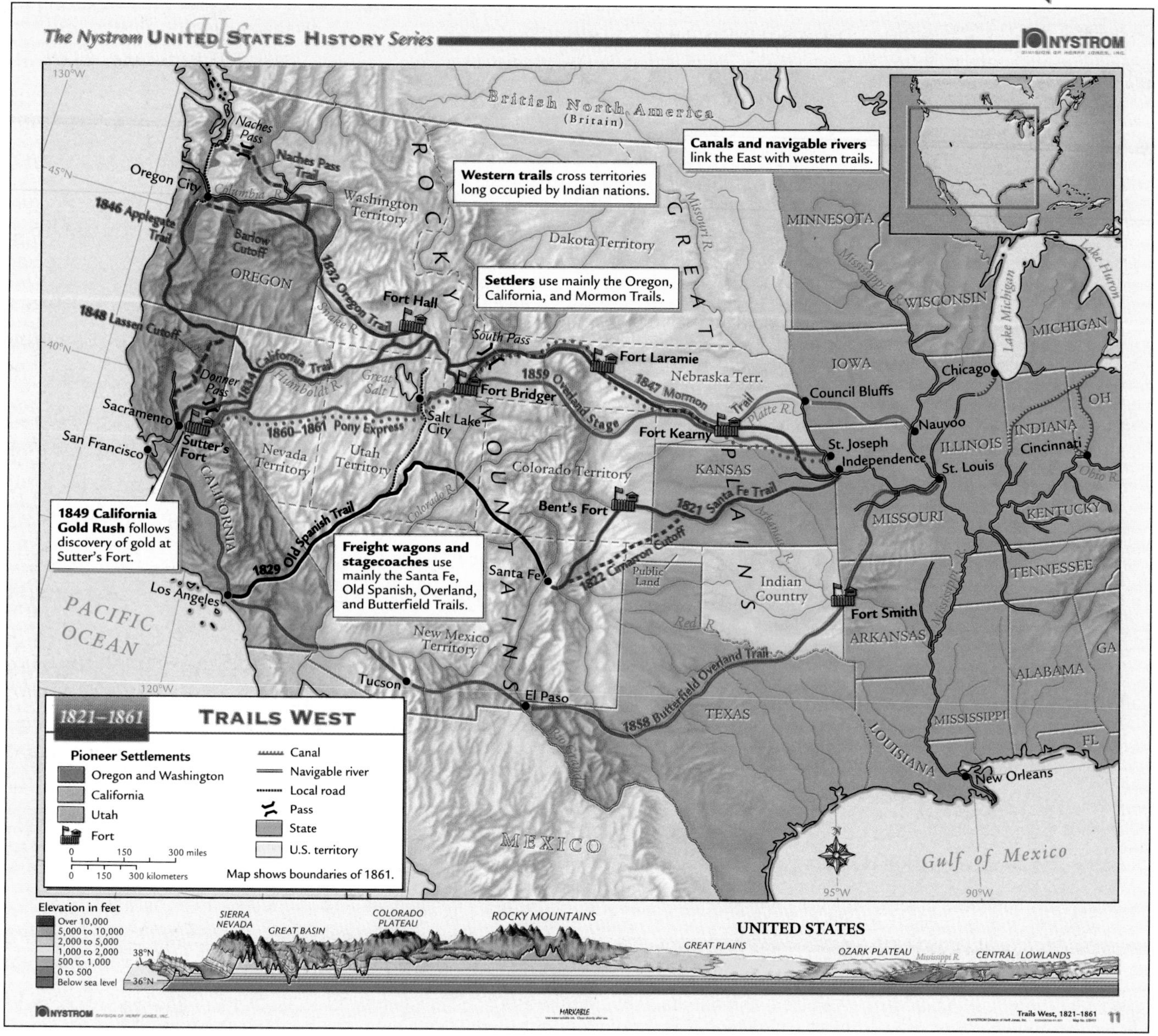

The Nystrom United States History Series
NYSTROM
1821–1861 TRAILS WEST
Pioneer Settlements
Oregon and Washington
California
Utah
Fort
Canal
Navigable river
Local road
Pass
State
U.S. territory
0 150 300 miles
0 150 300 kilometers
Map shows boundaries of 1861.
Canals and navigable rivers link the East with western trails.
Western trails cross territories long occupied by Indian nations.
Settlers use mainly the Oregon, California, and Mormon Trails.
1849 California Gold Rush follows discovery of gold at Sutter's Fort.
Freight wagons and stagecoaches use mainly the Santa Fe, Old Spanish, Overland, and Butterfield Trails.
British North America (Britain)
ROCKY MOUNTAINS
GREAT PLAINS
PACIFIC OCEAN
Gulf of Mexico
MEXICO
1846 Applegate Trail
1848 Lassen Cutoff
1832 Oregon Trail
1834 California Trail
1860–1861 Pony Express
1859 Overland Stage
1847 Mormon Trail
1821 Santa Fe Trail
1822 Cimarron Cutoff
1829 Old Spanish Trail
1858 Butterfield Overland Trail
Naches Pass Trail
Barlow Cutoff
Oregon City
Fort Hall
South Pass
Fort Laramie
Fort Bridger
Salt Lake City
Fort Kearny
Council Bluffs
St. Joseph
Independence
Nauvoo
Chicago
St. Louis
Cincinnati
Bent's Fort
Santa Fe
Fort Smith
Sacramento
San Francisco
Sutter's Fort
Los Angeles
Tucson
El Paso
New Orleans
Elevation in feet
Over 10,000
5,000 to 10,000
2,000 to 5,000
1,000 to 2,000
500 to 1,000
0 to 500
Below sea level
UNITED STATES
SIERRA NEVADA
GREAT BASIN
COLORADO PLATEAU
ROCKY MOUNTAINS
GREAT PLAINS
OZARK PLATEAU
CENTRAL LOWLANDS
Trails West, 1821–1861
11

From Trade Routes to Trailheads

Objective: *To give background on western settlements and transportation prior to widespread use of overland trails.*

Teaching Notes and Mapping Activity

You or your students can mark the following on the *Trails West* map and the *United States Cross Section.*

1. People of European descent were living in what would become the western United States long before any trails had been established.

   a. In the early 1800s, British and American fur trading companies established settlements in the Pacific Northwest. On the *Trails West* map, along the Columbia River, write **FUR TRADERS - 1810s**.

   b. California had been occupied by Spanish and Mexican ranchers since the late 1700s. In California, write **RANCHERS - 1770s**.

2. Most early settlers of the Pacific Coast region arrived by sea. Settlers in the Pacific Northwest and California usually purchased supplies from European or New England trading ships. Many Americans learned about the West from people who had traveled to the region by sea.

   a. Draw a ship in the Pacific Ocean west of Oregon.

   b. Draw another ship in the Pacific Ocean west of San Francisco.

   c. Eventually, traders established land routes to the Pacific Coast. These trade routes became the trails that were used by thousands of pioneers. Label the Oregon Trail, the California Trail, and the Old Spanish Trail **TRADE ROUTE**.

3. Unlike the Pacific Coast, the Utah Territory was of little interest to white settlers before trails were established. Because the region was harsh and dry, the Native Americans who had lived there for centuries were left in relative peace.

   a. Across the Utah Territory, write **NATIVE AMERICANS**.

   b. Below Native Americans, write **(DESERT)**.

4. When Americans decided to emigrate to Oregon or California, the most arduous part of their journey usually began at one of three main trailheads. These trailheads were located on the eastern edge of the Great Plains.

   a. Draw stars ★ over the city symbols that mark the towns of Council Bluffs, Iowa, and St. Joseph and Independence, Missouri.

   b. To the right of the legend, write ★ = **MAIN TRAILHEAD**.

5. For most travelers, the journey did not begin at the trailhead, it started further east. Pioneers traveled to the trailheads by river or rail. Once they reached the trailheads, they traveled by wagon, stagecoach, or horse.

   a. Draw an arrow along the Missouri River, from St. Louis to Independence.

   b. Draw arrows along the waterways from Chicago to Cincinnati, and from New Orleans to St. Louis.

   c. Draw an arrow from the easternmost point of the *United States Cross Section* to the eastern edge of the Great Plains.

   d. Label the arrow **TRAVEL BY RIVER AND RAIL**.

   e. Next, draw an arrow from the Great Plains to the Pacific Coast.

   f. Label the arrow **TRAVEL BY WAGON, STAGECOACH, OR HORSE**.

 Have students use the map scale in the legend to compute the distance of each of the journeys below:
   • Independence to Oregon City
   • Nauvoo to Salt Lake City
   • St. Joseph to Sacramento
   • St. Louis to Los Angeles

Correlates with:
● *The Nystrom Atlas of United States History,* pages 56–57
● *Mapping United States History,* To the Present, Lesson 18 To the Early 1909s, Lesson 26

Teaching Notes and Mapping Activity

You and your students can mark the following on the *Trails West* map, the Locator map, and the *United States Cross Section*.

1. The journey west took four to six months, and emigrants had to time their trips very carefully. Wagon trains had to leave in the spring within a three month window of time. If they left too early, there would be no grass on the prairie for their animals to eat. If they left too late, they would be faced with crossing mountain ranges during bad weather.

   a. On the Locator map, draw an arrow from the right edge of the red box to the Pacific Coast.

   b. Label the arrow **4 TO 6 MONTHS**.

   c. On the *United States Cross Section*, just east of the Great Plains, write **DEPART APRIL–JUNE**.

   d. On the cross section, across the Great Plains, write **GRASS FOR ANIMALS**.

2. Along each trail there were a number of forts. Some were military bases, others were trading posts. At forts, travelers could send mail, gain information, and most importantly, purchase supplies for their journey.

   a. On the *Trails West* map, label each of the forts **SUPPLIES**.

   b. Pioneers who started their journeys later than others ran the risk of forts being out of supplies. Add a question mark after each of your SUPPLIES labels.

3. Settlers heading west hoped to reach the biggest obstacle in their path—the Rocky Mountains—by midsummer. In July or August, they were likely to have the best weather for a mountain crossing, and much of the winter snow would have melted.

   a. On the cross section, below the Rocky Mountains, write **JULY–AUGUST**.

   b. South Pass made crossing the Rockies relatively easy, because the trail rose gradually. On the *Trails West* map, above the label for South Pass, write **EASY**.

4. West of the Rocky Mountains are the Great Basin and the Colorado Plateau. In these harsh, dry regions pioneers faced some of the most brutal terrain on their journey west. On the cross section, below the labels for the Great Basin and the Colorado Plateau, write **HARSH AND DRY**.

5. The mountain ranges in the far west were the last and sometimes most difficult barrier the pioneers faced. Neither the Sierra Nevada in California, nor the Cascade Range in Oregon and Washington, had a pass as easy to cross as South Pass in the Rockies. To make matters worse, by the time many wagon trains reached these ranges—in September and October—the weather was growing steadily worse.

   a. On the cross section, just above the label for the Sierra Nevada, write **CASCADE RANGE**.

   b. Across the terrain below these labels, write **BAD PASSES, POOR WEATHER**.

6. Emigrants hoped to arrive at their destinations by October or November, before winter set in. On the cross section, in the area west of the Sierra Nevada, write **ARRIVE OCT–NOV**.

 Have your students use the distances they computed in the last lesson to calculate the number of miles per day a wagon train would have to travel in order to complete each journey in:
- four months*
- five months*
- six months*

*You might want to mention to your students that many pioneers were religious and refused to travel on Sunday.

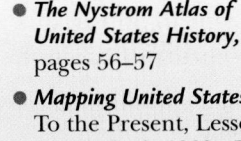

Correlates with:
- ***The Nystrom Atlas of United States History,*** pages 56–57
- ***Mapping United States History,*** To the Present, Lesson 18
  To the Early 1909s, Lesson 26

Seeking a Better Life

Objective: *To explain some of the reasons why the pioneers chose to make the difficult journey west.*

Teaching Notes and Mapping Activity

You and your students can mark the following on the *Trails West* map.

1. American settlers moved west for many different reasons. The first Americans to settle the Oregon Country were traders, hunters, and trappers who hoped to profit from the fur trade.

   a. On the *Trails West* map, point out the Oregon Trail. Trace it with your finger from trailhead to destination.

   b. Next, point out areas of settlement in Oregon and Washington. Show your students that the settlement areas are located along bodies of water.

   c. In the territory north of the Columbia River, write ① **TRADERS, HUNTERS, & TRAPPERS 1810s**.

   d. Later settlers to the Pacific Northwest came for religious reasons. In 1834 the first missionaries arrived, hoping to convert Native Americans to Christianity. Below ①, write ② **MISSIONARIES 1830s**.

   e. Still others came because of the opportunity to own land. Descriptions of the Oregon Country sparked large-scale emigration in the 1840s. These emigrants were primarily farmers and loggers. Below ②, write ③ **FARMERS & LOGGERS 1840s**.

2. The first U.S. citizens to settle in California were also traders. Americans had been trading goods at California ports since Mexico won its independence from Spain in 1821. In 1828 Abel Stearns became the first U.S. citizen to officially settle in California when he opened up a trading post in San Francisco.

   a. Point out the California Trail. Trace it from one of the trailheads to its final destination in Sacramento.

   b. Next, point out the areas of settlement in California. Show your students that many of California's settlement areas were also located along bodies of water.

   c. In California, just south of San Francisco, write ① **TRADERS 1820s–1830s**.

   d. In 1841 the first wagon train of settlers arrived in California. Until 1848, most of emigrants to California were farmers and small businessmen. Below ①, write ② **FARMERS & BUSINESSMEN 1840s**.

   e. In 1848 gold was discovered at Sutter's Fort. This sparked a huge influx of settlers. Below ②, write ③ **MINERS 1848**.

3. Like the Oregon missionaries, the first emigrants to the Utah Territory also came for religious reason. The Mormons, however, had been victims of religious persecution and came seeking a place to practice their religion freely. Their leader, Brigham Young, chose the harsh Utah desert because he felt its isolation offered Mormons just such a place.

   a. Point out the Mormon Trail and trace it with your finger. Show your students that the Mormon Trail covers much of the same route as the Oregon Trail, but is located on the opposite side of the Platte River.

   b. Next, point out the areas of settlement in Utah. Show your students that once again the settlement areas were located along bodies of water.

   c. In the Utah Territory, write **MORMONS (RELIGIOUS FREEDOM) 1847**.

    Have your students evaluate the different reasons settlers moved west and rank them in order of importance. Then have them write a paragraph explaining the order of their ranking.

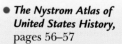

Correlates with:

- *The Nystrom Atlas of United States History,* pages 56–57

- *Mapping United States History,* To the Present, Lesson 18 To the Early 1909s, Lesson 26

WAR WITH MEXICO
1846–1848

Key Elements
★ *War With Mexico* map
★ Locator map
★ *Claiming the Southwest* timeline

Getting Started

To give students an overview of *War With Mexico,* ask them:

- What part of the world does the map show?

- What does the pink area represent? The green area? The striped area?

- What do the different colored arrows represent? What do the dotted arrows represent?

- What are some of the other symbols on the map? What do they represent?

- What is the title of the timeline? What events does it include?

- What period of time does the timeline cover?

Teaching Notes and Mapping Activities

~ Mexico Before the War
~ Prelude to Conflict
~ The Spoils of Manifest Destiny

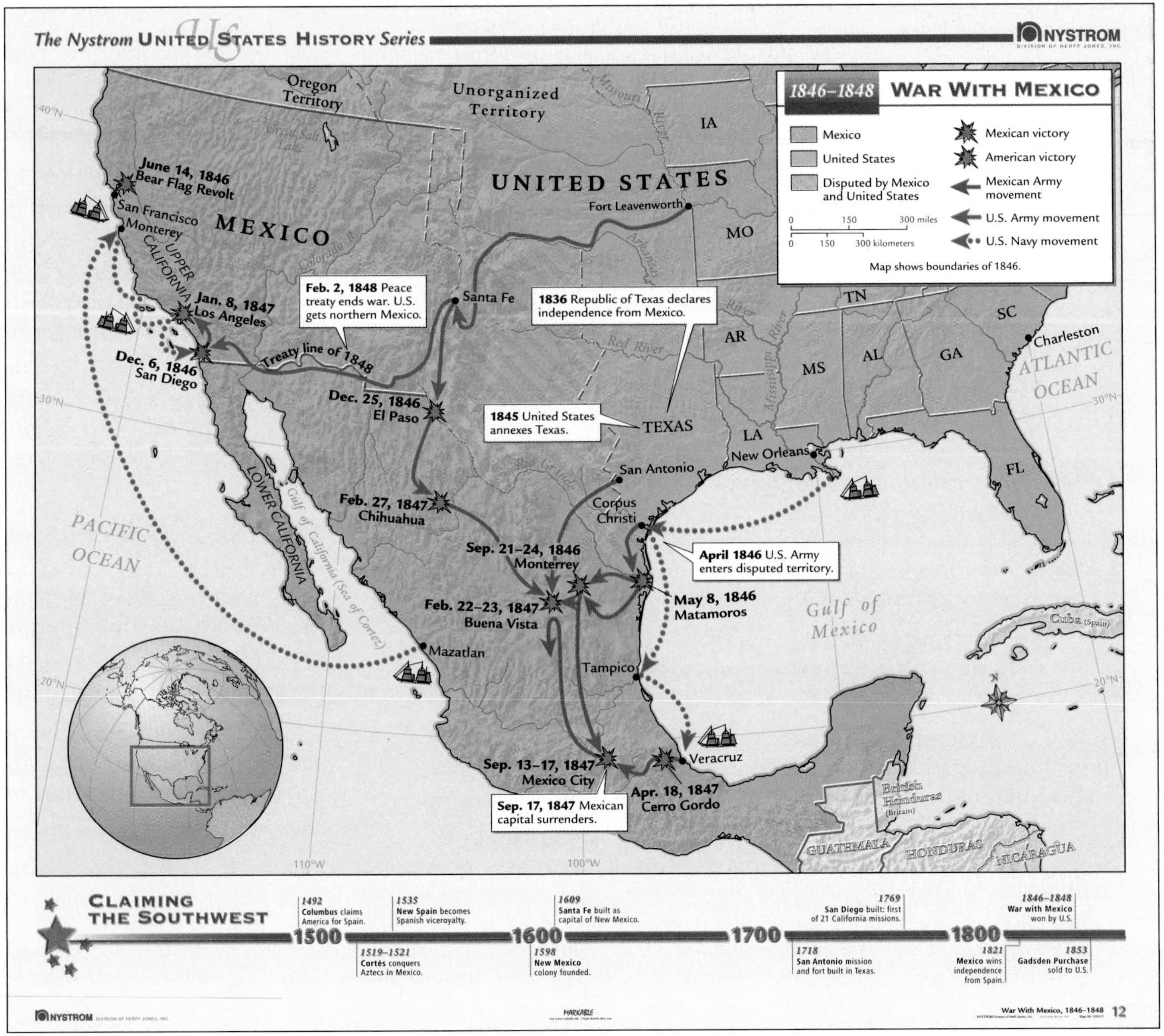

The Nystrom UNITED STATES HISTORY *Series*

NYSTROM
DIVISION OF HERFF JONES, INC.

1846–1848 WAR WITH MEXICO

- Mexico
- United States
- Disputed by Mexico and United States
- ✹ Mexican victory
- ✹ American victory
- ← Mexican Army movement
- ← U.S. Army movement
- •← U.S. Navy movement

0   150   300 miles
0   150   300 kilometers
Map shows boundaries of 1846.

UNITED STATES

MEXICO

Oregon Territory

Unorganized Territory

IA

Fort Leavenworth

MO

June 14, 1846 Bear Flag Revolt

San Francisco
Monterey
UPPER CALIFORNIA

Jan. 8, 1847 Los Angeles

Dec. 6, 1846 San Diego

Santa Fe

1836 Republic of Texas declares independence from Mexico.

Feb. 2, 1848 Peace treaty ends war. U.S. gets northern Mexico.

Treaty line of 1848

Dec. 25, 1846 El Paso

1845 United States annexes Texas.

TEXAS

TN

AR

MS   AL   GA

SC

Charleston

ATLANTIC OCEAN

LA

New Orleans

FL

San Antonio

Corpus Christi

April 1846 U.S. Army enters disputed territory.

PACIFIC OCEAN

LOWER CALIFORNIA

Gulf of California (Sea of Cortez)

Feb. 27, 1847 Chihuahua

Sep. 21–24, 1846 Monterrey

Feb. 22–23, 1847 Buena Vista

May 8, 1846 Matamoros

Gulf of Mexico

Cuba (Spain)

Mazatlan

Tampico

Sep. 13–17, 1847 Mexico City

Sep. 17, 1847 Mexican capital surrenders.

Apr. 18, 1847 Cerro Gordo

Veracruz

British Honduras (Britain)

GUATEMALA   HONDURAS   NICARAGUA

40°N
30°N
20°N
110°W   100°W

Great Salt Lake
Colorado R.
Missouri River
Arkansas River
Red River
Rio Grande

CLAIMING THE SOUTHWEST

1492 **Columbus** claims America for Spain.	*1535* **New Spain** becomes Spanish viceroyalty.

1519–1521 **Cortés** conquers Aztecs in Mexico.

1500

1609 **Santa Fe** built as capital of New Mexico.

1598 **New Mexico** colony founded.

1600

1700

1769 **San Diego** built: first of 21 California missions.

1718 **San Antonio** mission and fort built in Texas.

1800

1846–1848 **War with Mexico** won by U.S.

1821 **Mexico** wins independence from Spain.

1853 **Gadsden Purchase** sold to U.S.

NYSTROM DIVISION OF HERFF JONES, INC.

MARKABLE

War With Mexico, 1846–1848 **12**

Mexico Before the War

Objective: *To explain conditions in Mexico before the war and how they affected interaction with the United States.*

Teaching Notes and Mapping Activity

You or your students can mark the following on the *War With Mexico* map and the *Claiming the Southwest* timeline.

1. Spain originally held the territory that became the country of **Mexico**. Mexico won its independence from Spain in 1821.

   a. On the timeline, draw a box around the entry for 1821.

   b. Point out that in 1821, Mexico included the pink area, the disputed area, and all of Texas. On the map, draw a line along the boundary between Mexico and the United States in 1821.

2. The newly independent Mexico faced **many obstacles** in the years before the war. One of the main problems of the young country was an unstable government.

   a. Mexico City was the capital of the new country. Circle the label for Mexico City.

   b. In the Gulf of Mexico, write **1821–1845 UNSTABLE GOVT**. Draw an arrow from that label to the label for Mexico City.

   c. Mexico also had a very weak economy and a large national debt. Below UNSTABLE GOVT, write **WEAK ECONOMY**.

3. Another of Mexico's problems was its sparsely populated northern territories. Their distance from the rest of the country made it difficult for Mexico to take advantage of their resources.

   a. In 1821, only about 1% of all Mexicans lived north of El Paso. Below the boundary between Mexico and the Oregon Territory, write **SPARSELY POPULATED (1%)**.

   b. Only 3,000 Mexicans lived in **Upper California** in 1821. Below the label for Monterey, write **3,000**.

   c. There were only 2,500 Mexicans in **Texas** in 1821. Below the label for Texas, write **2,500**.

   d. **New Mexico** was the most populous of the northern territories.

In 1821 it was home to about 40,000 Mexicans. Below the label for Santa Fe, write **40,000**.

   e. Most Mexicans lived in the densely populated **south**. Across Mexico, between Monterrey and Mexico City, write **DENSELY POPULATED (99%)**.

4. Mexicans in the northern territories were isolated from the rest of the country.

   a. Starting south of San Diego, draw a dotted line southeast until it reaches the Gulf of Mexico south of Corpus Christi.

   b. Above the line, write **ISOLATED NORTH**.

5. The isolation of the North limited its trade and communication with the rest of the country. So Mexicans in the northern territories turned to the **United States** for supplies, commerce, and news.

   a. Circle the label for the United States.

   b. From the circled label, draw arrows pointing to the labels for San Francisco, Santa Fe, and Texas.

   c. Label each arrow **U.S. SETTLERS & TRADE**.

   d. Before 1840, most U.S. trade with California was by sea. In the Pacific Ocean west of San Francisco, write **U.S. TRADE**.

 Have students measure the distance between each of the cities below and Mexico City. Then ask how students think their distance from the capital affected their feeling of allegiance to Mexico?
   - San Francisco
   - Los Angeles
   - El Paso
   - Santa Fe
   - San Antonio

Correlates with:

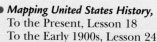

- *The Nystrom Atlas of United States History,* pages 54–55
- *Mapping United States History,* To the Present, Lesson 18 To the Early 1900s, Lesson 24

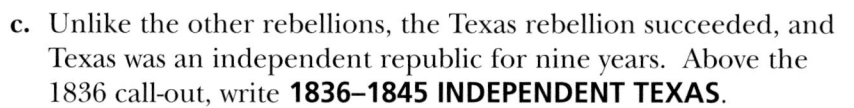

Teaching Notes and Mapping Activity

You and your students can mark the following on the *War With Mexico* map and the locator map.

1. In the 1800s, many people in the United States believed that it was their *Manifest Destiny* to inhabit the North American continent from the Atlantic Ocean to the Pacific Ocean.

   a. On the locator map, draw an arrow across the United States from the Atlantic to the Pacific.

   b. Label the arrow **MANIFEST DESTINY**.

   c. The United States believed that it was part of their Manifest Destiny to bring democracy and economic prosperity to the new lands they settled. Below MANIFEST DESTINY, write **DEMOCRACY** and **PROSPERITY**.

2. Mexico won independence from Spain at the same time that the United States was rapidly expanding. To create a buffer between itself and its growing neighbor, the Mexican government encouraged U.S. settlers to emigrate to **Texas**.

   a. Along the northern and eastern boundaries of Texas, write ① **BUFFER**.

   b. Below the label for Texas, write **U.S. SETTLERS**.

   c. To obtain land, settlers were required to swear allegiance to Mexico. In the eyes of the Mexican government, these settlers were Mexican citizens. Below U.S. SETTLERS, write = **MEXICAN CITIZENS?**

3. From 1821 to 1845, Mexico's unstable government and poor economy led many Mexicans to rebel against the government in the hopes of improving their situations.

   a. Across southern Mexico, between Mazatlan and Veracruz, write ② **MANY REBELLIONS**.

   b. In 1836, Texans also rebelled. Next to the 1836 call-out describing Texas' declaration of independence, write ③.

   c. Unlike the other rebellions, the Texas rebellion succeeded, and Texas was an independent republic for nine years. Above the 1836 call-out, write **1836–1845 INDEPENDENT TEXAS**.

4. In 1845, the United States annexed Texas. The Mexican government, which still considered Texas part of Mexico, saw this annexation as an act of war. Above to the call-out describing this annexation, write ④ **ACT OF WAR?**

5. The United States not only annexed Texas, it also claimed that the state's southern boundary was not the **Nueces River**, which ran through Corpus Christi, but the **Rio Grande**, which was about 150 miles south of the Nueces. Mexico disagreed.

   a. Compare the size of the territory north of the Nueces River with the size of the territory north of the Rio Grande.

   b. In April 1846, the U.S. Army crossed the Nueces River. Next to the call-out describing this event, write ⑤.

6. Mexico saw the U.S. action as an invasion of their country. Within a month, Mexican forces attacked a U.S. patrol and later fought the U.S. Army at Matamoros.

   a. Next to the label "May 8, 1846," write ⑥.

   b. It was only *after* several battles in the disputed territory that Congress officially declared war on Mexico. In the Gulf of Mexico, write ⑦ **U.S. DECLARES WAR**.

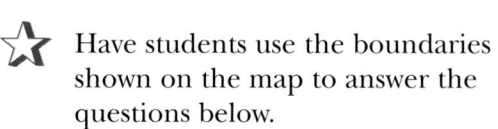

Have students use the boundaries shown on the map to answer the questions below.
- How many major battles took place in the United States?
- How many major battles took place in or near the disputed territory?
- How many major battles took place in Mexican territory?

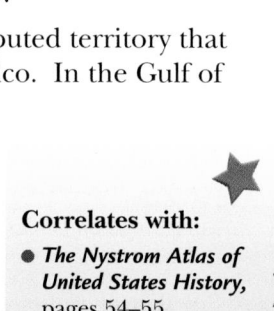
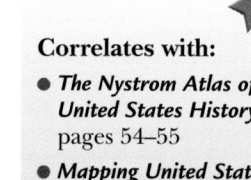
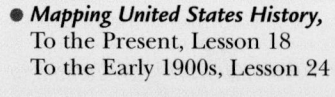

Correlates with:
- *The Nystrom Atlas of United States History,* pages 54–55
- *Mapping United States History,* To the Present, Lesson 18 To the Early 1900s, Lesson 24

The Spoils of Manifest Destiny

Objective: *To show how the consequences of the U.S.-Mexican War affected the territory acquired from Mexico.*

Teaching Notes and Mapping Activity

You and your students can mark the following on the *War With Mexico* map and the locator map.

1. With the victory over Mexico, the United States had achieved its *Manifest Destiny*. With the land gained from the war, the country extended from the Atlantic Ocean to the Pacific Ocean.

   a. On the locator map, write **MANIFEST DESTINY** across the United States.

   b. Point out the new boundary between the United States and Mexico—the Treaty line of 1848 and the Rio Grande. On the *War With Mexico* map, draw a line along this boundary.

   c. Draw a line through the label for Mexico.

   d. Label **MEXICO** south of the new boundary.

2. The new territory gave U.S. settlers more places to go where they could own their own land. U.S. settlers believed that it was part of their Manifest Destiny to bring democracy to these new lands.

   a. Circle the label for the United States.

   b. Draw an arrow from the label toward the new territory.

   c. Label the arrow **MORE SETTLERS**.

   d. Below MANIFEST DESTINY, write **DEMOCRACY**.

3. The U.S. settlers also believed that part of their Manifest Destiny involved bringing economic prosperity to the lands they settled. The newly acquired territory provided the United States with many economic opportunities.

   a. The land was very rich in minerals, particularly gold, silver, and copper. Across the new territory, write **GOLD**, **SILVER**, and **COPPER**.

   b. The land was also ideal for cattle ranching. Below GOLD, SILVER, and COPPER, write **CATTLE RANCHING**.

   c. California had important seaports, which improved U.S. ability to ship and trade goods throughout the world. Along the California coast, write **SHIPPING & TRADE**.

   d. All of these economic opportunities allowed U.S. settlers to achieve the prosperity that they assumed was part of their Manifest Destiny. Below DEMOCRACY, write **PROSPERITY**.

4. Despite its democratic intentions, Manifest Destiny meant taking lands that had been held by others. The former Mexican territories were not empty. Mexicans and Native Americans had been living there for centuries.

   a. In 1848, more than 75,000 Mexicans lived in the newly acquired territory. Below the label for the United States, write **75,000 MEXICANS**.

   b. There were at least 200,000 Native Americans living in the former Mexican territory in 1848. Below 75,000 MEXICANS, write **200,000+ NATIVE AMERICANS**.

5. U.S. settlers thought it was acceptable to take Mexican and Native American land, simply because these people were not white. Mexicans and Native Americans who found themselves living in U.S. territories also found that they had no rights whatsoever— Manifest Destiny did not apply to them. To the right of MANIFEST DESTINY, write **(ONLY FOR WHITES)**.

 Have your students use a contemporary map of the United States to answer the questions below.

  • Which U.S. states were all or partly formed from the territory acquired from Mexico in 1848?

  • List 5–10 major cities now located in the territory that once were part of Mexico.

Correlates with:

● *The Nystrom Atlas of United States History,* pages 54–55

● *Mapping United States History,* To the Present, Lesson 18 To the Early 1900s, Lesson 24

★ 13 SLAVERY DIVIDES THE NATION 1820–1857

Key Elements

★ *Missouri Compromise* map
★ *Compromise of 1850* map
★ *Kansas-Nebraska Act* map
★ *Dred Scott Decision* map

Getting Started

To give students an overview of *Slavery Divides the Nation,* ask them:

- The maps in *Slavery Divides the Nation* show the United States in which four years?

- What color are the slave states? The free states?

- What color are territories where slavery was banned?

- What color are territories where slavery was allowed by Congress? By the Supreme Court?

- What color are territories where the decision on slavery was left to the people of the territory?

- How did these decisions on slavery in the territories change over time?

Teaching Notes and Mapping Activities

～ The First Compromises
～ From Compromise to Conflict
～ Congress vs. Supreme Court

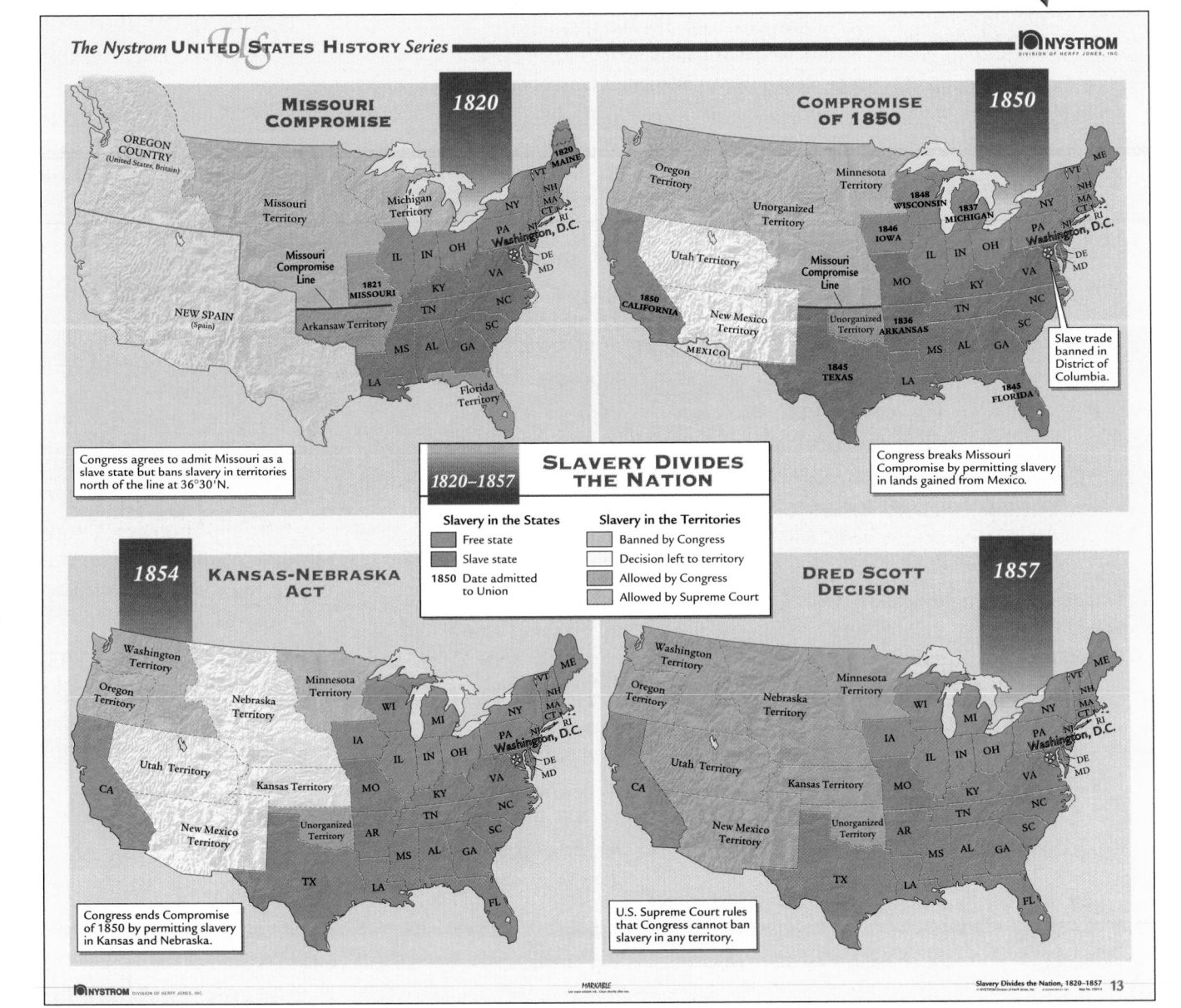

The Nystrom UNITED STATES HISTORY Series — NYSTROM

MISSOURI COMPROMISE — 1820

Congress agrees to admit Missouri as a slave state but bans slavery in territories north of the line at 36°30′N.

COMPROMISE OF 1850 — 1850

Congress breaks Missouri Compromise by permitting slavery in lands gained from Mexico.

Slave trade banned in District of Columbia.

SLAVERY DIVIDES THE NATION
1820–1857

Slavery in the States
- Free state
- Slave state
- 1850 Date admitted to Union

Slavery in the Territories
- Banned by Congress
- Decision left to territory
- Allowed by Congress
- Allowed by Supreme Court

1854 KANSAS-NEBRASKA ACT

Congress ends Compromise of 1850 by permitting slavery in Kansas and Nebraska.

DRED SCOTT DECISION — 1857

U.S. Supreme Court rules that Congress cannot ban slavery in any territory.

The First Compromises

Objective: *To show how the issue of slavery led to political compromises in 1820 and 1850.*

Teaching Notes and Mapping Activity

You or your students can mark the following on the *Missouri Compromise* map and the *Compromise of 1850* map.

1. The issue of slavery in the **territories** began with the **Louisiana Purchase** in 1803. At first, deciding which new states would allow slavery and which would be free was based on the boundaries formed by the Ohio and Mississippi Rivers.

   a. On the *Missouri Compromise* map, draw a line along the Ohio and Mississippi Rivers. Point out that they were accepted boundaries between slave states and free states.

   b. Louisiana fell outside these natural boundaries, but because it was located in the South, few contested its admission as a slave state. Find Louisiana on the map.

2. Conflict arose once territories west of the Mississippi began to apply for statehood. When Missouri applied for statehood in 1818, Congress took two years to find a solution. In 1820, Congress voted to ban slavery in territories north of 36° 30'N, but to allow slavery south of this line. Label the **Missouri Compromise** Line **36° 30'**.

3. Missouri was an exception to the new law, It was admitted as a slave state. Maine was added in 1820 as a free state, which gave slave and free states equal representation in the Senate.

   a. Underline the labels for Maine and Missouri.

   b. Across the **slave states**, write **12 STATES**. Across the **free states**, write **12 STATES**.

4. When new territory was acquired after the Mexican War, the slavery issue resurfaced. In 1850, Congress passed a series of bills designed to appease both slave and free states.

   a. On the *Compromise of 1850* map, write **SERIES OF BILLS** below the title of the map.

   b. First, California was admitted as a free state. In California, write ① **FREE STATE**.

5. California gave free states a majority in the Senate. To appease the South, Congress agreed that in Utah and New Mexico, settlers themselves would vote to decide the issue of slavery.

   a. This decision process was known as *popular sovereignty*. In the Utah and New Mexico Territories, write ② **POP. SOV.**

   b. In the *Slavery Divides the Nation* legend box, write **(SLAVERY POSSIBLE)** after "Decision left to territory."

6. Other aspects of the Compromise of 1850 included a ban on the slave trade in the District of Columbia and the creation of a stronger fugitive slave law.

   a. Northerners did not want the slave trade taking place in the nation's capital. Next to the call-out pointing to Washington, D.C., on the *Compromise of 1850* map, write ③.

   b. In return, Northern senators agreed to a law that committed free states to helping to capture and return runaway slaves. Across the eastern free states, write ④ **FUGITIVE SLAVE LAW**.

7. Many Northerners were furious about the Fugitive Slave Law. As a result, support for the Underground Railroad increased. Across the slave states, near their boundary with the free states, write **UNDERGROUND RAILROAD EXPANDS**.

 Have students use the 1820 and 1850 maps to answer the questions below:

- In how many territories was slavery banned in 1820? In 1850?
- In how many territories was slavery possible through popular sovereignty in 1820? In 1850?

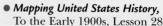

Correlates with:

- *The Nystrom Atlas of United States History,* pages 60–61
- *Mapping United States History,* To the Early 1900s, Lesson 28

From Compromise to Conflict

Objective: *To show some consequences of the continuing political compromises between free states and slave states.*

page 54

Teaching Notes and Mapping Activity

You and your students can mark the following on the *Slavery Divides the Nation* maps.

1. In 1854, Congress again compromised on the issue of slavery in the territories. For years, Southern senators obstructed the organization of the territories north of 36° 30'N, because their admission as free states would further diminish Southern power in the Senate. However, this tactic changed when proposals were made to build a railroad to the Pacific Ocean.

   a. Stephen Douglas, a senator from Illinois, wanted this railroad to begin in Chicago. On the 1850 map, write **RR** in Illinois.

   b. Draw an arrow from the RR in Illinois to the Pacific Coast in California and label it **NATIONAL RAILROAD**.

2. A national railroad could not be built through unorganized territory, so Douglas made a deal with Southern senators. If they would support the organization of the **Nebraska and Kansas Territories**, Douglas would support a bill to repeal the Missouri Compromise.

   a. On the 1850 map, circle the label for Unorganized Territory.

   b. On the 1854 map, circle the labels for the Nebraska and Kansas Territories

   c. Draw an arrow from the title of the *Kansas-Nebraska Act* map to the title of the *Missouri Compromise* map.

   d. Label the arrow **REPEALED**.

3. With the repeal of the Missouri Compromise, the new territories were open to the slavery through popular sovereignty.

   a. On the *Kansas-Nebraska Act* map, write **POP. SOV.** above the labels for the Kansas and Nebraska Territories.

   b. In the *Slavery Divides the Nation* legend box, write **(SLAVERY POSSIBLE)** after "Decision left to territory."

4. Douglas convinced many senators to support his bill by claiming that if the Unorganized Territory were divided into two parts, Nebraska would become a free territory, and Kansas would be a slave territory. This appealed to senators from both free and slave states.

   a. Draw an arrow from the free states to the Nebraska Territory. Label the arrow **FREE?**

   b. Draw an arrow from the slave states to the Kansas Territory. Label the arrow **SLAVE?**

5. Many Americans believed that popular sovereignty was the best way to decide on slavery in the territories. However, both pro- and anti-slavery forces rushed to settle Kansas. Soon violence erupted, and the territory became known as *Bleeding Kansas*. Below the label for the Kansas Territory, write **BLEEDING KANSAS**.

6. The controversy created by the **Kansas-Nebraska Act** led to the creation of a new political party in the United States. The Republican Party was created in 1854 in Michigan. Its main goal was to prevent the growth of slavery in the territories.

   a. Across Michigan, write **REPUBLICAN PARTY 1854**.

   b. Below REPUBLICAN PARTY, write **NO SLAVERY IN TERR.**

☆ Have students use the 1854 maps to answer the questions below:
  - In how many territories was slavery banned by Congress ?
  - In how many territories was slavery possible through popular sovereignty?
  - In 1854, which was greater—the amount of territory in which slavery was banned, or the amount of territory in which slavery was possible through popular sovereignty?

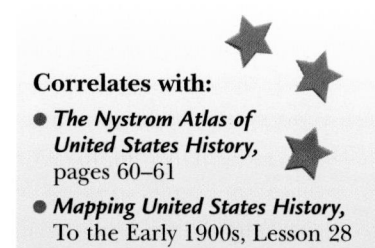

Correlates with:
- *The Nystrom Atlas of United States History,* pages 60–61
- *Mapping United States History,* To the Early 1900s, Lesson 28

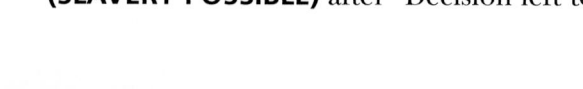

Congress v. Supreme Court

Objective: To show how the Supreme Court negated years of Congressional compromise on the issue of slavery.

Teaching Notes and Mapping Activity

You and your students can mark the following on the *Slavery Divides the Nation* maps.

1. As free and slave states created compromise after compromise, some Southerners argued that Congress did not have the power to make **laws concerning slavery** in the first place. In 1857, the Supreme Court ruled on this issue.

   a. Above the title of the *Dred Scott Decision* map, write **SUPREME COURT**.

   b. Above the titles of the other three maps, write **CONGRESS**.

2. **Dred Scott** was a slave owned by an army surgeon. In the 1830s, Scott's master moved from the slave state of Missouri to Illinois and then the Wisconsin Territory, but he eventually returned to Missouri. Scott's lawyers argued that his residence in free areas made him a free man.

   a. On the 1820 map, write ⚥ **DS** in Missouri. Then draw an arrow from the DS to Illinois.

   b. Draw a second arrow north from Illinois to Michigan Territory, from which Wisconsin was carved.

   c. Draw a third arrow back to Missouri.

3. The Dred Scott case reached the **U.S. Supreme Court** in 1857. At that time, a majority of the Supreme Court justices, including **Chief Justice Roger Taney**, were Southerners. Taney and the court ruled that as a slave, Dred Scott was not a person, but property. As property, he was not a U.S. citizen, had no rights, and therefore could not file a suit in a court of law.

   a. On the *Dred Scott Decision* map, write **SLAVE = PROPERTY** across the slave states.

   b. Below SLAVE = PROPERTY, write **SLAVE ≠ PERSON/U.S. CITIZEN**.

   c. Below PERSON/U.S. CITIZEN, write **NO RIGHTS**.

4. Scott's attorneys argued that Scott had lived in territories where slavery had been banned by the Missouri Compromise. Taney ruled that the Missouri Compromise was unconstitutional, because Congress had no right to pass laws that interfered with a **citizen's right to own property**—in this case, slaves.

   a. Draw arrows from the title for the *Dred Scott Decision* map to the titles of the other three maps.

   b. Across the titles of each of these three maps, write **UNCONSTITUTIONAL**.

   c. The Supreme Court decision made slavery legal in *all* the territories of the United States. Across the territories on the *Dred Scott Decision* map, write **PROPERTY (SLAVERY) PROTECTED BY CONSTITUTION**.

5. The Dred Scott decision was extremely controversial and served to further divide the United States. Some Northerners worried that Southerners would use the decision to force slavery on states that had already banned it. Others, like anti-slavery activist John Brown, saw the decision as a message that slavery could only be ended through violence.

   a. Across the northern free states, write **SLAVERY LEGAL?**

   b. Below SLAVERY LEGAL?, write **END SLAVERY THROUGH VIOLENCE?**

 Have your students compare all the maps. Then ask them to explain:
   - How each map shows the United States as a country literally divided by the issue of slavery.
   - How the maps show change over time regarding the issue of slavery.

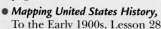

Correlates with:
- *The Nystrom Atlas of United States History,* pages 60–61
- *Mapping United States History,* To the Early 1900s, Lesson 28

SLAVERY AND THE ECONOMY
1860

Key Elements

★ *Slavery and the Economy* map
★ *Regional Populations* graph
★ *Cotton for the Textile Industry* graph

Getting Started

To give students an overview of *Slavery and the Economy,* ask them:

• What region of the world is shown on the map?

• What do the different-colored areas on the map represent?

• What do the different symbols on the map represent?

• Look at the *Regional Populations* graph. What three regions do they show?

• What information do the graphs show about each region?

• On the *Cotton for the Textile Industry* graph, what statistics are shown?

• What years does this graph cover?

Teaching Notes and Mapping Activities

~ North, South, and West in 1860
~ The Cotton Kingdom
~ The Industrial Empire

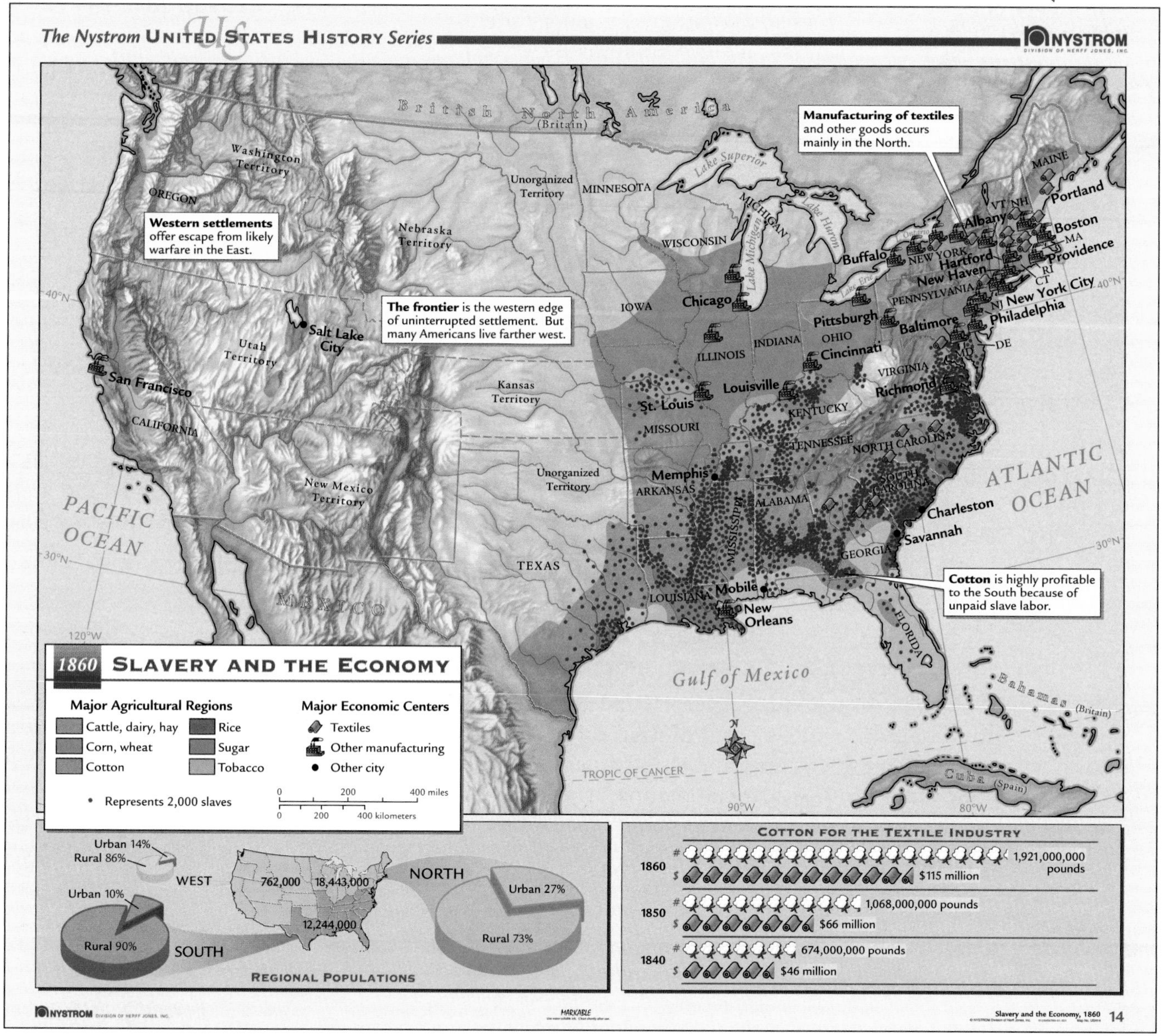

The Nystrom UNITED US STATES HISTORY *Series*

Manufacturing of textiles and other goods occurs mainly in the North.

Western settlements offer escape from likely warfare in the East.

The frontier is the western edge of uninterrupted settlement. But many Americans live farther west.

Cotton is highly profitable to the South because of unpaid slave labor.

1860 SLAVERY AND THE ECONOMY

Major Agricultural Regions
- Cattle, dairy, hay
- Corn, wheat
- Cotton
- Rice
- Sugar
- Tobacco

Major Economic Centers
- ◆ Textiles
- 🚂 Other manufacturing
- ● Other city

• Represents 2,000 slaves

0   200   400 miles
0   200   400 kilometers

REGIONAL POPULATIONS

WEST — Urban 14% / Rural 86%
762,000   18,443,000
SOUTH — Urban 10% / Rural 90%
12,244,000
NORTH — Urban 27% / Rural 73%

COTTON FOR THE TEXTILE INDUSTRY

Year	#	$
1860	1,921,000,000 pounds	$115 million
1850	1,068,000,000 pounds	$66 million
1840	674,000,000 pounds	$46 million

North, South, and West in 1860

Objective: *To provide an overview of the economies of different regions on the eve of the Civil War.*

Teaching Notes and Mapping Activity

You or your students can discuss the *Slavery and the Economy* map and the *Regional Populations* graph.

1. In 1860 the North, the South, and the West were all more rural than urban. Yet these three U.S. regions differed greatly. On the *Slavery and the Economy* map, draw lines along the boundaries separating the three regions. (See the *Regional Populations* graph.) Then have your students answer the questions below.

   a. Which states are part of the **North**?

   b. Which states are part of the **South**?

   c. Which states are part of the **West**? What are the other areas that make up the West?

2. The **agricultural economy** of each region was based on different combinations of agricultural products. Ask your students to look at the different agricultural regions on the map and then answer the questions below.

   a. In the North, what are the two major agricultural regions?

   b. In the South, what are the two most widespread agricultural regions? What other agricultural regions did the South have?

   c. What are the two main agricultural regions in the West?

3. Of all the regions, only the South had large numbers of **slaves**. Ask your students to look at the different agricultural regions in the South and then answer the questions below.

   a. Which agricultural regions had a high number of slaves?

   b. Which agricultural regions had few slaves?

4. Though the South produced all of the nation's **cotton**, most U.S. **textile mills**—which created fabric and clothing from cotton—were located in the North. Circle all the symbols for textile centers on the map and then ask the following questions.

   a. How many major textile mills were located in the South? In the North? In the West?

   b. In which of these regions was textile production a major economic activity?

5. The South had very few other major **manufacturing centers**. Draw boxes around symbols for manufacturing centers on the map and then ask the questions below.

   a. How many major manufacturing centers were located in the South? In the North? In the West?

   b. In which region was manufacturing a major part of the overall economy?

6. There were **population differences** in each region as well. Ask your students to look at the *Regional Populations* graph and then answer the questions below.

   a. What was the population of the South in 1860? What percentage of this population lived in cities?

   b. What was the population of the North in 1860? What percentage of this population lived in cities?

   c. What was the population of the West in 1860? What percentage of this population lived in cities?

 Have your students list the economic characteristics of each region and then answer the questions below:

- Which region do you think had the most diverse economy? Why?
- Which region had the largest percentage of its population involved in agriculture?
- Which region had the least amount of economic activity? Why?

Correlates with:

- **The Nystrom Atlas of United States History,** pages 62–63
- **Mapping United States History,** To the Present, Lesson 21 To the 1900s, Lesson 30

The Cotton Kingdom

Objective: *To illustrate the importance of cotton and slavery to Southern economy.*

Teaching Notes and Mapping Activity

You or your students can mark the following on the *Slavery and the Economy* map and the *Cotton for the Textile Industry* graph.

1. In 1860 the **most important crop in the South** was cotton. Southern cotton was made into fabric and clothing in the textile mills of both the North and Europe.

   a. Point out the growth of the Southern cotton industry on the *Cotton for the Textile Industry* graph.

   b. Circle two or three textile center symbols in the North.

   c. Draw arrows from the cotton-producing region in the South to the symbols that you circled. Label them **COTTON**.

   d. Now draw an arrow from the cotton-producing region to the Atlantic Ocean. Label it **COTTON - TO EUROPE**.

2. The South became so dependent on cotton that it grew few other crops. In fact, regions in which cotton was the main crop usually **had to import agricultural products** such as grain and beef from other areas.

   a. The **Deep South** imported wheat and corn from both the **Upper South** and the **North**. Draw an arrow from the green corn and wheat-growing region to the pink cotton-growing region. Label it **GRAIN**.

   b. Much of the beef eaten in the South came from **Texas**. Draw an arrow from the orange cattle-producing region in Texas to the pink cotton-producing region. Label it **BEEF**.

3. The South had **very little manufacturing** of any kind. Most manufactured goods used by Southerners, such as tools and weapons, were produced in the North.

   a. Circle two or three manufacturing symbols in the North.

   b. Draw arrows from the symbols you circled to the pink cotton-growing region in the South.

   c. Label the arrows **MFD. GOODS**.

4. Although there were some textile mills in the South, most of the clothing worn by Southerners came from fabric woven in the North.

   a. Circle another textile mill symbol in the North.

   b. Draw an arrow from the symbol you circled to the pink cotton-producing region in the South.

   c. Label the arrow **CLOTHING/FABRIC**.

5. From the sale of cotton, **Southerners invested profits** in what would help them increase production and earn even more money—**more slaves**. As the price of cotton went up, so did the price of the slaves they needed to grow and harvest the crop.

   a. In 1840 the average price of a slave was $750. On the 1840 line of the graph, write ☖ = **$750**.

   b. In 1850 the average price of a slave was $1000. On the 1850 line of the graph, write ☖ = **$1000**.

   c. In 1860 the average price of a slave was $1500. On the 1860 line of the graph, write ☖ = **$1500**.

   d. Historians estimate that in 1860 the South had between one and six billion dollars invested in slaves. Above the graph, write **INVESTED IN SLAVES = $1–6 BILLION**.

Ask students to answer these questions: What might have happened to the economy of the South if...
- ...the cotton crop failed or cotton prices dropped drastically?
- ...Europe and the North found another supplier of cotton?
- ...other regions refused to export grain and beef to the South?
- ...slaves were set free?

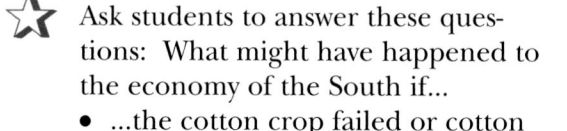

Correlates with:
- *The Nystrom Atlas of United States History,* pages 62–63
- *Mapping United States History,* To the Present, Lesson 21 To the 1900s, Lesson 30

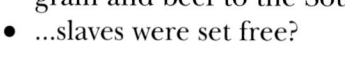

The Industrial Empire

Objective: *To illustrate the importance of manufacturing and trade to Northern economy.*

Teaching Notes and Mapping Activity

You or your students can mark the following on *Slavery and the Economy* map and the two graphs.

1. In 1860, the vast majority of U.S. **manufacturing** took place in **the North**. Most manufacturing centers were in the east, but northern industry extended as far west as Illinois. Manufacturing centers were linked by railroads.

   a. Choose a manufacturing center on the Atlantic Coast. Draw a line linking it to a center farther west.

   b. Draw a new line linking this second manufacturing center with one even farther west.

   c. Continue drawing lines linking northern manufacturing centers until the lines connect the Atlantic Coast manufacturing center to one of the centers in Illinois.

   d. Finally, link each manufacturing center along the route you have drawn to any other centers nearby.

2. **Railroads** helped northern industry. They transported grain, beef, and dairy products from rural areas to cities, and they transported manufactured goods and textiles produced in urban areas to distant farming communities.

   a. Look at the *Regional Populations* graph. On the North circle graph, across the Rural section, write **GRAIN**, **BEEF**, and **DAIRY**. Across the Urban section, write **MFD. GOODS** and **TEXTILES**.

   b. To show this transportation and trade pattern, draw a curving arrow from the labels for the agricultural products to the labels for the industrial products.

   c. Draw another curving arrow from the labels for the industrial products to the labels for the agricultural products.

3. Northern industry required raw materials, such as cotton, for its manufactured goods. Northern textile mills made large profits creating fabric and clothing from **Southern cotton**.

   a. Draw a line from the cotton-producing region in the South to two or three textile center symbols in the North.

   b. Southern cotton production was closely linked to profits made by the Northern textile industry. Ask your students to look at the *Cotton for the Textile Industry* graph.

   c. Write **ALL SOUTH** next to each line that shows the cotton production for that year.

   d. Write **MOSTLY NORTH** next to each line that shows the amount of money made by the textile industry each year.

4. Northern grain, textiles, and manufactured goods were shipped to both Europe and the South.

   a. In the Atlantic Ocean east of the manufacturing centers, draw a ship.

   b. From the ship draw an arrow pointing east. Label it **TO EUROPE**.

   c. Draw another arrow pointing south. Label it **TO THE SOUTH**.

5. Industrialists invested their profits in new machinery, raw materials, and land for new factories. In 1860, the United States had about one billion dollars invested in industry, most of it in the North. Above the Great Lakes, write **INVESTED IN INDUSTRY = $1 BILLION**.

 Ask students what might have happened to the North's economy if...
   - ...it could no longer get cotton from the South?
   - ...slaves were set free?

Correlates with:
- *The Nystrom Atlas of United States History,* pages 62–63
- *Mapping United States History,* To the Present, Lesson 21 To the 1900s, Lesson 30

THE UNION AND THE CONFEDERACY 1861–1865

Key Elements

★ *The Union and the Confederacy* map
★ *Populations* graphs
★ *National Resources* graph

Getting Started

To give students an overview of *The Union and the Confederacy,* ask them:

- What period of time does the map cover?
- What color are the states that are part of the Confederacy? Why?
- What color are the states that are part of the Union? Why?
- Did the Confederate States of America consist of free states or slave states?
- Did the United States of America consist of free states, slave states, or both? How can you tell?
- On the *Populations* graph, what do the colors represent?
- On the *Natural Resources* graph, what do blue and gray represent?

Teaching Notes and Mapping Activities

~ North vs. South: Different Perspectives

~ Patterns of Secession

~ Resources and the War Effort

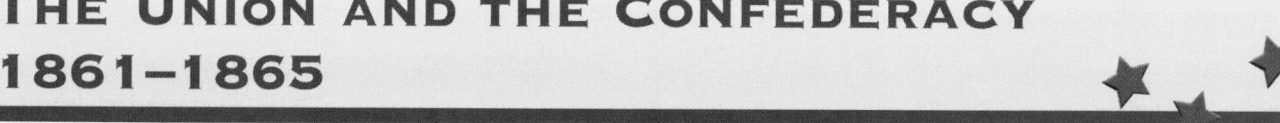

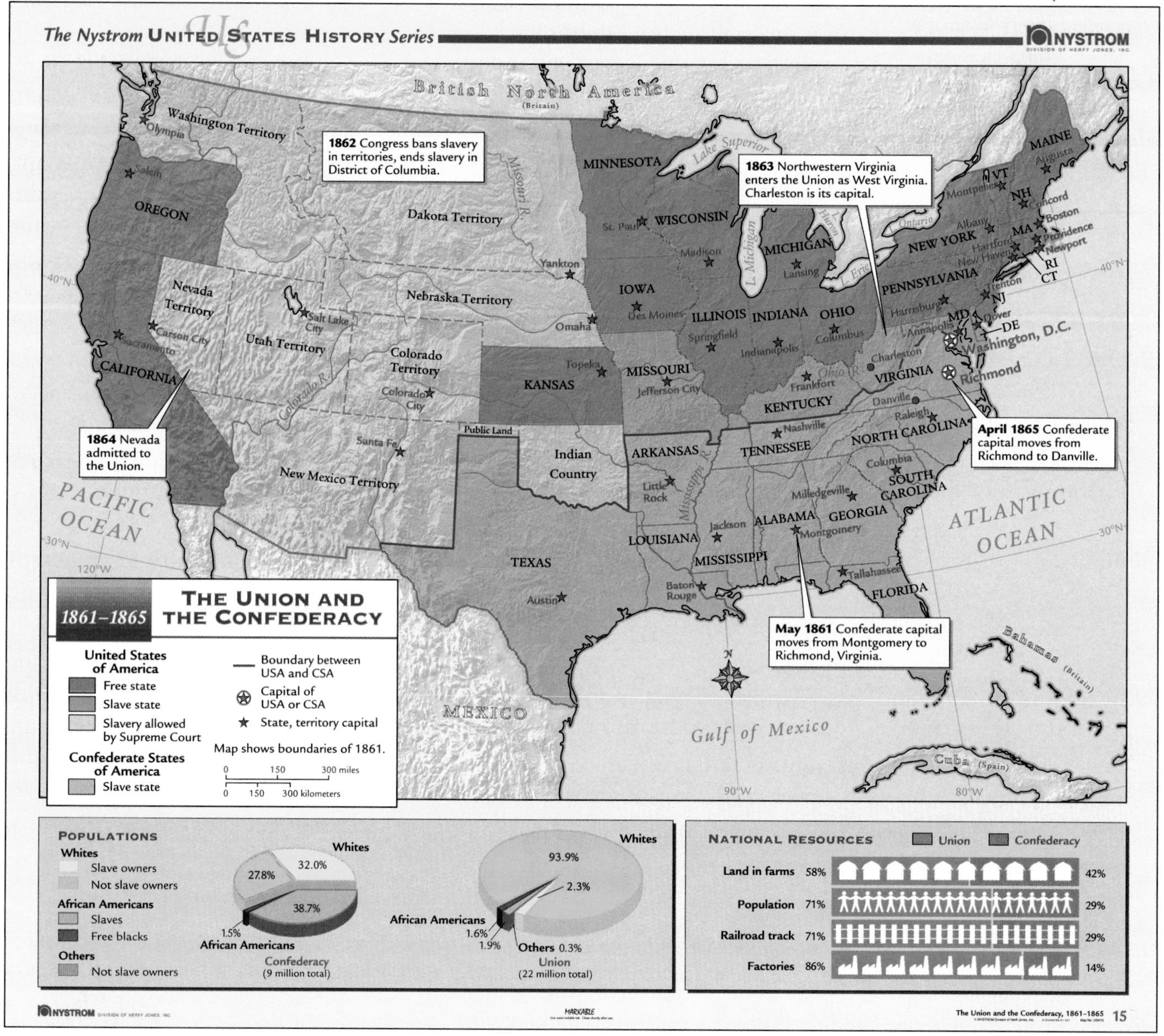

The Nystrom **UNITED STATES HISTORY** *Series* — **NYSTROM** DIVISION OF HERFF JONES, INC.

1862 Congress bans slavery in territories, ends slavery in District of Columbia.

1863 Northwestern Virginia enters the Union as West Virginia. Charleston is its capital.

1864 Nevada admitted to the Union.

April 1865 Confederate capital moves from Richmond to Danville.

May 1861 Confederate capital moves from Montgomery to Richmond, Virginia.

THE UNION AND THE CONFEDERACY
1861–1865

United States of America
- Free state
- Slave state
- Slavery allowed by Supreme Court

Confederate States of America
- Slave state

— Boundary between USA and CSA
⊛ Capital of USA or CSA
★ State, territory capital

Map shows boundaries of 1861.

0   150   300 miles
0   150   300 kilometers

POPULATIONS

Whites
- Slave owners
- Not slave owners

African Americans
- Slaves
- Free blacks

Others
- Not slave owners

Whites 32.0%
27.8%
38.7%
1.5%

Confederacy
(9 million total)

Whites 93.9%
2.3%
African Americans 1.6%
1.9%
Others 0.3%

Union
(22 million total)

NATIONAL RESOURCES   ■ Union   ■ Confederacy

	Union	Confederacy
Land in farms	58%	42%
Population	71%	29%
Railroad track	71%	29%
Factories	86%	14%

NYSTROM DIVISION OF HERFF JONES, INC.   HARKABLE   *The Union and the Confederacy, 1861–1865* **15**

North vs. South: Different Perspectives

Objective: *To note the different points of view held by Southerners and Northerners that led to the Civil War.*

Teaching Notes and Mapping Activity

You or your students can mark the following on *The Union and the Confederacy* map.

1. The division of the country into the **Union** (USA) and the **Confederacy** (CSA) was the culmination of years of tension between the North and the South.

   a. On the map, just above the Union states, write and underline **NORTH**.

   b. Trace the boundary line between the USA and CSA.

   c. Below the boundary line, write and underline **SOUTH**.

2. While the Civil War is commonly thought of as a war to end slavery, the situation was far more complicated than that. North and South had long been at odds over the issue of states' rights versus the power of the federal government.

   a. Most **Southerners** believed that individual states should be allowed to govern themselves with little or no interference from the federal government. Below SOUTH, write **STATES' RIGHTS**.

   b. Most **Northerners** believed that the federal government should have the final say over any laws passed in the states. Below NORTH, write **FEDERAL GOVERNMENT**.

3. **Slavery** did not cause the Civil War. However, it was the issue that brought the conflict between the Southern states and the federal government to a head.

   a. **Slave states** felt that they had the right to make their own laws concerning slavery. Below STATES' RIGHTS, write **STATES DECIDE SLAVERY**.

   b. **Free states** felt the federal government could overrule state laws on slavery, especially if the state laws violated the Constitution or affected other states. Below FEDERAL GOVERNMENT, write **FED GOVT DECIDES SLAVERY**.

4. When Abraham Lincoln, an anti-slavery Republican, was elected president in November 1860, many Southerners believed that the federal government would override existing state laws that allowed slavery. Their views on states' rights led many Southern states to leave the Union. They felt that each state had **the right to secede** if it wanted to do so.

   a. Below STATES DECIDE, write **SECESSION LEGAL**.

   b. Northerners felt that no state could simply decide to leave the Union. Below FED GOVT DECIDES, write **SECESSION ILLEGAL**.

5. Because Southerners believed states had the right to secede from the Union, they viewed the **formation of the Confederate States of America** as a legal act. To many Northerners, the formation of the Confederacy was both criminal and treasonous.

   a. Seceding **Southerners** believed themselves to be citizens of a new nation. Below SECESSION LEGAL, write **CSA = NEW NATION**.

   b. **Northerners**, on the other hand, saw the Confederacy as a group of states in rebellion against their government. Below SECESSION ILLEGAL, write **CSA = STATES IN REBELLION**.

6. You may want to point out to your students that on this map, the Union and Confederacy are the same colors as the uniforms of the two armies— blue and gray.

 The different perspectives of the North and South even led to different names for the Civil War. Have students discuss why they think most Northerners referred to the conflict as the Civil War or The War Between the States, and Southerners called it The War of Northern Aggression.

Correlates with:
- *The Nystrom Atlas of United States History,* pages 64–65
- *Mapping United States History,* To the Present, Lessons 20–21 To the Early 1900s, Lesson 29–30

Patterns of Secession

Objective: *To sequence the secession of different slave states and to identify those that did not secede.*

Teaching Notes and Mapping Activity

You or your students can mark the following on
The Union and the Confederacy map.

1. The Confederate States of America did not spring up overnight, nor did all the Southern states **secede** immediately after Abraham Lincoln was elected. **South Carolina**, the first state to secede, did so a month after Lincoln was elected.

   a. Outline the state of South Carolina.

   b. In South Carolina, write ① **DEC. 1860**.

2. In January 1861, five more Southern states—**Mississippi**, **Florida**, **Alabama**, **Georgia**, and **Louisiana**—followed South Carolina's example and seceded from the Union. (States are named in chronological order of secession.)

   a. Outline the group of states listed above.

   b. Across these five states, write ② **JAN. 1861**.

3. Two months later, **Texas** joined the states of the Deep South, seceding in March 1861.

   a. Outline Texas

   b. Across Texas, write ③ **MAR. 1861**.

4. For states of the Upper South, the election of Lincoln was not a legitimate reason to secede from the Union, but an attack on Southern states was. **Virginia**, **Arkansas**, **North Carolina**, and **Tennessee** joined the Confederate States of America only *after* U.S. troops fired on Fort Sumter, a federal military installation held by Confederate forces in South Carolina.

   a. Outline the group of Southern states above, the last to secede.

   b. Across this group of states, write ④ **APR. 1861 (AFTER FT. SUMTER)**.

   c. Have your students read the May 1861 call-out. Point out that the Confederate capital was moved to Virginia after the state seceded.

5. Not all slave states chose to secede. The northernmost slaves states—**Missouri**, **Kentucky**, **Maryland**, and **Delaware**—chose to stay with the Union.

   a. Outline each of the states listed above.

   b. In each of the slave states that did not secede, write the letter **U** for Union.

6. Both Missouri and Kentucky had groups of people who favored secession. These groups set up separate state governments and sent delegates to the Confederate Congress.

   a. In Missouri and Kentucky, write and circle the letter **C** for Confederacy.

   b. Draw arrows from each of the circled letters pointing to the Confederate capital in Richmond, Virginia.

7. Not everyone in the Confederate states favored secession. Virginia, in particular, was divided. When the Virginia state legislature voted to secede, many western counties rejected the vote and immediately declared themselves independent from Virginia. These counties quickly banded together, welcomed Union troops, and filed for statehood. In 1863 **West Virginia** was admitted to the Union.

   a. Outline West Virginia.

   b. Read the call-out pointing to West Virginia. Above the call-out, write **1861 - REJECTED SECESSION**.

☆ Ask your students to look at the map and then explain why they think:

- ...the states in the Deep South were the first to secede?
- ...the states in the Upper South waited to secede?
- ...the northernmost slave states did not secede?

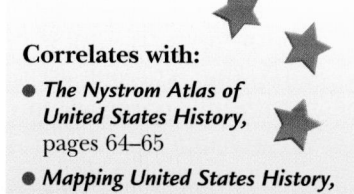

Correlates with:

- ***The Nystrom Atlas of United States History,*** pages 64–65
- ***Mapping United States History,*** To the Present, Lessons 20–21 To the Early 1900s, Lessons 29–30

Resources and the War Effort

Objective: *To evaluate Union and Confederate resources and how they affected the war effort of each side.*

Teaching Notes and Mapping Activity

You or your students can mark the following on *The Union and the Confederacy* map and the two graphs.

1. A nation's **resources** have a huge impact on its ability to wage war. A difference in resources ultimately determined the outcome of the Civil War. For example, even though the Union had only slightly more land in farms than the Confederacy, the products of these farms gave the Union a huge advantage.

   a. Review the *Slavery and the Economy* map (USH14) with your students. Have them identify the major **agricultural products** of the Union and the Confederacy.

   b. The Union's major agricultural products were foodstuffs. At the top of *The Union and the Confederacy* map, across the Union states, write ⚘ ☒ = **GRAINS, BEEF, DAIRY**.

   c. The major agricultural product of the Confederacy was cotton. Just below the boundary between the USA and CSA, write ❀ = **COTTON**.

   d. Have your students look at the *National Resources* graph. Across the Union farm symbols on the "Land in farms" bar, write **FOOD**.

   e. Across the Confederate farm symbols, write **COTTON**.

2. Not only did the Union have more people than the Confederacy, but a higher percentage of the its **population** could be counted on to support the war effort.

   a. In the North, most of the population supported the war effort of the Union. Across the Union *Populations* graph, write **SUPPORTIVE**.

   b. However, in the South, only most whites supported the war efforts of the Confederacy. On the Confederacy *Populations* graph, write **SUPPORTIVE** across the orange and yellow portions.

   c. The Confederacy could not count on slaves or free blacks to support its war effort. Across the red and brown portions of the graph, write **NO**.

   d. Slaves made up nearly 40% of the Confederate population. On the *National Resources* graph, draw **X**'s over three of the Confederate population symbols.

3. The Union had a significant advantage over the Confederacy in miles of **railroad track**. Railroads are valuable during wartime, because they allow an army to quickly transport troops, weapons, and supplies over long distances.

   a. Point out to your students the difference between the Union and the Confederacy on the "Railroad track" bar of the *National Resources* graph.

   b. On the map, below GRAINS, BEEF, DAIRY, write ┼┼┼┼┼ = **TRANSPORT ADVANTAGE**.

4. **Factories** are also extremely important to a nation's war effort. They manufacture weapons, ammunition, and tools, as well as other necessities, such as canned foods, clothing, and shoes.

   a. Point out to your students the difference between the Union and the Confederacy on the "Factories" bar of the *National Resources* graph.

   b. On the map, below TRANSPORT ADVANTAGE, write ⌂ = **SUPPLIES ADVANTAGE**.

 Ask students to explain...
   - ...why grains, beef, and dairy products are more valuable than cotton during war.
   - ...why the South's slave population would not support the Confederate war effort.
   - ...how factories offer a military advantage.

Correlates with:
- *The Nystrom Atlas of United States History,* pages 64–65
- *Mapping United States History,* To the Present, Lesson 20–21 To the Early 1900s, Lesson 29–30

16

CIVIL WAR
1861–1865

Key Elements
★ *Civil War* map
★ *Areas of Control* maps
★ Locator map

Getting Started
To give students an overview of *Civil War*, ask them:
- What is the title of the main map?
- What part of the United States is shown on this map?
- On all of these maps, what do the blue areas represent?
- What do the gray areas represent?
- What do the ship symbols represent?
- What symbol marks a Union victory? A Confederate victory? A battle with no clear victor?
- What is the title of the series of smaller maps?
- What do the smaller maps show?

Teaching Notes and Mapping Activities
~ Union Strategy
~ Confederate Strategy
~ The Bitter End

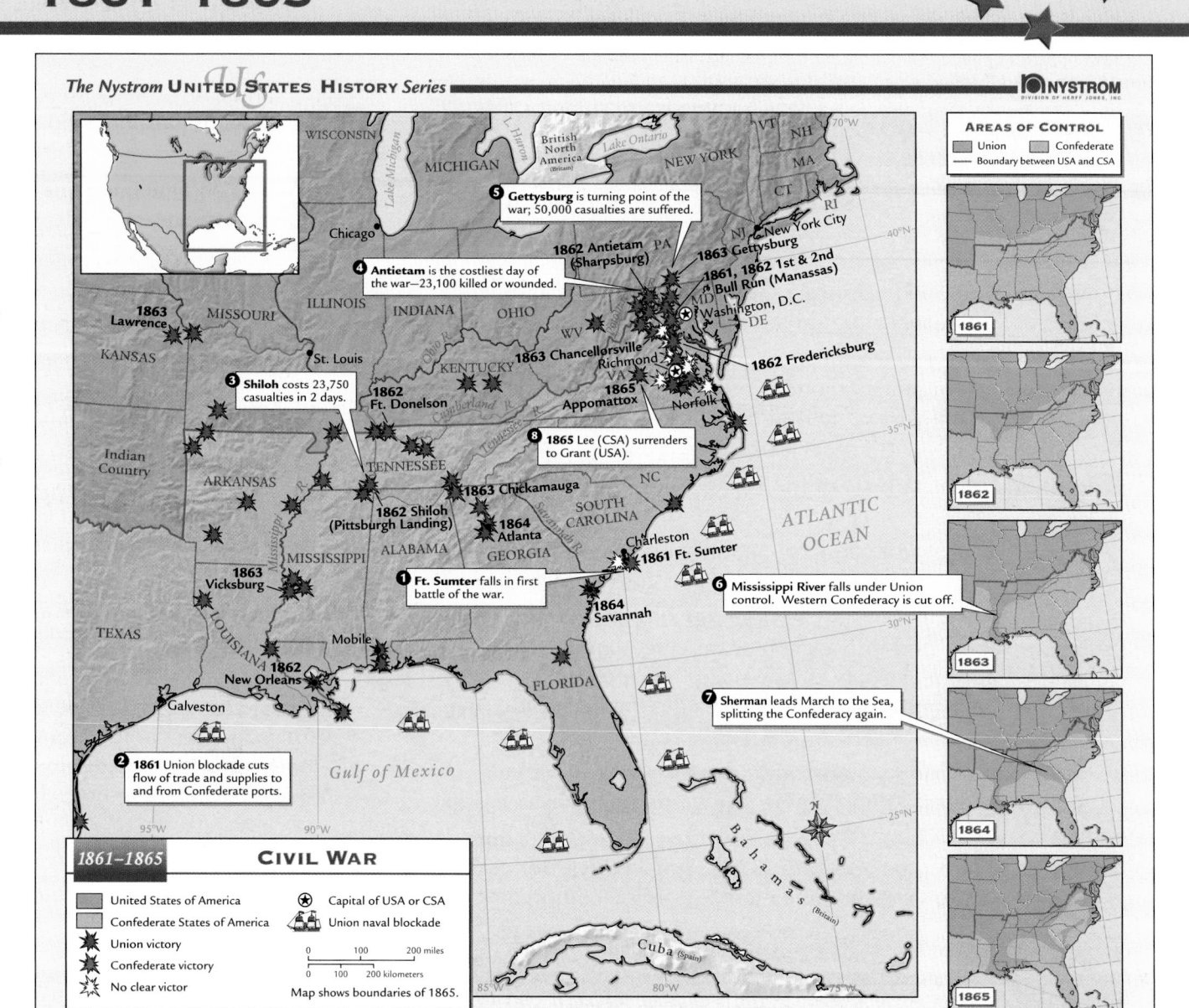

Union Strategy

Objective: *To map Union strategy for defeating the Confederacy during the Civil War.*

Teaching Notes and Mapping Activity

You or your students can mark the following on the *Civil War* and *Areas of Control* maps.

1. The North fought the Civil War to prevent the South from leaving the Union. Northerners did not think of the Confederacy as a separate country, but as states in rebellion against the federal government. In the top margin of the map, write **CONFEDERACY = U.S. STATES IN REBELLION.**

2. To prevent the Confederate states from seceding, the Union decided it would would have to invade and conquer the South. To accomplish this goal, Union generals devised the **Anaconda Plan**, named after a snake that slowly squeezes the life out of its prey.

   a. First, Union forces would cut off the South's supplies with a naval blockade. On the *Areas of Control 1861* map, draw one snake in the Gulf of Mexico and another in the Atlantic Ocean.

   b. The Union army would then move south, tightening its grip as it advanced, until the South surrendered. On the *Areas of Control 1861* map, draw a snake along the boundary between the Union and the Confederacy.

3. The North planned to begin squeezing the Confederacy by gaining **control of important rivers**, which the South used for trade and transportation.

   a. The Union launched attacks from the Ohio River. On the *Civil War* map, draw an arrow along the Cumberland River from the Ohio River to Ft. Donelson.

   b. Draw an arrow along the Tennessee River from the Ohio River to the Union victory symbol just west of Ft. Donelson.

   c. These victories allowed Union General Ulysses S. Grant to march his army farther south. Draw an arrow along the Tennessee River until it reaches Shiloh.

   d. After defeating the Confederates at Shiloh, Grant turned west. Draw an arrow west from Shiloh to the Mississippi River just below 35°N.

   e. Below the arrows from the Tennessee River to the Mississippi River, write **GRANT**.

   f. Other Union troops moved down the Mississippi to join Grant's forces. From St. Louis, draw an arrow along the Mississippi until it meets the arrow marking Grant's path.

   g. Grant continued south and, after much fighting, captured **Vicksburg** in 1863. Starting at the point where the two arrows meet, draw a new arrow south along the Mississippi, until it reaches Vicksburg.

4. As the army attacked from the north, the **U.S. Navy** moved in from the south. In 1862, Admiral David Farragut captured New Orleans.

   a. Draw an arrow north along the Mississippi River from the Gulf of Mexico to New Orleans. Label the arrow **FARRAGUT**.

   b. Union forces continued up the Mississippi and joined with Grant's army at Vicksburg. Draw an arrow north along the Mississippi River, from New Orleans to Vicksburg.

   c. By gaining control of the Mississippi, the Union had divided the Confederacy. On the *Areas of Control 1863* map, draw a snake along the Mississippi River.

 Have your students compare the Civil War map with the Slavery and the Economy map (USH14).
- Why do you think Northern generals favored the Anaconda Plan?
- What effect do you think the Anaconda Plan had on the South?

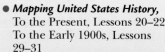

Correlates with:
- *The Nystrom Atlas of United States History,* pages 64–68
- *Mapping United States History,* To the Present, Lessons 20–22 To the Early 1900s, Lessons 29–31

Confederate Strategy

Objective: *To map Confederate strategy for gaining independence during the Civil War.*

Teaching Notes and Mapping Activity

You or your students can mark the following on the *Civil War* map.

1. The South fought the Civil War for the right to leave the United States. Confederates considered themselves part of a new nation. In the top margin of the map, write **CONFEDERACY = NEW & INDEPENDENT COUNTRY**.

2. The Confederates' main military goal was to **defend their homeland**. Much of their defensive efforts took place in Virginia, which had more battles than any other state during the Civil War—over 2,000.

   a. The Confederate capital was less than 100 miles from the U.S. capital, which made it a prime target for Union forces. Draw a line between Richmond, Virginia, and Washington, D.C., and label it **< 100 MILES**.

   b. The **two best Confederate generals**—Robert E. Lee and Thomas "Stonewall" Jackson—had the task of defending Virginia. South of Richmond, write **ROBERT E. LEE** and **STONEWALL JACKSON**.

3. Lee's strategy was to **fight defensively** and make the war costly for the North. Confederates hoped that if the Union suffered enough losses, it would give up and let the Confederate states exist in peace.

   a. Most of the South's victories between 1861 and 1863 came by **repelling Union attacks**. Find the Confederate victories listed below and underline their labels.
   - First Bull Run
   - Fredericksburg
   - Second Bull Run
   - Chancellorsville

   b. Mark each Confederate victory with a **D** for defensive.

   c. The South won at Chancellorsville, but **Stonewall Jackson died** from battle injures. Draw a line through the label for STONEWALL JACKSON and write **1863** next to it.

4. Another Southern strategy was to **win the support of other countries**. Confederates hoped that battlefield victories would encourage European countries to recognize their independence and assist them against the Union.

   a. England and France were two countries the Confederates hoped would help them. In the Atlantic Ocean east of the Confederate States, write **ENGLAND?** and **FRANCE?**.

   b. Lee believed that an **offensive victory** would sway the countries of Europe. In 1862 he invaded the North but was forced to retreat after the **Battle of Antietam**. Mark this Confederate loss with an **O** for offensive.

   c. In 1863, Lee again invaded the North. His armies were defeated at the **Battle of Gettysburg**. Mark this Confederate loss with an **O** for offensive.

   d. After Gettysburg, the South's hopes for help from Europe were dashed. Draw a line through your labels for ENGLAND and FRANCE and write **1863** next to each.

5. You might want to tell your students that even before Gettysburg, European countries were not inclined to help the Confederacy. The **Emancipation Proclamation** led Europe to see the war as a conflict over slavery, and most Europeans favored abolition.

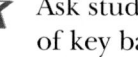 Ask students to compare the number of key battles that took place in the United States with the number that took place in the Confederate states.
- Where did most of these battles take place?
- How did Confederate strategy affect the location of the battles?
- How did Union strategy affect the location of the battles?

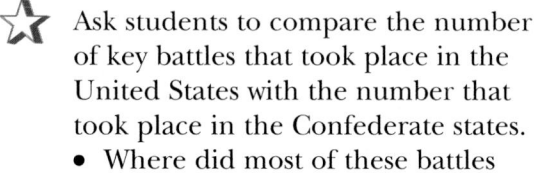
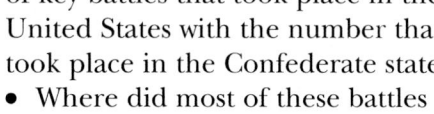

Correlates with:
- *The Nystrom Atlas of United States History,* pages 64–68
- *Mapping United States History,* To the Present, Lessons 20–22 To the Early 1900s, Lessons 29–31

The Bitter End

Objective: *To map the military campaigns that led to the end of the Civil War.*

Teaching Notes and Mapping Activity

You or your students can mark the following on the *Civil War* map.

1. By the middle of 1863, the Union had gained control of the Mississippi River, successfully dividing the Confederacy.

   a. Draw a line along the Mississippi River from St. Louis to the Gulf of Mexico. Along the line, write **UNION**.

   b. After Vicksburg, Grant was put in charge of the Union army in the East. North of Washington, D.C, write **GRANT**.

2. Grant's new job was to accomplish what no other Union general had been able to do—defeat Robert E. Lee in Virginia. To do this, Grant launched the **Overland Campaign**.

   a. Lee repelled Grant's first three attacks. But after each battle, instead of retreating, Grant marched his army around Lee's and continued south. Draw a line connecting the three "No clear victor" symbols north of Richmond.

   b. At **Cold Harbor**, Grant's attack was again repelled by Lee's forces. Continue your line southeast to the "No clear victor" symbol east of Richmond.

   c. Grant then attacked **Petersburg**, a supply center for Richmond. Lee again stopped Grant, but the Union army surrounded Petersburg and blockaded the city. Draw an arrow south of Richmond, from Cold Harbor to the "No Clear Victor" symbol west of the Confederate capital.

   d. Grant's strategy was simple: The North had more men. It could afford great losses. East of the arrow marking Grant's path of attack, write **UNION CASUALTIES 60,000+**.

   e. Lee outmaneuvered Grant, but he lost men in each battle. Unlike the Union, the Confederacy had no reinforcements to replace the dead and wounded. Below UNION CASUALTIES, write **CONFEDERATE CASUALTIES 30,000+**.

3. While Grant fought Lee in Virginia, Union forces in the West worked to divide the South. Near the end of 1863, Union forces won a decisive victory at **Chattanooga**. From Ft. Donelson, draw an arrow southeast through the two Union victory symbols along the Cumberland River until it reaches the Union victory symbol on the Tennessee River just north of Chickamauga.

4. From Chattanooga, Union forces continued to push towards the sea. In September 1864, Union General William T. Sherman captured Atlanta, Georgia.

   a. Draw an arrow from Chattanooga-Chickamauga to Atlanta.

   b. From Atlanta, Sherman began his **March to the Sea**. Draw an arrow from Atlanta to Savannah.

   c. Sherman's goal was to destroy as many Confederate resources as possible. Below the arrow, write **SHERMAN**.

   d. After capturing Savannah, Sherman's army marched north to join with Grant's forces in Virginia. From Savannah, draw an arrow pointing north and label it **SHERMAN**.

5. Sherman's campaign isolated Lee from the rest of the South. Lee and his men abandoned Petersburg and attempted to outrun Grant's army, but his soldiers were starving and exhausted, and they lacked ammunition. Seven days after the fall of Petersburg, Lee surrendered to Grant, effectively ending the Civil War.

   a. Draw an arrow from Petersburg to **Appomattox** and label it **LEE**.

   b. Read and outline Call-out ❽.

 Have your students use the call-outs and the dates of major battles on the Civil War map to create a timeline of the Civil War.

Correlates with:

- *The Nystrom Atlas of United States History,* pages 64–68
- *Mapping United States History,* To the Present, Lessons 20–22 To the Early 1900s, Lessons 29–31

17

INDIAN WARS
1622–1890

Key Elements

★ *Indian Wars* map
★ *Indian Policy* timeline

Getting Started

To give students an overview of *Indian Wars*, ask them:

- What is the title of this map?
- What years does the map cover?
- What do the yellow and orange colors show on this map?
- What does the green color represent?
- What do the red, white, and blue symbols represent?
- What are the words in black capital letters?
- What is the title of the timeline?
- When was Indian Territory established?
- Look on the map. Where was Indian Territory?

Teaching Notes and Mapping Activities

~ Indian Lands
~ Indian Policy
~ Battles in the West

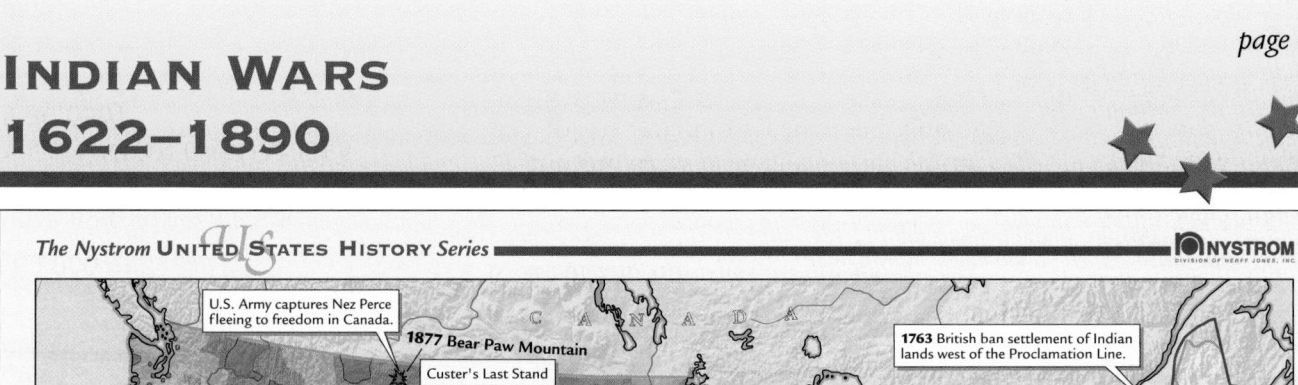

The Nystrom UNITED STATES HISTORY Series

NYSTROM
DIVISION OF HERFF JONES, INC.

U.S. Army captures Nez Perce fleeing to freedom in Canada.

1877 Bear Paw Mountain

Custer's Last Stand

1763 British ban settlement of Indian lands west of the Proclamation Line.

1876 Little Bighorn

1877 Big Hole

1876 Rosebud

CROW

NEZ PERCE

1877 Chief Joseph's route

SHOSHONE

1865–68 Red Cloud War

1866 Fetterman Fight

DAKOTA (SIOUX)

1862 Santee Uprising

OJIBWAY CHIPPEWA

WINNEBAGO

OTTAWA

1763 Fort Detroit

IROQUOIS

1675–76 King Philip's War

PEQUOT

1636–37 Pequot War

MODOC

1890 Wounded Knee

Last armed fight of Indian Wars

CHEYENNE

SHOSHONE

1872–73 Modoc War

1832 Black Hawk War

SAUK

FOX

POTAWATOMI

WYANDOT

MIAMI

DELAWARE

SHAWNEE

1794 Fallen Timbers

1879 Milk Creek

ARAPAHO

UTE

1811 Tippecanoe

KICKAPOO

KASKASKIA

1774 Point Pleasant

POWHATAN

1860 Pyramid Lake

PAIUTE

PAWNEE

1622–44 Jamestown

1864 Sand Creek

CHEYENNE

1838–39

Trail of Tears

NAVAJO

1864 Canyon de Chelly

KIOWA

1680–92 Pueblo Revolt

MOHAVE

1874–75 Red River War

COMANCHE

CHICKASAW

CHEROKEE

Thousands of Cherokee die on forced march west.

PACIFIC OCEAN

APACHE

Geronimo surrenders.

1886 Skeleton Canyon

1830–1850 Indians from east of the Mississippi are relocated to Indian Territory.

1813–14 Creek War

CREEK

CHOCTAW

1817–18 First Seminole War

SEMINOLE

1835–42 Second Seminole War

1685–88 Fort St. Louis

KARANKAWA

Gulf of Mexico

1855–58 Third Seminole War

ATLANTIC OCEAN

BAHAMAS

MEXICO

CUBA

1622–1890 **INDIAN WARS**

Lands Lost by Indians
- 1622–1774
- 1775–1819
- 1820–1849
- 1850–1864
- 1865–1889

Lands Defined by U.S. Government
- Indian Territory, 1850
- Indian reservation, 1890

Major Conflicts
- ✸ Indian victory
- ✸ Indian defeat
- ✸ No clear victor

UTE Indian nation

Map shows present boundaries.

0   100   200 miles
0   100   200 kilometers

INDIAN POLICY

1750   1800   1850   1900

1787 Northwest Ordinance includes promise never to take Indian lands.

1824 U.S. Bureau of Indian Affairs is established.

1854 Kansas-Nebraska Act opens Indian treaty lands of 1830 to white settlement.

1871 Indian Appropriation Act ends treaty-making with Indian nations.

1924 Indian Citizenship Act defines all Native Americans as U.S. citizens.

1763 Proclamation Line prevents colonial settlements on Indian lands.

1802 Indian Territory is established.

1830 Indian Removal Act moves Indians west of the Mississippi.

1887 Dawes Severalty Act ends legal standing of tribes until 1934.

1907 Indian Territory becomes state of Oklahoma.

NYSTROM DIVISION OF HERFF JONES, INC.

Indian Wars, 1622–1890 **17**

Indian Lands

Objective: *To show the progressive loss of Indian land between 1622 and 1890.*

Teaching Notes and Mapping Activity

You or your students can mark the following on the *Indian Wars* map.

1. Before 1622 there were just a few European settlements in what would become the United States. Native Americans were the main inhabitants.

   a. Point out several Indian nations named on the map.

   b. Indians had millions of miles of land available to them. In Mexico and the Gulf of Mexico, write **BEFORE 1622: 3,000,000 SQ. MI.**

2. Between 1622 and 1774, England established 13 colonies along the Atlantic coast. Settlers also started crossing the Appalachian Mountains. The Spanish and French were settling near the Mississippi River delta and the Gulf of Mexico. Indians were pushed out, bought out, or chose to leave these regions.

   a. Indians lost land represented by the light yellow areas. Identify the Indian nations of these areas.

   b. Draw a few arrows from the light yellow areas to land still available for Indians.

3. Between 1775 and 1819, the 13 English colonies won their independence. They became the United States. By 1819, pioneers began to settle along the Ohio River and southern Mississippi River valleys. Again, Indians were pushed out, bought out, or chose to leave those regions.

   a. Indians lost land in the yellow areas. Identify the Indian nations in these areas.

   b. Draw a few arrows from the yellow areas to land still available for Indians.

4. Between 1820 and 1849, more and more settlers moved into the Northwest Territory around the Great Lakes. Indians living east of the Mississippi River were relocated to Indian Territory in the west.

   a. Indians lost land in the dark yellow areas. Identify the Indian nations in these areas.

   b. Draw a few arrows from the dark yellow areas to land still available for Indians.

5. Between 1850 and 1864, settlers moved to California, Oregon, and Utah. Gold and silver were also discovered in areas of the west. Indians in these areas often were pushed out.

   a. Indians lost land in the orange areas. Identify the Indian nations in these areas.

   b. Draw a few arrows from the orange areas to land still available for Indians.

6. Between 1865 and 1889, Indians were forced onto reservations. Indians rebelled and wars broke out.

   a. Indians lost land in the dark orange areas. Identify the Indian nations in these areas.

   b. Draw a few arrows from the dark orange areas to land still available for Indians.

7. By 1890 Indians were living on reservations.

   a. Outline a few of the reservations.

   b. Indians had lost most of their land. In Mexico and the Gulf of Mexico, write **1890: 70,000 SQ. MI.**

 Have students use a road map to locate any Indian reservations in your state or region. Discuss how they affect the area.

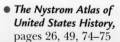
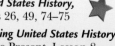

Correlates with:

● *The Nystrom Atlas of United States History,* pages 26, 49, 74–75

● *Mapping United States History* To the Present, Lesson 8 To the Early 1900s, Lessons 10, 23, 36

Indian Policy

Objective: *To understand how government policies regarding Indians had an impact on where they lived.*

Teaching Notes and Mapping Activity

You or your students can mark the following on the *Indian Wars* map.

1. After the French and Indian War, Great Britain gained land from the Appalachian Mountains to the Mississippi River. As settlers moved west of the Appalachians, Indians rebelled. To prevent another war, King George III established the **Proclamation Line of 1763**. Land west of the line was reserved for Indians.

   a. On the *Indian Policy* timeline, point to and read the description for 1763.

   b. The Proclamation Line followed the Appalachian Mountains. On the map, trace the line.

   c. Between the Mississippi River and the Proclamation Line write **RESERVED FOR INDIANS 1763**.

2. After the American Revolution, the Proclamation Line no longer applied. As settlers moved west of the Appalachians, the government set up guidelines for the treatment of Indians.

   a. Outline the Northwest Territory: draw a line along the Ohio/Pennsylvania boundary to the Ohio River. Follow the Ohio to the Mississippi. Trace the Mississippi north to its source.

   b. Label the area between the two rivers **NW TERRITORY**.

   c. The Northwest Ordinance included the **first U.S. Indian policy**. On the timeline, read the 1787 entry.

   d. The ordinance promised never to take Indian lands without their consent. On the map, above the Northwest Territory, write **CANNOT TAKE W/O INDIAN CONSENT 1787**.

3. In the 1830s, Indians living east of the Mississippi River were moved to Indian Territory west of the Mississippi. They were told this land would be theirs "as long as the rivers shall run and the grass shall grow."

   a. On the timeline, read the 1830 entry.

   b. No one thought the Great Plains land was worth much. Some called it the "Great American Desert." On the map, outline the Indian Territory. Above it, write **INDIAN TERR 1830**.

   c. Over 70,000 Indians were forced to leave their homes and move to Indian Territory. Many died on the journey. Trace the **Trail of Tears**.

   d. Also draw arrows from the Chickasaw, Creek, Choctaw, and Seminole nations to the Indian Territory.

4. After a few years, white settlers wanted to live west of the Mississippi. The **Kansas-Nebraska Act** divided the Indian Territory. The northern section became part of Kansas and Nebraska.

   a. On the timeline, read the 1854 entry.

   b. On the map, in Indian Territory, draw a line along the boundary between Kansas and Oklahoma.

   c. Label the land below the line **INDIAN 1854**.

5. By 1887 most Indians were living on reservations owned by the tribes. The **Dawes Severalty Act** divided up the reservation land into 40- to 160-acre plots and distributed the land to individual Indians. Any remaining land was sold to white settlers.

   a. On the timeline, read the 1887 entry.

   b. Outline one of the larger reservations in the West.

   c. By 1932 two-thirds of what were Indian reservations were held by whites. Divide the reservation into three sections. Label one section **I 1932**.

 Have students use the timeline to research the impact of Indian policies on Native American ways of life.

Correlates with:
- *The Nystrom Atlas of United States History,* pages 37, 49
- *Mapping United States History* To the Early 1900s, Lesson 23

Battles in the West

Objective: *To identify reasons why Indian wars were fought using the Sioux Indian nation as an example.*

Teaching Notes and Mapping Activity

You or your students can mark the following on the *Indian Wars* map.

1. Indian wars were fought for a variety of reasons. For example, in the 1860s, the Santee **Sioux** were living on a reservation in Minnesota. They faced starvation after a poor harvest. However, government trading posts refused to give them food and supplies until a delayed government check arrived. Meanwhile, white settlers began moving onto Sioux land.

   a. Sioux raiding parties began attacking settlers in western Minnesota. Above the **Santee Uprising** label write ⬠ **SETTLERS**.

   b. The army captured 2,000 Sioux and tried and hung 38 of them. The Sioux were moved to a smaller reservation in South Dakota. From the Santee Uprising west to the South Dakota border, draw an arrow.

2. Another group of Sioux were living in Wyoming Territory. They became upset when the government began building a road through their favorite hunting ground.

   a. The road followed the **Bozeman Trail**. From southeast Wyoming to southwest Montana, draw a dotted line.

   b. The Sioux, led by Red Cloud, fought the army over the construction of the road. Below **Red Cloud's War**, write –⬭– **ROAD**.

   c. Farther north, 80 soldiers were ambushed and killed. Underline **Fetterman Fight**.

   d. The government finally gave up their plans for the road. The Sioux were given a large reservation in the Black Hills. From Fetterman Fight to the southwest corner of South Dakota, draw an arrow.

3. The Sioux were content living in the Black Hills. Then in 1874 **gold** was discovered on their land. Thousands of miners poured onto their reservation. The government offered to buy the Black Hills for $6 million. The Sioux refused because the land was sacred to them. In South Dakota, write ⛏ **MINERS**.

4. Thousands of discontented Sioux left their reservation to join other Indian nations in Montana. There, government agents were concerned that Indians would interfere with construction of the **Northern Pacific Railroad**.

   a. Optional: On *The Nystrom United States History Series 18* wall map or transparency, trace the North Pacific Railroad's route.

   b. Fighting between Indians and government troops broke out at **Rosebud** and later at **Little Bighorn**. Above Custer's Last Stand, write ╫╫╫╫ **RAILROADS**.

5. The last major battle in the Indian wars was fought in South Dakota. Sioux, who were living on a reservation, were practicing the **Ghost Dance** religion. They hoped that they could drive white settlers from their lands with this ceremonial dance. Government troops worried that there would be war. In the **Wounded Knee Massacre**, hundreds of Native American men, women, and children were killed. Below Wounded Knee, write ♫ **RELIGION**.

 Have students research battles involving other Indian nations in the Indian wars. Then, on the map, beside each battle, ask them to write the reason why the battle was fought.

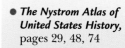

Correlates with:
- *The Nystrom Atlas of United States History,* pages 29, 48, 74
- *Mapping United States History To the Early 1900s,* Lessons 23, 36

18 RAILROADS TRANSFORM THE WEST 1860–1893

Key Elements

★ *1869* map
★ *1893* map
★ Locator map
★ *Miles of Railroad Track* graph
★ *Population in the West* graph
★ *Farmland in the West* graph

Getting Started

To give students an overview of *Railroads Transform the West,* ask them:

- What are the names of the two main maps?
- What do the yellow regions on these maps represent?
- What do the green arrows represent?
- What other symbols can be found on the maps? What do they represent?
- What are the titles of the three graphs? What does each show?
- What does the group of states outlined in red represent on the small map between *Population in the West* and *Farmland in the West?*

Teaching Notes and Mapping Activities

~ Railroads Link the Nation
~ The Growing Cattle Kingdom
~ The West Fuels U.S. Industry

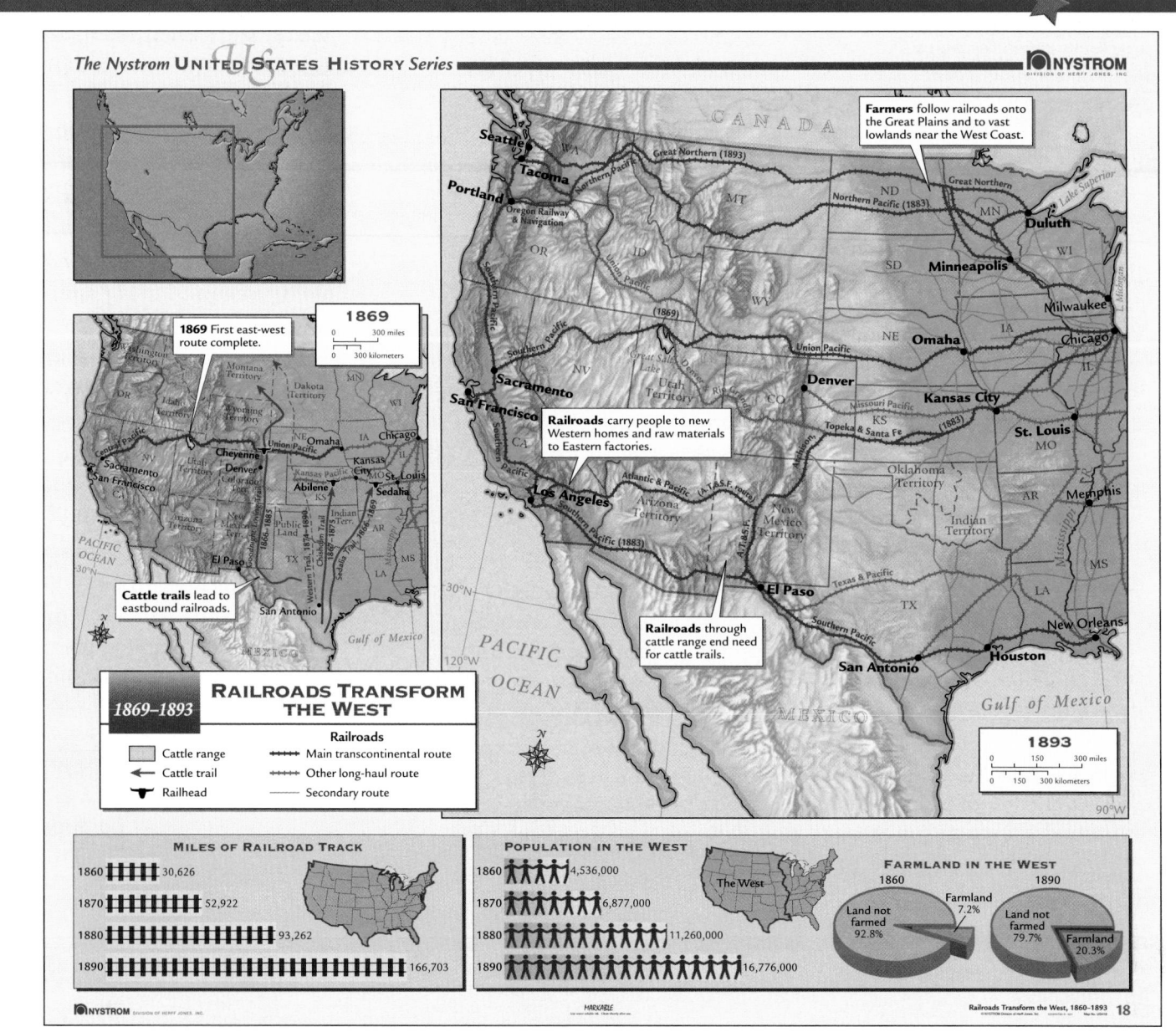

The Nystrom UNITED STATES HISTORY Series

NYSTROM DIVISION OF HERFF JONES, INC.

Farmers follow railroads onto the Great Plains and to vast lowlands near the West Coast.

1869 First east-west route complete.

1869 0 — 300 miles / 0 — 300 kilometers

Cattle trails lead to eastbound railroads.

Railroads carry people to new Western homes and raw materials to Eastern factories.

Railroads through cattle range end need for cattle trails.

RAILROADS TRANSFORM THE WEST
1869–1893

Railroads
- Cattle range — Main transcontinental route
- Cattle trail — Other long-haul route
- Railhead — Secondary route

1893 0 — 150 — 300 miles / 0 — 150 — 300 kilometers

MILES OF RAILROAD TRACK

Year	Miles
1860	30,626
1870	52,922
1880	93,262
1890	166,703

POPULATION IN THE WEST

Year	Population
1860	4,536,000
1870	6,877,000
1880	11,260,000
1890	16,776,000

The West

FARMLAND IN THE WEST

1860
Land not farmed 92.8%
Farmland 7.2%

1890
Land not farmed 79.7%
Farmland 20.3%

HARCABLE

NYSTROM DIVISION OF HERFF JONES, INC.

Railroads Transform the West, 1860–1893 **18**

Railroads Link the Nation

Objective: *To show the completion of some major U.S. railroads in the West in chronological order.*

Teaching Notes and Mapping Activity

You or your students can mark the following on the *1893* map.

1. The **first transcontinental railroad** in the United States was completed in 1869, but workers had been building it for years. Most of those who built the railroads were immigrants.

   a. In 1863 the **Central Pacific** Railroad Company began laying track in Sacramento, California. On the *1893* map, draw an arrow along the Southern Pacific line from Sacramento to the Great Salt Lake. [Use both maps to show your students that the Central Pacific eventually became the Southern Pacific.]

   b. Most Central Pacific Railway workers were Chinese immigrants. Label your Central Pacific Railway arrow **CHINESE**.

   c. In 1865 the **Union Pacific** Railroad Company began laying track in Omaha, Nebraska. Draw an arrow along the Union Pacific Railway line from Omaha to the Great Salt Lake.

   d. Most Union Pacific Railroad workers were Irish immigrants. Label your Union Pacific Railway arrow **IRISH**.

2. The **Southern Pacific** Railroad Company built a route that linked Northern and Southern California.

   a. Draw an arrow along the Southern Pacific Railroad from Sacramento to Los Angeles. Label it **1882**.

   b. A year later the railroad linked California to southern cities by a route that ran across the deserts of the Southwest. Draw a new arrow along the Southern Pacific railway from Los Angeles to New Orleans, Louisiana.

   c. By 1887 the company had built a railroad connecting California to Oregon. Along the Southern Pacific railroad from Sacramento to Portland, draw an arrow and label it **1887**.

3. The **Atchison, Topeka, and Santa Fe** Railway Company (A.T.&S.F.) also built a route across the Southwest. By 1883 the A.T.&S.F. Railroad connected Kansas City, Missouri, to El Paso, Texas.

   a. Draw an arrow along the A.T.&S.F. railroad line from Kansas City to El Paso.

   b. The A.T.&S.F. joined with the Atlantic & Pacific to create a new route to Los Angeles, which was completed in 1887. Draw an arrow along the Atlantic & Pacific Railroad from Los Angeles to the A.T.&S.F railroad line. Label the arrow **1887**.

4. In 1883 the **Northern Pacific** Railroad connected the Great Lakes region to the Pacific Northwest.

   a. Draw an arrow along the Northern Pacific and the Oregon Railway & Navigation lines from Duluth, Minnesota, to Portland.

   b. A year later, the **Oregon Short Line** linked the Union Pacific railroad to the Northern Pacific. Draw an arrow along the red Union Pacific line from Oregon to the purple Union Pacific line in Wyoming. Label it **OR SHORT LINE 1884**.

   c. By 1888 a route connecting the Puget Sound area to the Northern Pacific was completed. Along the railroad that connects Tacoma, Washington, to the Northern Pacific line, draw an arrow. Label it **1888**.

5. To remind students that travel occurred in both directions, make all your arrows two-way.

 Have your students devise travel routes for the following trips:
   - Minneapolis to Los Angeles
   - New Orleans to Denver
   - St. Louis to Portland
   - Chicago to El Paso

Correlates with:
- *The Nystrom Atlas of United States History,* pages 72–73
- *Mapping United States History,* To the Present, Lesson 25 To the Early 1900s, Lesson 35

The Growing Cattle Kingdom

Objective: *To map the increasing number of cattle in the different states and territories of the West.*

Teaching Notes and Mapping Activity

You or your students can mark the following on the *1869* map, the *1893* map, and the *Farmland in the West* graph.

1. Before the Civil War, only a small number of ranchers were **raising cattle in the West**, most of them in California and Texas.

   a. **Texas** cattle were usually driven to railheads and then shipped east. In 1860 Texas had more than 3 million cattle. On the *1869* map, write � = **3 MILLION** in Texas.

   b. **California** cattle were used mainly to feed a population that had been growing since the Gold Rush. California had over 1 million cattle. Write ☐ = **1 MILLION** in California.

   c. Point out the cattle trails and railheads to your students.

2. People in other states and territories in the West were also raising cattle. As in California, most of these animals were used to feed the local population.

   a. On the *1869* map, write ☐ = and the 1860 cattle population in each state and territory listed below.

   - Washington Territory   25,000
   - Oregon   145,000
   - Utah Territory   13,000
   - New Mexico Territory   63,000
   - Nebraska   25,000
   - Kansas   72,000

   b. In many territories, the cattle population was unknown, because so few Americans had settled in these regions by 1860. Draw a question mark **?** in the remaining territories of the West.

3. By the 1880s, railroads crisscrossed the West, the region's population had more than doubled, and the cattle industry was booming. Western ranchers were making large profits selling cattle to regions that could not raise their own.

   a. Point out the nation's increase in railroad track on the *Miles of Railroad Track* graph and the population increase in the West between on the *Population of the West* graph.

   b. On the *1893* map, write ☐ = and the 1880s cattle population in each of the western states and territories listed below.

   - Washington   200,000
   - Oregon   600,000
   - California   815,000
   - Idaho   200,000
   - Nevada   216,000
   - Utah Territory   130,000
   - Arizona   135,000
   - Montana   428,000
   - Wyoming   500,000
   - Colorado   800,000
   - New Mexico   135,000
   - Dakotas   206,000
   - Nebraska   1.1 million
   - Kansas   1.5 million
   - Texas   5 million

   c. In 1890 it was estimated that 44 percent of U.S. land not farmed was being used to raise cattle. Most of this land was in the West. On the "Land not farmed" portion of the 1890 *Farmland in the West* graph, write **44% CATTLE RANCHING**.

   d. Tell your students that as the cattle population increased, the bison population decreased. In 1800 there were 40 million bison in America, but by 1890 only a few thousand remained.

   Point out to your students that, unlike other states and territories, the cattle population in California dropped. Have them make a list of reasons why this might have happened.

Correlates with:

- **The Nystrom Atlas of United States History,** pages 72–73

- **Mapping United States History,** To the Present, Lesson 25 To the Early 1900s, Lesson 35

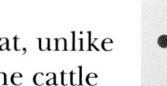

The West Fuels U.S. Industry

Objective: *To show the important role of the West in the industrialization of the United States.*

Teaching Notes and Mapping Activity

You or your students can mark the following on the *1893* map and the small map of western states.

1. **The West** played an integral role in the industrialization of the United States. By the 1890s the agricultural products of the West were **feeding the factory workers** of the East.

   a. **Ranches** throughout the West supplied beef for the cities of the East. On the *1893* map, point out the extent of the western cattle range to your students.

   b. In the red-outlined part of the small map between the population and farmland graphs, write **BEEF**.

2. The **Great Plains** became the nation's breadbasket. Farms there supplied **grain** used throughout the United States.

   a. On the *1893* map, across eastern Montana, North Dakota, South Dakota, and western Minnesota, write **WHEAT**.

   b. Across eastern Nebraska and Iowa, write **CORN**.

   c. Across eastern Colorado, Kansas, and Missouri, write **CORN & WHEAT**.

   d. Below BEEF on the small map of the West, write **GRAIN**.

3. Other areas of the West supplied fruits and vegetables. For example, citrus fruits were grown in California.

   a. On the *1893* map, south of San Francisco, write **FRUITS**.

   b. Below GRAIN on the small map of the West, write **FRUITS & VEGETABLES**.

4. The West also provided many **raw materials** used to produce manufactured goods.

   a. The Pacific Northwest provided lumber. On the *1893* map, from Northern California to Washington, write **LUMBER**.

   b. Below FRUITS & VEGETABLES on the small map of the West, write **LUMBER**.

5. **Mountain and desert regions** of the West supplied the Industrial East with many of the minerals needed for manufacturing.

   a. On the *1893* map, write the word **MINERALS** in each of the locations listed below.
   - along the Sierra Nevada range
   - in Nevada northeast of Sacramento
   - across southern Arizona and New Mexico
   - along the northern part of the Idaho-Montana border
   - south of the Great Salt Lake
   - along the Rocky Mountains

   b. Below LUMBER on the small map of the West, write **MINERALS**.

6. While the West specialized in producing food and raw materials, **the East** produced manufactured goods. Most of the manufactured goods used in the West were produced in the East.

   a. Across the Eastern states on the small map, write **MFD. GOODS**.

   b. To illustrate the interdependency of the two regions, draw a looping arrow ⟿ from the goods produced in the West to the states of the East.

   c. Draw another looping arrow ⟿ from the label MFD. GOODS to the states of the West.

   d. Railroads also contributed to industrialization. Point out the proximity of railway lines to production centers.

 Have your students create a list of railroad routes which different regions might have used to exchange goods. Also list which goods might be transported over these routes.

Correlates with:
- *The Nystrom Atlas of United States History,* pages 72–73
- *Mapping United States History,* To the Present, Lesson 25 To the Early 1900s, Lesson 35

Key Elements

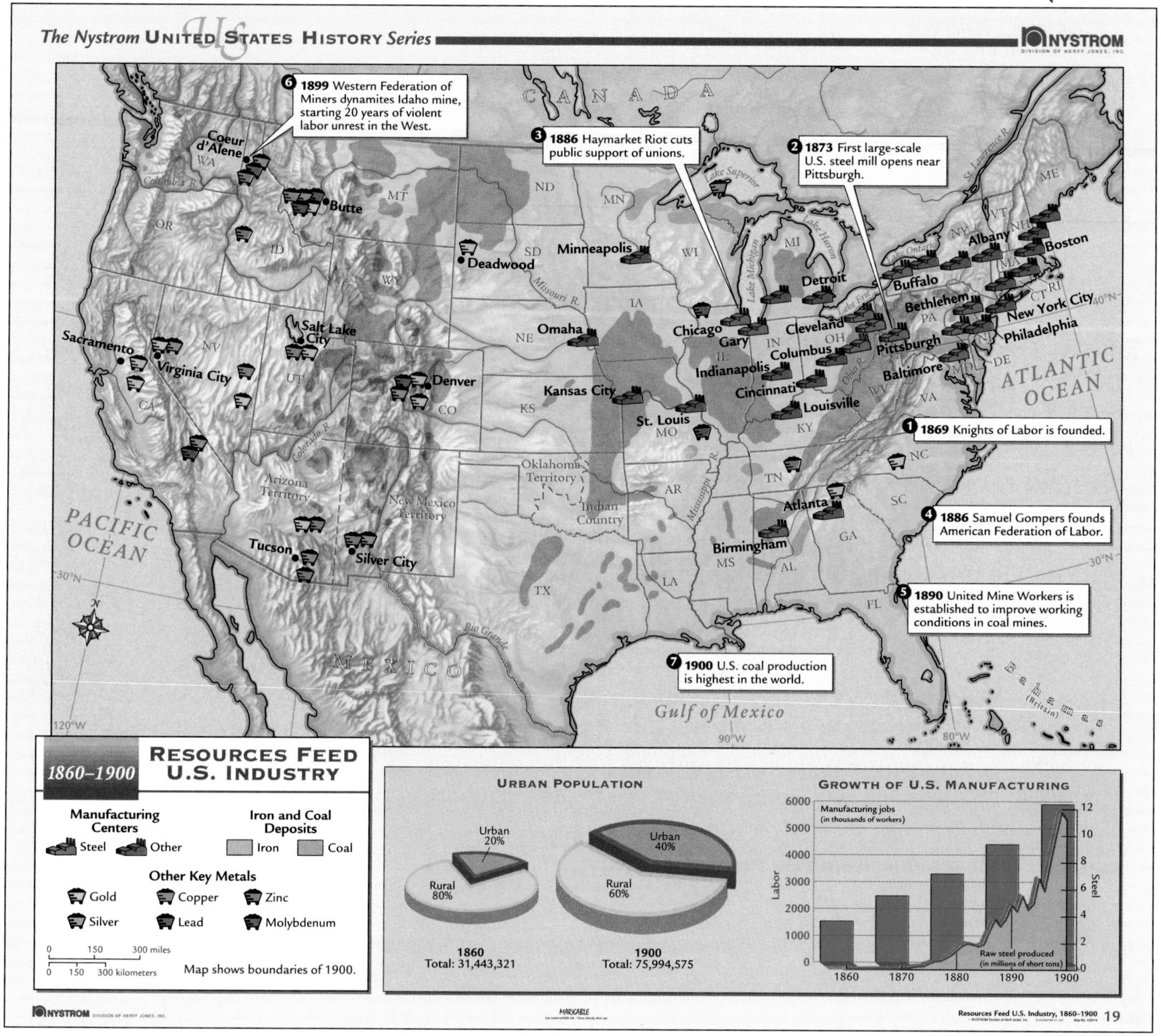

★ *Resources Feed U.S. Industry* map
★ *Urban Population* graphs
★ *Growth of U.S. Manufacturing* graph

Getting Started

To give students an overview of *Resources Feed U.S. Industry,* ask them:

- What is the title of this map?
- What years does this map cover?
- What do the areas of color on the map represent?
- What do the building symbols represent? the coal car symbols?
- Look at the *Urban Population* graphs. What percent of the population was urban in 1860? in 1900?
- Look at the *Growth of U.S. Manufacturing* graph. How much did the number of manufacturing jobs grow between 1860 and 1900? How much did steel production increase?

Teaching Notes and Mapping Activities

～ Mining Grows in the West
～ Manufacturing Grows in the East
～ Labor Unrest

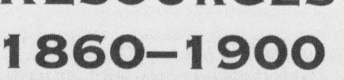

The Nystrom **UNITED STATES HISTORY** *Series* — **NYSTROM** DIVISION OF HERFF JONES, INC.

6 **1899** Western Federation of Miners dynamites Idaho mine, starting 20 years of violent labor unrest in the West.

3 **1886** Haymarket Riot cuts public support of unions.

2 **1873** First large-scale U.S. steel mill opens near Pittsburgh.

1 **1869** Knights of Labor is founded.

4 **1886** Samuel Gompers founds American Federation of Labor.

5 **1890** United Mine Workers is established to improve working conditions in coal mines.

7 **1900** U.S. coal production is highest in the world.

RESOURCES FEED U.S. INDUSTRY
1860–1900

Manufacturing Centers
Steel   Other

Iron and Coal Deposits
Iron   Coal

Other Key Metals
Gold   Copper   Zinc
Silver   Lead   Molybdenum

0   150   300 miles
0   150   300 kilometers   Map shows boundaries of 1900.

URBAN POPULATION

Urban 20%
Rural 80%
1860
Total: 31,443,321

Urban 40%
Rural 60%
1900
Total: 75,994,575

GROWTH OF U.S. MANUFACTURING

Manufacturing jobs (in thousands of workers)

Raw steel produced (in millions of short tons)

1860 1870 1880 1890 1900

NYSTROM DIVISION OF HERFF JONES, INC.   MARKABLE   **Resources Feed U.S. Industry, 1860–1900** 19

Mining Grows in the West

Objective: *To demonstrate how mining affected the settlement of the West.*

Teaching Notes and Mapping Activity

You or your students can mark the following on the *Resources Feed U.S. Industry* map.

1. The prospect of finding **gold** brought people from all over the world to the West.

   a. One famous gold rush began in 1849 in **California** at **Sutter's Mill**. Near Sacramento, label the two gold symbols **G**.

   b. By 1864 gold in the rivers and on the surface of the land was exhausted. Corporations and their hydraulic mining equipment took over deep underground mining. Some miners stayed in California. Others moved to nearby states. From Sacramento to the Nevada border, draw an arrow.

2. While searching for gold in **Nevada**, prospectors discovered the largest **silver** deposit in the United States—the **Comstock Lode**. The mine flourished from 1858 to 1865 and from 1873 to 1882.

   a. In Nevada, near Virginia City, label the gold symbol **G** and the silver symbol **S**.

   b. When the government limited the use of silver in its coins, the value of silver dropped, mines closed, and miners left Nevada. From Nevada to Montana, draw an arrow.

3. In 1864 prospectors in **Montana** searched for silver. Instead, they uncovered one of the world's richest **copper** deposits, the **Anaconda Mine**. Copper conducts electricity. It was used in electric lights and in telephones and telegraphs. Demand for copper increased in the late 1800s. In Montana, near Butte, label the copper symbol **C**.

4. In 1865 federal troops discovered gold in **Bingham Canyon** located in **Utah**. Utah was settled by the Mormons. The government hoped that a flood of non-Mormon miners would come to lessen the Mormon influence in the territory. However, few came. In Utah, near Salt Lake City, label the gold symbol **G**.

5. Few settlers lived in **Colorado** until gold was discovered there.

   a. The gold rush in 1859 brought about 100,000 people to the **Denver** and **Pikes Peak** area. In Colorado, label the two gold symbols **G**.

   b. Silver deposits were discovered in **Leadville** and **Aspen**. However, like Nevada, mines closed when silver prices dropped. Label the silver symbol **S**.

   c. In 1879 another mineral was found in Colorado—**molybdenum**—but no one knew what to do with it. Thirty-five years later, the Germans used molybdenum in their weapons. The mineral made steel stronger and corrosion resistant. Demand for the mineral increased sharply. Label the molybdenum symbol **M**.

6. In the 1870s, government troops discovered gold on Indian lands in the **Black Hills** of **South Dakota**. Thousands of prospectors invaded the area, in the last major gold rush in the continental United States. Indians fought the miners, but eventually moved to a new reservation. In South Dakota, label the gold symbol **G**.

7. Other mines were established across the West. However, after 40 years of prospecting, most of the region was still unsettled.

   a. In 1900 only 28 percent of the nation's people lived west of the Mississippi. From the Pacific Ocean to the Mississippi River, draw an arrow . Label it **28% OF POP**.

   b. From the Mississippi River to the Atlantic Ocean, also draw an arrow . Label it **72% OF POP**.

Correlates with:
- *The Nystrom Atlas of United States History,* pages 76
- *Mapping United States History* To the Early 1900s, Lesson 37

⭐ Have students research a state in the west. Have them determine if mining is still a big industry in the state.

Objective: *To show how manufacturing changed between 1860 and 1900.*

Teaching Notes and Mapping Activity

You or your students can mark the following on the *Resources Feed U.S. Industry* map.

1. In 1860 the **manufacturing centers** in the United States were concentrated in the **East**.

   a. Optional: Use *The Nystrom United States History Series 14* wall map or transparency to locate manufacturing centers in 1860.

   b. Most industrial centers were located along the **northeast** coast. On the *Resources Feed U.S. Industry* map, point to the manufacturing centers between Boston and Philadelphia. Next to them, in the Atlantic Ocean, write **1860**.

   c. Many of these manufacturing centers were textile mills that wove cloth. Below 1860, write **TEXTILES**.

2. In 1860 **iron** was the most commonly used industrial metal. Iron was strong, but it was also heavy. Steel was strong too, but it was lighter than iron. In 1860 steel was very expensive. Under 1860, add **IRON**.

3. After 1860 new methods were developed to make **steel** more economical to produce.

   a. In 1873 the first large-scale steel mill opened in the United States. Callout ❷ identifies it. Circle this mill.

   b. Soon there were thousands of steel mills in the United States. Point to several steel manufacturing centers on the map.

   c. On the *Growth of U.S. Manufacturing* graph, from 1860 to 1900, trace the line showing tons of raw steel produced.

4. Steel is made from **raw materials** that come from all over the United States.

   a. **Iron ore** is needed to make steel. The largest iron ore deposit in North America is in Minnesota. On the map, label it **I**. Also label two other large iron deposits.

   b. **Coal** is used to heat the iron ore. Label three coal deposits **C**.

   c. Other minerals are added to steel. For example, a **zinc** coating, called galvanizing, is often added to prevent rusting. Label two zinc deposits with a **Z**.

5. Steel was used to build machines, steamships, and a variety of other products.

   a. In the late 1800s, there was a huge demand for steel rails. Over 130,000 miles of **railroad tracks** were laid between 1860 and 1890. From Chicago to Sacramento, draw a railroad track symbol 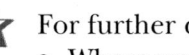.

   b. Steel was also used to build **skyscrapers**. The first skyscraper was built in the late 1800s. Near Chicago, draw a skyscraper.

6. In 1900 the United States was first in the world in factory production.

   a. Draw a line along the Mississippi River.

   b. Along the Kentucky/Tennessee boundary and the northern boundary of Virginia, draw a line.

   c. Northern and eastern states produced 85 percent of the country's industrial output. Count the number of manufacturing centers north and east of the lines you drew. Write that number in the region.

   d. Then count and record the number of manufacturing centers in the southeast and in the west.

☆ For further discussion:
   - Where were most of the steel manufacturing centers located?
   - Where were these centers in relation to coal and iron deposits?
   - Look at the two graphs. Is there a relationship between urban population and the number of manufacturing jobs? What is it?

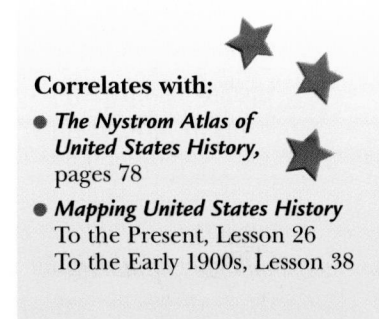

Correlates with:
- ***The Nystrom Atlas of United States History,*** pages 78
- ***Mapping United States History*** To the Present, Lesson 26 To the Early 1900s, Lesson 38

Labor Unrest

Objective: *To identify ways American workers fought for better working conditions in the late 1800s.*

Teaching Notes and Mapping Activity

You or your students can mark the following on the *Resources Feed U.S. Industry* map.

1. Between 1860 and 1900, the number of **manufacturing jobs** in the United States almost quadrupled. On the *Growth of U.S. Manufacturing* graph, outline the bars for 1860 and 1900.

2. In the late 1800s, working conditions in the nation's factories and mines were terrible. Some workers formed **labor unions** to fight for safer working conditions and shorter work days.

   a. In 1869 the **Knights of Labor** was founded in Philadelphia. This union fought for 8-hour work days and equal pay for equal work. It also fought against child labor. On the map, near Philadelphia, write **U** for union.

   b. In 1886 the **American Federation of Labor** (AFL) was founded. The union encouraged consumers to support union labor by looking for the union label on goods they purchased. The union also fought for 8-hour work days, 5-day work weeks, and safer working conditions. Next to callout ❹, write **U**.

   c. Men and children worked in mines. Hours were long and accidents, cave-ins, and explosions were common. In 1890 the **United Mine Workers** was organized in Columbus, Ohio. It fought for better working conditions. On Columbus, write **U**.

3. **Striking** was one way unions fought for better working conditions.

   a. In 1886 workers at the **McCormick Harvester Plant** went on strike because their pay had been cut. They also wanted to work 8 hours a day, instead of 10. Near Chicago, write **S** for strike.

   b. The company hired strikebreakers to take the place of striking workers. Outside the factory, strikers attacked strikebreakers and police started shooting in response. A few strikers were killed. Draw a conflict symbol ✸ around the S.

   c. The next day, strikers held a labor meeting at **Haymarket Square** to protest the police action. At the end of the peaceful meeting, about 180 police officers marched in the square, a bomb was thrown, and a riot broke out. Seven police officers were killed and union leaders were blamed. Public support for unions dropped. Draw a second conflict symbols ✸ around the S.

4. In 1892 workers at the **Carnegie Steel Company** in Homestead, Pennsylvania, also went on strike.

   a. These workers were also protesting a pay cut. Near Pittsburgh, write **S** for strike.

   b. The plant manager refused to talk with the strikers. He hired armed guards to protect the plant. Violence broke out and over 20 people were killed. After that, most workers quit the union and returned to work. The strike failed. Draw a conflict symbol ✸ around the S.

5. In 1894 there were an estimated 1,400 labor strikes. Workers continued to protest low wages and poor working conditions. On several manufacturing centers, write **S** for strike.

6. Strikes occasionally turned violent. In 1899 the **Western Federation of Miners** dynamited a mine in Idaho. Draw a conflict symbol ✸ near Coeur d'Alene.

 For further discussion:
- How would you feel if you had to work 10 hours a day, six days a week, in a factory at your age? When would you have time for school? time to play?
- Do you think workers have a right to strike for better working conditions?

Correlates with:
- ● *The Nystrom Atlas of United States History,* page 79

IMMIGRANTS
1895–1929

20

Key Elements

★ *Immigrants* map

★ *Immigration by Region of Origin* circle graphs

★ *Immigration to the United States* line graph

Getting Started

To give students an overview of *Immigrants,* ask them:

• What is the title of this map?

• What years does it cover?

• What do the arrows represent?

• Why are the arrows different colors? different widths?

• Why are the names of some ethnic groups in all capital letters and others are not?

• What does the line graph show? Which section matches the dates on the map?

• What do the circle graphs show? How to the colors relate to the map?

Teaching Notes and Mapping Activities

～ Why Immigrants Came

～ Top Regions of Origin

～ Immigration Rates

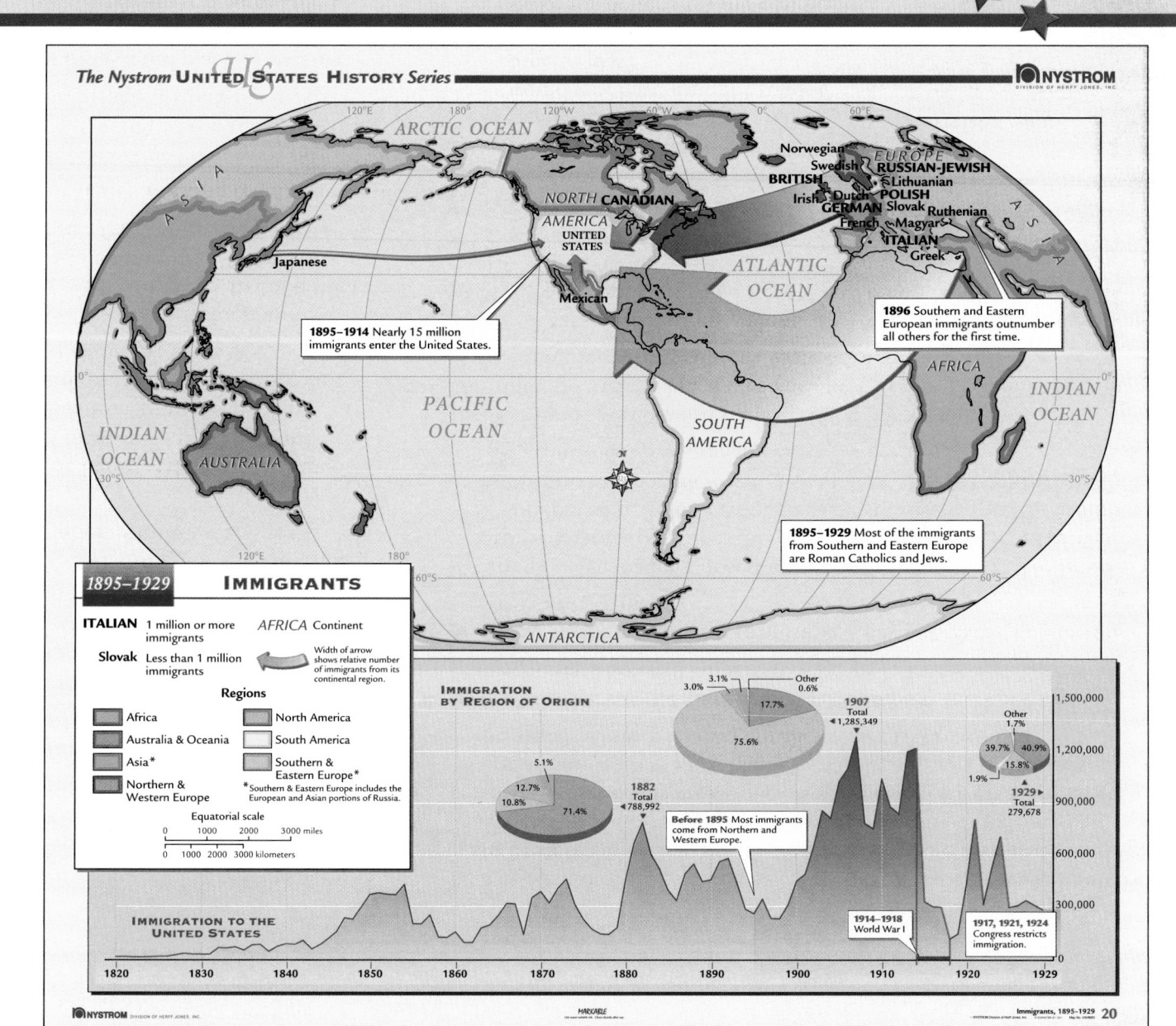

The Nystrom UNITED STATES HISTORY Series

1895–1914 Nearly 15 million immigrants enter the United States.

1896 Southern and Eastern European immigrants outnumber all others for the first time.

1895–1929 Most of the immigrants from Southern and Eastern Europe are Roman Catholics and Jews.

1895–1929 IMMIGRANTS

ITALIAN 1 million or more immigrants

Slovak Less than 1 million immigrants

AFRICA Continent

Width of arrow shows relative number of immigrants from its continental region.

Regions

- Africa
- Australia & Oceania
- Asia*
- Northern & Western Europe
- North America
- South America
- Southern & Eastern Europe*

*Southern & Eastern Europe includes the European and Asian portions of Russia.

Equatorial scale
0   1000   2000   3000 miles
0   1000 2000 3000 kilometers

IMMIGRATION BY REGION OF ORIGIN

1907 Total 1,285,349
3.1%
3.0%
Other 0.6%
17.7%
75.6%

1882 Total 788,992
5.1%
12.7%
10.8%
71.4%

Before 1895 Most immigrants come from Northern and Western Europe.

1929 Total 279,678
39.7%
40.9%
15.8%
1.9%
Other 1.7%

IMMIGRATION TO THE UNITED STATES

1914–1918 World War I

1917, 1921, 1924 Congress restricts immigration.

1820 1830 1840 1850 1860 1870 1880 1890 1900 1910 1920 1929

1,500,000
1,200,000
900,000
600,000
300,000

Immigrants, 1895–1929 **20**

Why Immigrants Came

Objective: *To identify major reasons for immigration to the United States.*

Teaching Notes and Mapping Activity

You or your students can mark the following on the *Immigrants* map.

1. Between 1895 and 1929, immigrants came to the United States for a variety of reasons. One reason was to **escape poverty**. In the 1800s, in Norway, there was a shortage of good farmland. Food was in short supply. **Norwegians** left their homeland.

   a. North of Norway, draw a poverty symbol **¢**.

   b. Now draw an arrow from Norway to the United States.

2. People also moved to the United States to escape **overcrowding**. For example, the population of the small island of Sicily more than tripled between 1800 and 1900. Millions left Sicily and southern Italy for America. **Italians** became one of the largest groups of new immigrants in the early 1900s.

   a. Across Italy, draw a cluster of stick figures.

   b. Then draw an arrow from Italy to the United States.

3. Some people immigrated to the United States to escape **religious persecution**. In Russia, **Jews** were forced to live in a region called the Pale of Settlement. Many were not allowed to own land or hold certain jobs. When *pogroms* (lootings, beatings, and killings) against Jews began, hundreds of thousands fled to America.

   a. To the right of the Russian-Jewish label, draw this symbol ✡.

   b. Then draw an arrow from Russia to the United States.

4. Other people immigrated to the United States to escape **political repression**. Between 1795 and 1914, Poland was divided up among three nations: Russia, Prussia (Germany), and Austria-Hungary. In the Russian section, all social and political activities were prohibited. In the Prussian section, **Poles** were forced to speak German.

   a. East of Poland, write **PR** for political repression.

   b. Then draw an arrow from Poland to the United States.

5. People immigrated to the United States to escape **war**. For example, the Mexican Revolution of 1910 drove many **Mexicans** across the U.S.–Mexico boundary. Political upheaval continued for years.

   a. On Mexico, draw a war symbol ✺.

   b. Then trace the arrow from Mexico to the United States.

6. Many immigrants came to the United States because they heard it was the land of opportunity. One out of every 10 **Greeks** left their homeland looking for a **better life**.

   a. On the United States, draw a better life symbol ☺.

   b. Then draw an arrow from Greece to the United States.

7. Many **Japanese** men came to the United States as contract workers. They immigrated because of **jobs**.

   a. On the United States, draw a jobs symbol ✎.

   b. Then trace the arrow from Japan to the United States.

   c. Later, many of these men wanted Japanese wives. Many marriages were arranged on the basis of photos alone. Thousands of **picture brides** immigrated to America. Draw a second arrow from Japan to the United States and label it **BRIDES**.

 For further discussion:
- Do you know any Norwegian Americans? Italian Americans? Russian Americans? Polish Americans? Mexican Americans? Japanese Americans?
- When did their families come to the United States? Why?

Correlates with:
- *The Nystrom Atlas of United States History,* pages 82–83

Teaching Notes and Mapping Activity

You or your students can mark the following on the *Immigration to the United States* line graph, *Immigration by Region of Origin* circle graphs, and the *Immigrants* map.

1. The year **1882** was a big year for immigration. More immigrants came to the United States that year than any other year between 1820 and 1895.

   a. Point to the *Immigration to the United States* line graph.
   - Trace the line from 1820 to 1895.
   - Then put an **X** on the peak for 1882.

   b. Find the *Immigration by Region of Origin* circle graph for 1882.
   - Look at the pattern on the graph.
   - Then outline the largest section of the graph and have students name the region.

   c. On the *Immigrants* map, have students locate the Northern and Western Europe region. Point out that it is the same color as its section of the circle graph.
   - Ask students to name immigrant groups from that region (British, German, etc.).
   - In the arrow for that region, write **1882**.
   - These immigrants came from the same countries as the early European settlers in the United States. They were often called Old Immigrants. Above the arrow, write **OLD IMMIGRANTS**.

2. The year **1907** was an even bigger year for immigration. That record wasn't surpassed until the late 1900s.

   a. Point to the *Immigration to the United States* line graph.
   - Trace the line from 1882 to 1907.
   - Then put an **X** on 1907.

   b. Find the *Immigration by Region of Origin* circle graph for 1907.
   - Look at the pattern on the graph.
   - Then outline the largest section of the graph and have students name the region.

   c. On the *Immigrants* map, have students locate the Southern and Eastern Europe region.
   - Ask students to name immigrant groups from that region.
   - In the arrow for that region, write **1907**.
   - These immigrants came from different countries than the earlier European settlers in the United States. So they were often called New Immigrants. Below the arrow, write **NEW IMMIGRANTS**.

3. The year **1929** did not attract as many immigrants.

   a. Point to the *Immigration to the United States* line graph.
   - Trace the line from 1907 to 1929.
   - Then put an **X** on 1929.

   b. Find the *Immigration by Region of Origin* circle graph for 1929.
   - Look at the pattern on the graph.
   - Then outline the two largest sections of the graph and have students names the regions.

   c. On the *Immigrants* map, have students locate the North American and the Northern and Western Europe regions.
   - Ask students to name immigrant groups from both regions.
   - In the arrow from Canada, write **1929**.
   - In the arrow from Northern and Western Europe, add **1929**.
   - Some of these immigrants were neighbors, others were Old Immigrants. Above the arrow from Canada, write **NEIGHBORS**.

⭐ Have students redraw the circle graphs for 1882, 1907, and 1929 as bar graphs. See if any other comparisons can be made.

Correlates with:
- **The Nystrom Atlas of United States History,** pages 82–83

Immigration Rates

Objective: *To identify factors that caused immigration rates to rise and fall.*

Teaching Notes and Mapping Activity

You or your students can mark the following on the *Immigration to the United States* line graph.

1. Immigration rates rise and fall over the years.

   a. With your finger, from 1820 to 1929, trace the immigration line graph.

   b. Have students point out some years with high immigration rates. Label these with plus **+** signs.

   c. Also have students point out some years with low immigration rates. Label these with minus **–** signs.

2. Immigration rates change for a variety of reasons. One of them is **war**. Immigration usually falls during time of war. Travel is difficult and often dangerous.

   a. The **Civil War** was fought between 1860 and 1865. Along the date line, between these years, write a **W** for war.

   b. World War I was fought between 1914 and 1918. Between those years, write **W**.

3. Immigration also falls during times of economic **depression**. During a depression, money and jobs are scarce.

   a. There was a severe depression in **1837**. Along the timeline, above 1837, write **D** for depression.

   b. Severe depressions also occurred during the following years. Along the timeline, mark each with a **D**.
   - 1873
   - 1893
   - 1907
   - 1929

4. Immigration often drops a a result of new immigration **laws**.

   a. An immigration law was passed in 1875. It prevented convicts and prostitutes from entering the country.
   - On the line graph, mark 1875 with a **▼**.
   - Above the **▼**, write **NO CONVICTS.**

   b. In the mid 1800s, thousands of Chinese workers came to the United States to help build railroads and work the mines. In 1882, the **Chinese Exclusion Act** was passed. It prevented more Chinese immigrants from entering the country.
   - On the line graph, mark 1882 with a **▼**.
   - Above the **▼**, write **NO CHINESE**.

   c. In 1917, another immigration law was passed.
   - It required adult immigrants to show that they could read and write. To the left of 1917, write **LITERACY TESTS**.
   - It also excluded most Asians. Below LITERACY TESTS, add **ASIANS EXCLUDED**.

   d. In 1921, Congress set a limit on the number of immigrants from specific regions that could enter the United States each year. These quotas were based on the nationalities of foreign-born people in the United States in 1910. Above 1921, write **QUOTAS**.

   e. The **Immigration Act of 1924** limited immigration from the Eastern Hemisphere by basing quotas on the 1920 U.S. population. These quotas insured that most immigrants would come from northern and western Europe. Next to 1924, write **S + E EUROPE QUOTAS**.

 Have students list the pros and cons of setting immigration quotas.

Correlates with:
- *The Nystrom Atlas of United States History,* pages 82–83

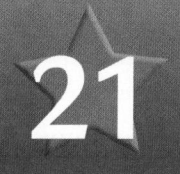

21

WORLD WAR I IN EUROPE 1914–1918

Key Elements

★ *World War I in Europe* map
★ Locator map
★ *Military Resources* graph
★ *Military Deaths* graph

Getting Started

To give students an overview of *World War I in Europe*, ask them:

- What is the title of this map?
- What part of the world is shown on this map?
- What years does the map cover?
- What do the three main colors on the map represent?
- What do the yellow lines show?
- What does the red symbol represent?
- On the *Military Resources* graph, what does the purple color represent? the orange color?
- Which side had more troops?
- On the *Military Deaths* graph, which side had more deaths?

Teaching Notes and Mapping Activities

~ Alliances Draw Europe into War
~ The Western Front
~ The Eastern Front

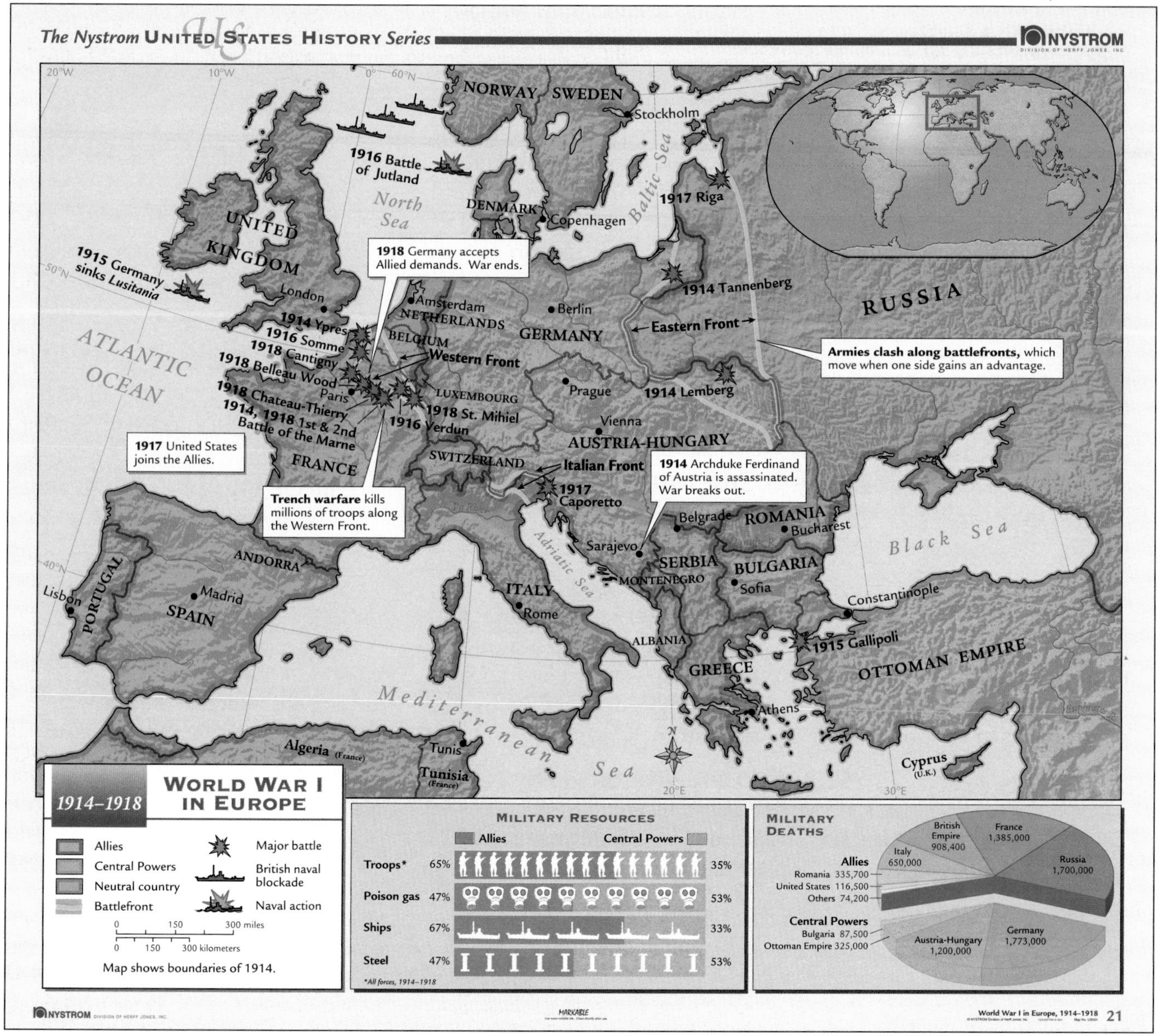
The Nystrom United States History Series
NYSTROM
DIVISION OF HERFF JONES, INC.
NORWAY
SWEDEN
Stockholm
1916 Battle of Jutland
North Sea
DENMARK
Copenhagen
Baltic Sea
1917 Riga
UNITED KINGDOM
London
1915 Germany sinks Lusitania
1918 Germany accepts Allied demands. War ends.
Amsterdam
NETHERLANDS
BELGIUM
Berlin
GERMANY
1914 Tannenberg
Eastern Front
RUSSIA
Armies clash along battlefronts, which move when one side gains an advantage.
1914 Ypres
1916 Somme
1918 Cantigny
1918 Belleau Wood
Paris
1918 Chateau-Thierry
1914, 1918 1st & 2nd Battle of the Marne
Western Front
LUXEMBOURG
1918 St. Mihiel
1916 Verdun
Prague
1914 Lemberg
Vienna
AUSTRIA-HUNGARY
ATLANTIC OCEAN
1917 United States joins the Allies.
FRANCE
SWITZERLAND
Italian Front
1917 Caporetto
1914 Archduke Ferdinand of Austria is assassinated. War breaks out.
Trench warfare kills millions of troops along the Western Front.
Belgrade
ROMANIA
Bucharest
Black Sea
Sarajevo
SERBIA
BULGARIA
Sofia
MONTENEGRO
Adriatic Sea
ANDORRA
Lisbon
PORTUGAL
Madrid
SPAIN
ITALY
Rome
Constantinople
ALBANIA
1915 Gallipoli
OTTOMAN EMPIRE
GREECE
Athens
Mediterranean Sea
Algeria (France)
Tunis
Tunisia (France)
Cyprus (U.K.)
20°W
10°W
0°
60°N
50°N
40°N
20°E
30°E
N
WORLD WAR I IN EUROPE
1914–1918
Allies
Central Powers
Neutral country
Battlefront
Major battle
British naval blockade
Naval action
0 150 300 miles
0 150 300 kilometers
Map shows boundaries of 1914.
MILITARY RESOURCES
Allies
Central Powers
Troops* 65% 35%
Poison gas 47% 53%
Ships 67% 33%
Steel 47% 53%
*All forces, 1914–1918
MILITARY DEATHS
Allies
Italy 650,000
British Empire 908,400
France 1,385,000
Russia 1,700,000
Romania 335,700
United States 116,500
Others 74,200
Central Powers
Bulgaria 87,500
Ottoman Empire 325,000
Austria-Hungary 1,200,000
Germany 1,773,000
NYSTROM DIVISION OF HERFF JONES, INC.
MARKABLE
World War I in Europe, 1914–1918 21

Alliances Draw Europe into War

Objective: *To identify Central Power and Allied countries and the alliances that brought them to war.*

Teaching Notes and Mapping Activity

You or your students can mark the following on the *World War I in Europe* map.

1. Between 1870 and 1914, the countries of Europe entered into a number of alliances. For example, Germany, Austria-Hungary, and Italy formed the **Triple Alliance**. They agreed to come to the aid of each other if attacked by two or more countries.

   a. On Germany, Austria-Hungary, and Italy, write **TA**.

   b. Connect the TAs with three lines.

2. Next, Kaiser Wilhelm II of Germany, Emperor Charles of Austria-Hungary, and Tsar Nicholas II of Russia (Kaiser Wilhelm's cousin) formed the **Three Emperors' League**. They each agreed to remain neutral if the others went to war.

   a. On Germany, Austria-Hungary, and Russia, write **TEL**.

   b. Connect the TELs with three lines.

3. Later, France and Russia formed an alliance. They agreed to help each other if attacked by Germany.

   a. On France and Russia, write **A** for alliance.

   b. Connect the As with a line.

4. Russia and Serbia had been longtime friends.

   a. On Russia and Serbia, write **F** for friends

   b. Connect the Fs with a line.

5. In the early 1900s, the United Kingdom, France, and Russia formed the **Triple Entente**. (King George V of England and Tsar Nicholas II of Russia were cousins.) The three countries opened discussions for joint military efforts.

   a. On the United Kingdom, France, and Russia, write **TE**.

   b. Connect the TEs with three lines.

6. On June 28, 1914, Austria-Hungary's archduke, Franz Ferdinand, was **assassinated** by a Serbian terrorist. Draw a conflict symbol on Sarajevo.

7. One month later, Austria-Hungary declared **war** on Serbia.

   a. In the upper left corner of the map, write and underline **ALLIES**. Below that, write **SERBIA**.

   b. In the upper right corner of the map, write and underline **CENTRAL POWERS**. Below that, write **AUSTRIA-HUNGARY**.

8. The alliances went into effect. Germany supported Austria-Hungary. To the list of Central Powers, add **GERMANY**.

9. Russia announced that it would stand behind Serbia and send in troops. To the list of Allies, add **RUSSIA**.

10. Germany then declared war on Russia and France. To the list of Allies, add **FRANCE**.

11. Germany invaded neutral Belgium on its way to France. This caused the United Kingdom to declare war on Germany. To the list of Allies, add **BELGIUM** and **UNITED KINGDOM**.

12. By the end of the war, most countries in Europe and the world had chosen sides.

    a. Use the information on the map to add to the list of Allies and Central Powers.

    b. The United States joined the Allies in 1917. Add **UNITED STATES** to the list.

 Ask students to use the *Military Resources* graph to compare resources available to the Allies and the Central Powers. Did either side have an advantage?

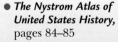

Correlates with:
- *The Nystrom Atlas of United States History,* pages 84–85
- *Mapping United States History* To the Present, Lesson 29 To the Early 1900s, Lesson 43

The Western Front

Objective: *To sequence battles fought along the Western Front.*

Teaching Notes and Mapping Activity

You or your students can mark the following on the *World War I in Europe* map.

1. World War I was fought across Europe. France and the United Kingdom fought Germany on battlefields in France and Belgium. These battlefields became known as the **Western Front**.

   a. On the map, underline the words *Western Front*.

   b. Trace the yellow lines representing the front.

2. On September 6, 1914, French and German troops fought near the Marne River, east of Paris. This Allied victory stopped the German invasion of France and ended German hopes for a speedy victory. Label the **1st Battle of the Marne** ①.

3. Both the Allies and the Central Powers raced to the sea. Each wanted control of the ports along the English Channel. From mid-October to mid-November, they fought near **Ypres** in Belgium. The Allies were able to stop Germany's march to the channel. Label Ypres ②.

4. Soldiers dug **trenches** along the Western Front. They ate, slept, fought, and died in these muddy holes. Because of the trenches, the Western Front hardly moved for 3 ½ years. Along the far Western Front trench line, from Ypres to the German border, write **3 ½ YRS**.

5. In spring of 1915, the Allies and Central Powers fought again at Ypres. This was the first time **poison gas** was used. Near Ypres, draw a gas mask.

6. In February of 1916, the Allies and Central Powers fought at **Verdun** in France. The battle went on for months. The city of Verdun was almost destroyed, and each side suffered roughly 300,000 casualties. Label Verdun ③.

7. On July 1, 1916, British and German troops fought at **Somme**. Britain suffered almost 60,000 casualties in one day. Fighting again went on for months. The Allies gained just 7 miles.

   a. Label Somme ④.

   b. The British introduced **tanks** at this battle. Near Somme, draw a tank.

8. In the spring of 1917, French troops mutinied. They protested what they felt were pointless deaths and horrible living conditions. In southern France, write **TROOPS MUTINY**.

9. On April 6, 1917, the **United States declared war** on Germany. By late June, American troops began arriving in France. In the Atlantic Ocean, draw a ship and label it **U.S.**

10. The war went on for another year.

    a. In late May 1918, American troops fought their first major battle of the war at **Cantigny**. Label it ⑤.

    b. At the same time, the Allies stopped a German advance just 50 miles from Paris. Label **Chateau-Thierry** ⑥.

    c. In June, the Allies drove the Germans out of **Belleau Wood**. Label it ⑦.

    d. In July, the **2nd Battle of the Marne** was a turning point for the Allies. Label it ⑧.

    e. In September, the Allies easily won **St. Mihiel**. Label it ⑨.

11. In the fall of 1918, widespread riots broke out in Germany. Kaiser Wilhelm gave up his throne. On Germany, write **CENTRAL POWERS SURRENDER**.

☆ Have students make a model of a World War I trench.

☆ Ask students to find out what the following are: U-boats, doughboys, zeppelins, mustard gas, dogfights, aces, Big Berthas.

Correlates with:

● *The Nystrom Atlas of United States History,* pages 84–85

● *Mapping United States History* To the Present, Lesson 29 To the Early 1900s, Lesson 43

The Eastern Front

Objective: *To sequence events that occurred on the Eastern Front.*

Teaching Notes and Mapping Activity

You or your students can mark the following on the *World War I in Europe* map.

1. World War I was fought across Europe. Germany and Austria-Hungary fought Russia on battlefields in all three countries. These battlefields became known as the **Eastern Front**.

   a. Underline the words *Eastern Front*.

   b. Trace the yellow lines representing the front.

2. Germany was surprised at how fast Russia had mobilized its troops. By late August 1914, two Russian armies had entered Germany.

   a. From Russia to **Tannenberg**, draw an arrow.

   b. However, by August 31, German troops had surrounded one of the Russian armies. Over 90 percent of this army was captured or killed. Label Tannenberg ①.

   c. The other Russian army was also defeated. The Russians were chased out of Germany. From northeast Germany to the far eastern battlefront line, draw an arrow.

3. In August and September of 1914, Russian troops invaded northeastern Austria-Hungary. The Russians were able to defeat Austria-Hungary's poorly equipped and poorly organized army.

   a. From Russia to the battlefront line that runs through Austria-Hungary, draw an arrow.

   b. Label the battle of **Lemberg** ②.

4. After Austria-Hungary's defeat, the Germans took control of the Eastern Front. By May of 1915, they had gained hundreds of miles of Russian territory. The Russian army in the south was crushed.

   a. From the battlefront line that runs through Austria-Hungary to the far eastern battlefront, draw an arrow.

   b. The Central Powers captured **Poland**, **Lithuania**, and part of

Latvia. Label the land between the two battlefronts **CP**.

5. In 1916 **Romania** joined the Allies.

   a. Romanian troops tried to invade neighboring Austria-Hungary. From Romania north to Austria-Hungary, draw an arrow.

   b. They were quickly driven back by the Central Powers, who took control of Romania's oil and wheat fields. Draw an arrow back to Romania. Then label Romania **CP**.

6. By 1917, the Russian people were tired of war. Food and fuel were in short supply. Over a million troops had died. On March 15, Tsar Nicholas II was forced to give up his throne.

   a. On Russia, write **TSAR ABDICATES**.

   b. The Central Powers transported Vladimir Lenin to Russia. They hoped that Lenin, a Russian revolutionary, would incite Russians to rebel against their government. From Switzerland to Russia, draw an arrow. Label it **LENIN**.

7. Civil war broke out in Russia. Germany took advantage of the situation and forced the Russians from the city of **Riga**. Label the city ③.

8. Late in 1917, the new Russian government surrendered to the Central Powers. The war on the Eastern Front ended, freeing up German troops to fight on the Western Front. Fighting on the Western Front continued for another year. On the Eastern Front, write **RUSSIA SURRENDERS**.

 Have students make a timeline of events and battles in World War I. Have them include battles on both the Eastern and Western Fronts.

 Ask students to research battles on other fronts and explain their affect on the war.

Correlates with:

- *The Nystrom Atlas of United States History,* pages 84–85
- *Mapping United States History* To the Present, Lesson 29 To the Early 1900s, Lesson 43

GREAT DEPRESSION AND DUST BOWL
1929–1940

Key Elements

★ *Great Depression and Dust Bowl* map
★ *Bank Failures* graph
★ *Stock Market Crash* graph
★ *Severe Droughts Strike* graph

Getting Started

To give students an overview of *Great Depression and Dust Bowl*, ask them:

- What is the title of this map?
- What does the brown color represent? the orange?
- What do the symbols on the map represent?
- Look at the *Bank Failures* graph. Which year had the highest number of bank failures?
- Look at the *Stock Market Crash* graph. When did the stock market crash?
- Look at the *Severe Droughts Strike* graph. Which year had the most land hit by drought?

Teaching Notes and Mapping Activities

~ The Great Depression
~ Drought and the Dust Bowl
~ Migration East and West

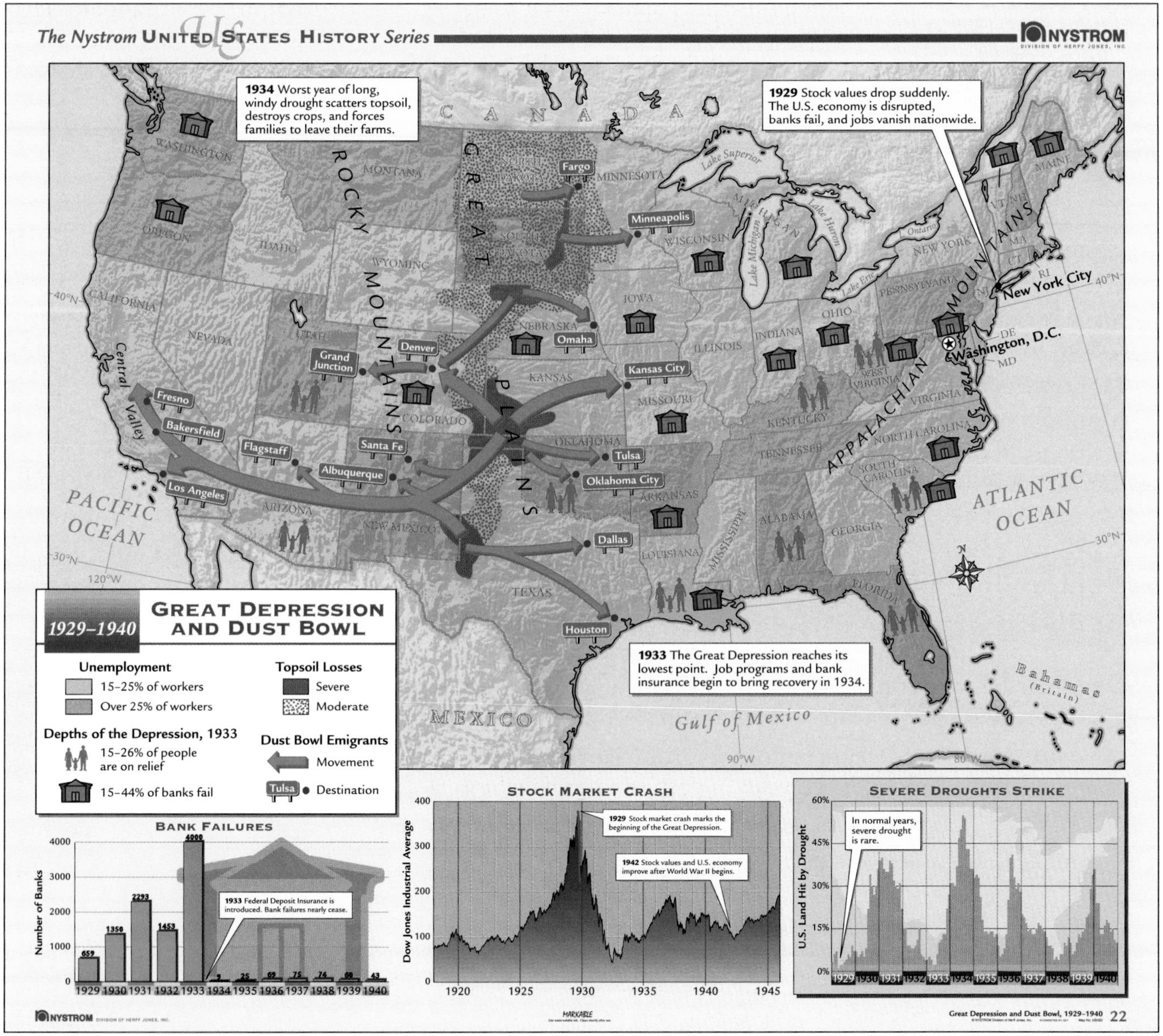

The Nystrom **UNITED STATES HISTORY** *Series*

NYSTROM
DIVISION OF HERFF JONES, INC

1934 Worst year of long, windy drought scatters topsoil, destroys crops, and forces families to leave their farms.

1929 Stock values drop suddenly. The U.S. economy is disrupted, banks fail, and jobs vanish nationwide.

1933 The Great Depression reaches its lowest point. Job programs and bank insurance begin to bring recovery in 1934.

GREAT DEPRESSION AND DUST BOWL
1929–1940

Unemployment
- 15–25% of workers
- Over 25% of workers

Topsoil Losses
- Severe
- Moderate

Depths of the Depression, 1933
- 15–26% of people are on relief
- 15–44% of banks fail

Dust Bowl Emigrants
- Movement
- Tulsa ● Destination

BANK FAILURES

Number of Banks

- 1929: 659
- 1930: 1350
- 1931: 2293
- 1932: 1453
- 1933: 4000
- 1934: 9
- 1935: 26
- 1936: 69
- 1937: 75
- 1938: 74
- 1939: 60
- 1940: 43

1933 Federal Deposit Insurance is introduced. Bank failures nearly cease.

STOCK MARKET CRASH

Dow Jones Industrial Average

1929 Stock market crash marks the beginning of the Great Depression.

1942 Stock values and U.S. economy improve after World War II begins.

SEVERE DROUGHTS STRIKE

U.S. Land Hit by Drought

In normal years, severe drought is rare.

Great Depression and Dust Bowl, 1929–1940   22

NYSTROM DIVISION OF HERFF JONES, INC.

The Great Depression

Objective: *To examine the impact the 1929 stock market crash had on the economy.*

Teaching Notes and Mapping Activity

You or your students can mark the following on the *Great Depression and Dust Bowl* map.

1. The 1920s were a time of prosperity. Businesses grew and the stock market steadily climbed. On the *Stock Market Crash* graph, from 1920 to 1929, trace the line with an arrow pointing up.

2. On Thursday, October 24, 1929, stock values dropped. Values fell again a few days later. People panicked and sold a record number of stocks. The **stock market crashed** and the Great Depression began.

   a. On the stock market graph, label the red line **BLACK THURSDAY**.

   b. Stock values continued to fall for the next three years. On the graph, from 1929 to 1933, trace the line with an arrow pointing down.

3. Following the stock market crash, factories, businesses, and stores closed. Millions were left **unemployed**. By 1933, one out of every four American workers was out of work.

   a. On the map, have students identify any states with an unemployment rate of less than 15%. (There are none.)

   b. Then have students name states where the unemployment rate was 15-25%.

   c. Now have students identify states where the unemployment rate was over 25%. Label each with **U**.

4. Most people without jobs couldn't afford to pay their rent or mortgages. They lost their homes. During the Depression, many of the homeless built shacks in garbage dumps and along railroad tracks. They called these shabby communities Hooverville, named after the president they blamed for their financial problems. Many cities had Hoovervilles. Near Washington, D.C., write **HOOVERVILLE**.

5. Banks invested in the stock market. They loaned people money. But many jobless people couldn't afford to pay their bank loans.

   a. Between 1929 and 1933, almost 10,000 **banks failed**. Bank failures reached an all-time high in 1933. On the *Bank Failures* graph, outline the bar for 1933.

   b. When banks failed, people lost all the money they had in the bank. On the map, have students identify states in which 15–44% of the banks failed. Draw a line under each of their bank symbols.

   c. In 1933, the government introduced the Federal Deposit Insurance Corporation (FDIC), which insured bank deposits. The FDIC increased faith in banks because people felt their money was safe. On the graph, compare the number of bank failures before and after FDIC. Above the bars for 1934–1940, write **FDIC**.

6. By 1933, over a million families were on Federal **relief**. Many more were poor, but too proud to accept help from the government. On the map, circle the relief symbols.

7. The United States pulled out of the Depression in 1942. That year, the U.S. entered World War II and the economy began to improve.

   a. On the *Stock Market Crash* graph, trace the line from 1933 to 1942.

   b. From 1942 to 1946, trace line with an arrow pointing up.

 For further discussion:
   - Which states had high levels of unemployment, bank failures, *and* people on relief?
   - Why do you think some states were hit harder by the depression than others?

Correlates with:

- *The Nystrom Atlas of United States History,* pages 90
- *Mapping United States History* To the Present, Lesson 32

Drought and the Dust Bowl

Objective: *To identify the Dust Bowl region and the factors that caused this environmental disaster.*

Teaching Notes and Mapping Activity

You or your students can mark the following on the *Great Depression and Dust Bowl* map.

1. Before settlers arrived, the **Great Plains** was mostly grassland. The **wild grasses** had a deep root system that helped hold soil in place. Along the Great Plains, draw about 20 grass symbols **I**.

2. In the late 1800s, settlers began to farm the Great Plains.

   a. Some settlers raised **cattle** on the grassland. On the Great Plains, draw several cattle symbols ☿.

   b. Other settlers planted crops. In the 1870s, a variety of **wheat** was introduced that grew well on the plains. Change five of the grass symbols to wheat symbols ⚶.

   c. During World War I, millions of acres of grassland were plowed under and wheat was planted. Tractors made plowing easier and the war made wheat profitable. Change 13 of the remaining grass symbols to wheat symbols ⚶.

3. In 1931, it barely rained on the Great Plains. Plants started to wither. A **drought** began.

   a. Look at the *Severe Droughts Strikes* graph. The year 1929 was normal—severe drought was rare. Underline 1929.

   b. At the 5% level, draw a dotted line across the graph.

   c. With your finger, trace the bars—comparing 1929 with 1931, 1934, and 1936.

   d. In 1936, the drought extended from the Rockies to the Appalachians. On the map, put one hand on the Rocky Mountains and the other on the Appalachian Mountains.

4. Wind is normal on the plains. But when it was combined with droughts, hot summers, overgrazing, and the replacement of deep-rooted grass with shallow-rooted wheat, the result was **dust storms**.

   a. Wind often blows from the west. West of the Rockies, draw a large arrow pointing east.

   b. Dust storms destroyed crops. They ruined cars and trucks. They could bury houses and cattle under mounds of topsoil. Over two of your cattle symbols, draw ⇒.

   c. Some severe dust storms blew topsoil all the way to the Atlantic Ocean. In fact, one storm in 1934 carried 350 million short tons of dirt to the East Coast. In the Atlantic Ocean, draw a topsoil symbol ⁛.

5. After years of drought and dust storms, millions of acres of the Great Plains were ruined. Crops and farms were destroyed. People were forced to move.

   a. With your finger, circle areas of moderate and severe topsoil loss.

   b. Now, with a marker, circle the entire area.

   c. Above your circle, write **DUST BOWL**.

6. In 1935 the government established the **Soil Conservation Service**. This service taught farmers planting techniques that could protect the soil. They also planted 18,500 miles of trees to break the winds. By 1938 they had reduced blowing soil by 65%. In the Dust Bowl, draw several tree symbols ♀.

☆ Have students conduct an experiment on soil loss. Have them blow a fan across two containers of plants with dry soil. Behind one of the containers, erect some type of wind barrier. Measure the amount of soil blown off each container.

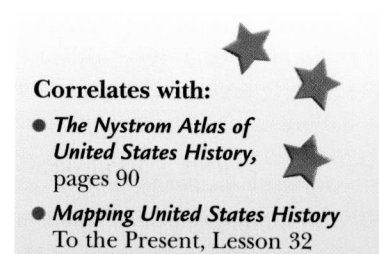

Correlates with:
- *The Nystrom Atlas of United States History,* pages 90
- *Mapping United States History To the Present,* Lesson 32

Migration East and West

Objective: *To trace migration routes during the Depression and Dust Bowl years.*

Teaching Notes and Mapping Activity

You or your students can mark the following on the *Great Depression and Dust Bowl* map.

1. During some years of the Depression, one-quarter of the nation was unemployed. Some jobless people rode the rails in freight cars and explored the country. Some called these travelers hobos.

   a. From New York City to San Francisco (in California, near the first e in Central Valley), draw a railroad symbol ┼┼┼┼┼.

   b. Label the line **HOBO**.

2. During the Depression, the Great Plains turned into a **Dust Bowl**. Years of drought and strong winds sent topsoil flying, destroying crops and damaging homes.

   a. With your finger, outline areas that had moderate topsoil loss.

   b. With a marker, outline areas that had severe topsoil loss.

3. After years of drought and no crops, families had a difficult time making ends meet. Some found work in **nearby cities**, so they could keep making payments on their farms.

   a. Trace arrows from areas that had severe topsoil loss to nearby cities.

   b. Have students name cities that Dust Bowl victims migrated to.

4. Other families lost their farms. Some of them heard there was work in **California**. Millions traveled west on Route 66.

   a. From western Oklahoma to California, trace the arrow.

   b. Migrants from Oklahoma, Texas, Arkansas, and Missouri moved to California. Although only about 20 percent were from Oklahoma, all the **migrants** were often lumped together and called Okies. Label the arrow **OKIES**.

5. Some of the Dust Bowl migrants found work in **factories**. Near Los Angeles, draw a factory symbol 🏭.

6. Other migrants hoped to find work **picking fruit** and other crops.

   a. California's Central Valley was a major agricultural area. Point to Central Valley.

   b. Working and living conditions for many of the migrants were terrible. Work was physically hard, hours were long, pay was low. Migrants set up temporary camps along irrigation ditches in fields. They were called **squatter camps**. These camps were very unsanitary. In Central Valley, draw several tents.

7. Several thousand people from the Great Plains migrated to California. The state was flooded with poor families. There wasn't enough work for all of them. Some were turned back at the California border. They were forced to return home. From California to the Great Plains, draw another arrow.

8. The government set up camps for some of the migrant families. One of them, Arvin Federal Camp in southern California, was called Weedpatch. It had showers, a laundry, tents and cabins, and a school for the children. Near Bakersfield, write **WEEDPATCH**.

9. By 1940, the drought had ended.

   a. Some families returned to the Great Plains. From California to the Great Plains, draw a second arrow.

   b. Other families settled permanently in California. In California, draw several home symbols ⌂.

 Show students photos of migrant workers from the Great Plains. Have students choose a person from one of those photos and write a paragraph describing what that person might be experiencing.

Correlates with:
● *The Nystrom Atlas of United States History,* pages 90
● *Mapping United States History* To the Present, Lesson 33

23

WORLD WAR II IN EUROPE
1939–1942

Key Elements
★ *World War II in Europe* map
★ *Battle of Britain* map
★ Locator map
★ *Military Resources* graph

Getting Started

To give students an overview of *World War II in Europe,* ask them:

- What is the title of the main map?
- What part of the world is shown on this map?
- What do the four main map colors represent?
- What do the arrows show?
- What does the smaller map show?
- What do the symbols represent?
- Look at the *Military Resources* graph. Which side had the most resources?

Teaching Notes and Mapping Activities
~ German Expansion
~ The Battle of Britain
~ Battles in Europe

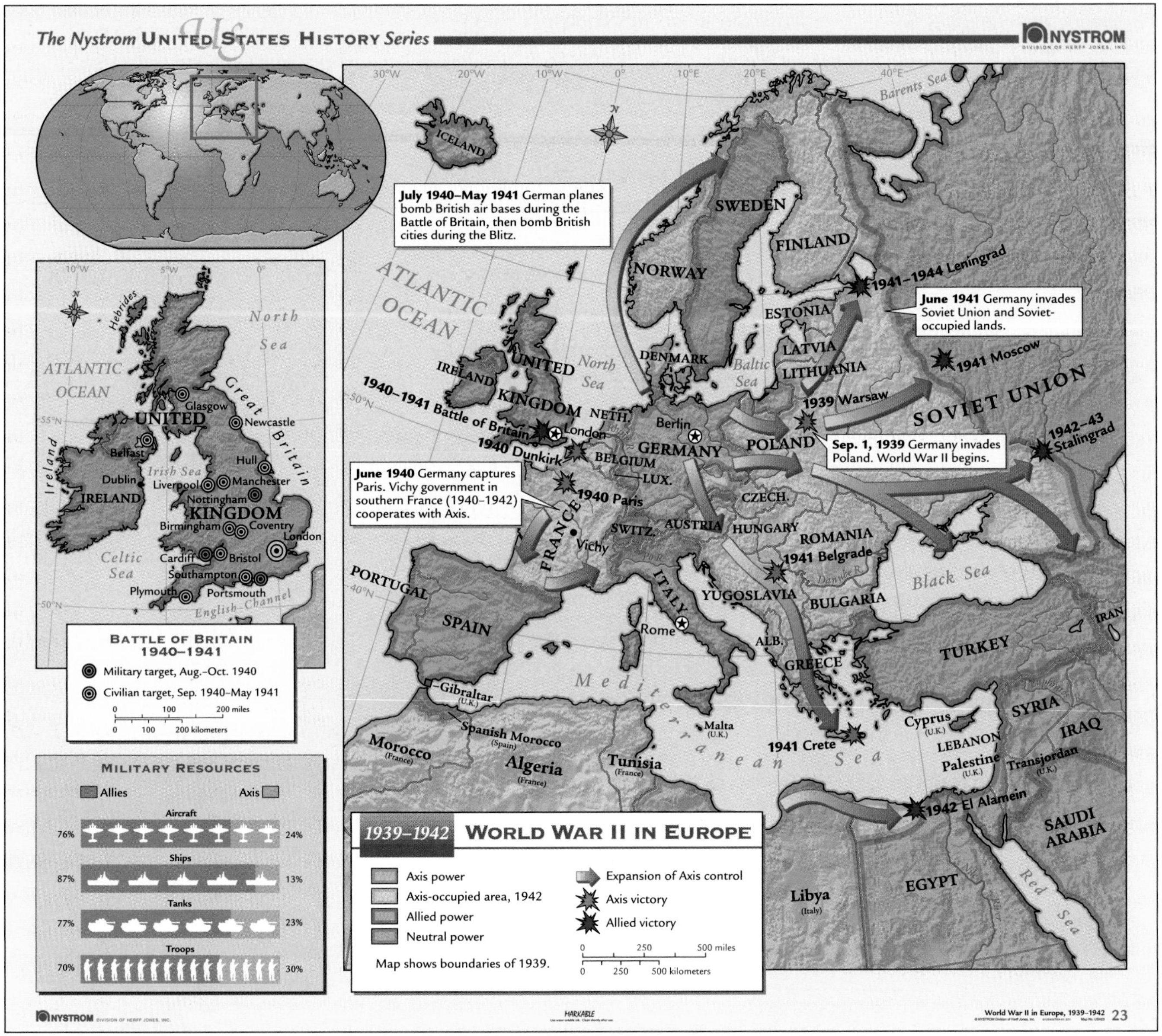

The Nystrom **UNITED STATES HISTORY Series** | **NYSTROM** DIVISION OF HERFF JONES, INC.

July 1940–May 1941 German planes bomb British air bases during the Battle of Britain, then bomb British cities during the Blitz.

1941–1944 Leningrad

June 1941 Germany invades Soviet Union and Soviet-occupied lands.

1941 Moscow

1940–1941 Battle of Britain

1939 Warsaw

Sep. 1, 1939 Germany invades Poland. World War II begins.

1942–43 Stalingrad

1940 Dunkirk

June 1940 Germany captures Paris. Vichy government in southern France (1940–1942) cooperates with Axis.

1940 Paris

1941 Belgrade

1941 Crete

1942 El Alamein

BATTLE OF BRITAIN 1940–1941
◎ Military target, Aug.–Oct. 1940
◎ Civilian target, Sep. 1940–May 1941
0   100   200 miles
0   100   200 kilometers

MILITARY RESOURCES

	Allies	Axis
Aircraft	76%	24%
Ships	87%	13%
Tanks	77%	23%
Troops	70%	30%

1939–1942 WORLD WAR II IN EUROPE

- Axis power
- Axis-occupied area, 1942
- Allied power
- Neutral power

- Expansion of Axis control
- Axis victory
- Allied victory

Map shows boundaries of 1939.

0   250   500 miles
0   250   500 kilometers

German Expansion

Objective: *To identify areas overtaken by Germany between 1935 and 1940.*

Teaching Notes and Mapping Activity

You or your students can mark the following on the *World War II in Europe* map.

1. The **Treaty of Versailles** ended World War I. It punished Germany severely. The treaty blamed Germany for causing the war. It forced Germany to give up territory in Europe, as well as colonies in Africa and Asia.

   a. Outline Germany's boundaries. (Be sure to include the section north of Poland)

   b. After World War I, Germany lost territory to the following countries. Mark each with a dot ●.
   - France
   - Denmark
   - Poland
   - Belgium
   - Czechoslovakia

2. In 1933 **Adolph Hitler** was appointed chancellor of Germany. He began a program of expansion aimed first at regaining territory lost in World War I.

   a. Give the map a title. Across the top of the map, write **GERMAN EXPANSION**.

   b. In 1935 Hitler took back the **Saar Valley** coalfields that Germany had lost to France. In Germany, near Luxembourg, write **1935**.

   c. In 1936 Hitler took back the **Rhineland**. In western Germany, write **1936**.

3. In March of 1938, German troops took over neighboring **Austria**. Some Austrians welcomed unification with Germany. On Austria, write **1938**.

4. Hitler also wanted control of neighboring **Czechoslovakia**.

   a. In March of 1938, German troops invaded **Sudetenland**, a region of Czechoslovakia bordering Germany. The Sudetenland had a large German population. Label western Czechoslovakia **1938**.

   b. After invading Sudetenland, Hitler signed the **Munich Agreement**. He promised the United Kingdom and France that he would take no more land. A year later, Hitler broke his promise and invaded the rest of Czechoslovakia. Label eastern Czechoslovakia **1939**.

5. Concerned about German expansion, the United Kingdom and France pledged to help **Poland** if it was invaded.

   a. On September 2, 1939, Germany invaded Poland. Trace the arrows from Germany to Poland.

   b. In response, the United Kingdom and France declared **war** on Germany. However, they did little to help Poland. On Poland, write **1939**.

6. Germany relied on iron ore from Sweden. The ore was shipped out of Norway. In April of 1940, Germany invaded **Norway**. It also captured **Denmark**. On both countries, write **1940**.

7. The following month, Germany invaded the Low Countries. **Luxembourg** surrendered in one day, the **Netherlands** in five days, and **Belgium** in 18. Across the region, write **1940**.

8. Next Germany launched a major attack on **France**. By June 14, 1940, German troops had marched into Paris.

   a. Germany took over the northern two-thirds of France. Label it **1940**.

   b. Southern France, while under French control, cooperated with the Germans. Circle **Vichy**.

9. Outline the area under German control in 1940.

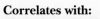

Correlates with:
- *The Nystrom Atlas of United States History,* pages 92–93
- *Mapping United States History To the Present,* Lesson 34

 Have students compare territory controlled by Germany in 1935, 1940, and 1945.

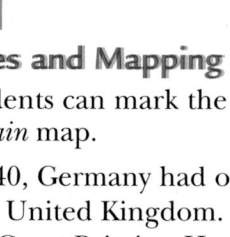

The Battle of Britain

Objective: *To recognize Germany's changing strategy in this significant air battle.*

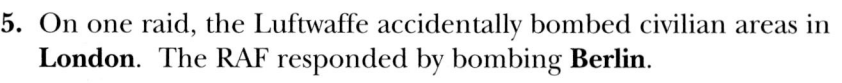

Teaching Notes and Mapping Activity

You or your students can mark the following on the *Battle of Britain* map.

1. By July of 1940, Germany had only one enemy to worry about in Europe—the United Kingdom. Hitler launched **Operation Sea Lion** against Great Britain. However, before Germany could invade Britain by sea, it had to destroy Britain's air force.

   a. On the *World War II in Europe* map, label Germany with a **G** and Great Britain with a **B**.

   b. Point out the seas and channel that separate the United Kingdom from the rest of Europe.

2. In summer of 1940, Germany's air force, the **Luftwaffe**, had roughly four times more aircraft than Britain's **Royal Air Force** (RAF).

   a. On the *Military Resources* graph, draw a box around the two Axis aircraft symbols. Above them, write **LUFT**.

   b. Also draw a box around half of an Allies aircraft symbol. Above it, write **RAF**.

3. On July 10, 1940, the Luftwaffe began Operation Sea Lion. They targeted British **ships** in the English Channel and **radar stations**. At that time, Britain had one of the most advanced early warning systems in the world.

   a. Above the *Battle of Britain* map, write **OPERATION SEA LION**.

   b. In the English Channel, draw two ships.

   c. On the southern coast of Britain, draw a radar.

4. By August, the Germans thought they had destroyed Britain's early warning system. The Luftwaffe then began to aggressively target **RAF aircraft** on the ground and in the air. Many RAF airfields were badly damaged. Along Britain's southern coast and near London, draw aircraft symbols ✈.

5. On one raid, the Luftwaffe accidentally bombed civilian areas in **London**. The RAF responded by bombing **Berlin**.

   a. On the *World War II in Europe* map, around London and Berlin, draw bombing symbols ✳.

   b. Many parents in British cities were concerned about the safety of their children. So they sent their children to live in rural areas. On the *Battle of Britain* map, draw arrows away from cities.

6. In September of 1940, Hitler changed his strategy. This time he directed the Luftwaffe to intentionally bomb cities. For 57 consecutive nights, London was bombed. People slept under tables, in air raid shelters, and in subway tunnels. The British called this the **Blitz**. Circle civilian targets on the map.

7. Bombing continued off and on until May of 1941. However, the RAF shot down Luftwaffe aircraft faster than German factories could produce more planes. Hitler realized that he could not bomb Great Britain into surrendering. Operation Sea Lion was abandoned. Draw a line through OPERATION SEA LION.

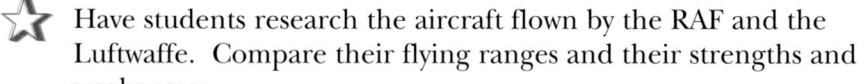 Have students research the aircraft flown by the RAF and the Luftwaffe. Compare their flying ranges and their strengths and weaknesses.

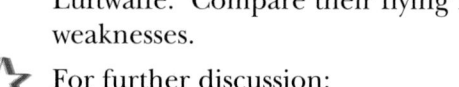 For further discussion:
- Who won the Battle of Britain? How?
- Why was the war in Great Britain different from the war in France or Poland?
- What do you think it was like living in London during the Blitz?

Correlates with:
- *The Nystrom Atlas of United States History,* pages 92–93
- *Mapping United States History* To the Present, Lesson 34

Battles in Europe

Objective: To sequence battles in the early years of World War II.

Teaching Notes and Mapping Activity

You or your students can mark the following on the *World War II in Europe* map.

1. World War II began with the Axis invasion of **Poland** in 1939.

   a. Germany invaded Poland from the west and the Soviet Union invaded Poland from the east. Trace the arrows from Germany to Poland. From the Soviet Union to Poland, draw another arrow.

   b. Although the Polish army was large, it was no match for the German *blitzkrieg*, or lightning war, in which planes, tanks, and armies all attacked Poland at once. On Poland, write **BLITZKRIEG**.

   c. After a three-week siege, Warsaw fell to the Germans. Near **Warsaw**, write ①.

2. The German army also staged a blitzkrieg against the Low Countries. Allied troops from Britain and France rushed to help **Belgium**. When Belgium surrendered, the troops were trapped and retreated to the French port of **Dunkirk**. To rescue the defeated Allies, the United Kingdom sent hundreds of boats—destroyers, yachts, ferries, and fishing boats. From May 26 to June 4, 1940, the boats evacuated 338,000 troops.

   a. In the England Channel, draw several small boat symbols ⬟.

   b. Near Dunkirk, write ②.

3. In June of 1940, the Germans marched toward **Paris**. To save the city from destruction, the French government declared Paris an open city. German troops entered the French capital without a fight. Near Paris, write ③.

4. In 1941, the Germans set their sights on the Balkans.

   a. They forced **Bulgaria**, **Hungary**, and **Romania** to join the Axis. Label each with **AX** for Axis.

   b. **Yugoslavia** refused to join the Axis Powers. On April 6, 1941, German planes bombed **Belgrade** for 1 ½ hours, killing more than 17,000 people. German troops then marched into the city. Trace the arrow from Germany to Belgrade.

   c. By Easter, the city had surrendered. Near Belgrade, write ④.

5. **Italy** had become an Axis power in 1940. In 1941 Italy launched a campaign to conquer **Greece**.

   a. The Italian troops soon were losing. The Germans rushed to help. Trace the arrow from Belgrade to Greece.

   b. The Axis troops forced the British (who came to help the Greeks) to **Crete**. There thousands of German paratroopers participated in the first **airborne invasion** in history. Near Crete, draw paratrooper symbols ⊖.

   c. Near Crete, write ⑤.

6. Germany and the Soviet Union had agreed in 1939 not to go to war against each other. However, in 1941 when the Germans launched **Operation Barbarossa** against the Soviets, they became enemies.

   a. Germans surrounded **Moscow**. Axis troops were winning. Then winter set in. Temperatures dropped and tanks broke down. Soviets forced the Germans to retreat 100 miles from Moscow. Near Moscow, write ⑥.

   b. In 1942 German and Soviet troops fought each other in **Stalingrad** for months. Then winter arrived. Thousands of Germans froze or starved each day. Near Stalingrad, write ⑦.

Correlates with:
- ● *The Nystrom Atlas of United States History,* pages 92–93
- ● *Mapping United States History* To the Present, Lesson 34

 Have students use the information on the *Military Resources* graph to create a circle graph for each resource.

WORLD WAR II IN EUROPE 1942–1945

Key Elements

★ *World War II in Europe* map

★ *D-Day* map

★ Locator map

★ *Lives Lost to Total War* graphs

Getting Started

To give students an overview of *World War II in Europe,* ask them:

- What is the title of the main map?
- What part of the world is shown on this map?
- What do the four main colors on this map represent?
- What is the title of the smaller map?
- What part of the main map does it show?
- Look at the *Lives Lost to Total War* graph. How many people died in each war?

Teaching Notes and Mapping Activities

~ Battles in Africa and Southern Europe

~ The D-Day Invasion

~ Battles in Northern Europe

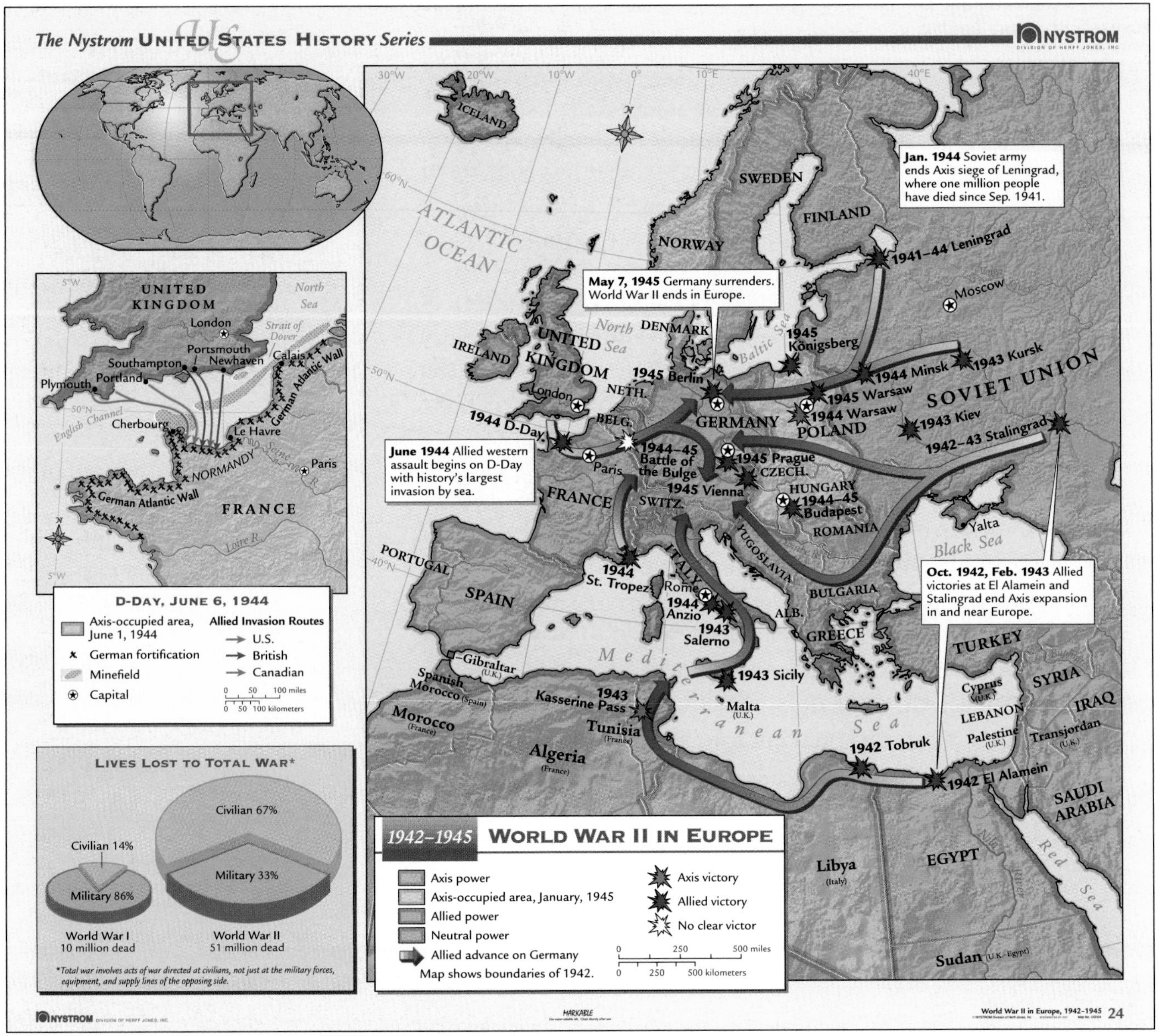

The Nystrom UNITED STATES HISTORY Series

D-DAY, JUNE 6, 1944

- Axis-occupied area, June 1, 1944
- ✕ German fortification
- Minefield
- ⊛ Capital

Allied Invasion Routes
- → U.S.
- → British
- → Canadian

0   50   100 miles
0   50   100 kilometers

UNITED KINGDOM

Plymouth · Portland · Southampton · Portsmouth · Newhaven · London · Calais · Dover · Strait of Dover

North Sea

Cherbourg · Le Havre · NORMANDY · German Atlantic Wall · Seine R. · Paris

FRANCE

English Channel · Loire R.

LIVES LOST TO TOTAL WAR*

Civilian 14%
Military 86%

World War I
10 million dead

Civilian 67%
Military 33%

World War II
51 million dead

*Total war involves acts of war directed at civilians, not just at the military forces, equipment, and supply lines of the opposing side.

Main map

ICELAND

ATLANTIC OCEAN

Jan. 1944 Soviet army ends Axis siege of Leningrad, where one million people have died since Sep. 1941.

SWEDEN · FINLAND · NORWAY

Moscow

1941–44 Leningrad

May 7, 1945 Germany surrenders. World War II ends in Europe.

NORTH Sea · DENMARK · Baltic Sea · 1945 Königsberg · 1944 Minsk · 1943 Kursk

IRELAND · UNITED KINGDOM · London · NETH. · 1945 Berlin · 1945 Warsaw · 1944 Warsaw · SOVIET UNION

1944 D-Day · BELG. · GERMANY · POLAND · 1943 Kiev

June 1944 Allied western assault begins on D-Day with history's largest invasion by sea.

Paris · 1944–45 Battle of the Bulge · 1945 Prague · CZECH. · 1942–43 Stalingrad

FRANCE · SWITZ. · 1945 Vienna · HUNGARY · 1944–45 Budapest · ROMANIA · Yalta

PORTUGAL · SPAIN · 1944 St. Tropez · ITALY · Rome · 1944 Anzio · 1943 Salerno · YUGOSLAVIA · BULGARIA · ALB. · GREECE · Black Sea

Oct. 1942, Feb. 1943 Allied victories at El Alamein and Stalingrad end Axis expansion in and near Europe.

Gibraltar · Spanish Morocco (Spain) · 1943 Kasserine Pass · 1943 Sicily · Malta (U.K.) · Mediterranean Sea · TURKEY · Cyprus (U.K.) · SYRIA · IRAQ

Morocco (France) · Tunisia (France) · 1942 Tobruk · LEBANON · Palestine (U.K.) · Transjordan (U.K.)

Algeria (France) · 1942 El Alamein · SAUDI ARABIA

Libya (Italy) · EGYPT · Red Sea

Sudan (U.K.-Egypt)

1942–1945 WORLD WAR II IN EUROPE

- Axis power
- Axis-occupied area, January, 1945
- Allied power
- Neutral power
- → Allied advance on Germany

- ✸ Axis victory
- ✸ Allied victory
- ✸ No clear victor

0   250   500 miles
0   250   500 kilometers

Map shows boundaries of 1942.

World War II in Europe, 1942–1945   **24**

Battles in Africa and Southern Europe

Objective: *To trace Allied advances through North Africa and Italy.*

Teaching Notes and Mapping Activity

You or your students can mark the following on the *World War II in Europe* map.

1. For two years, Axis and Allied troops fought in North Africa. The British struggled to prevent the Germans from reaching the Suez Canal and oil fields in the Middle East.

   a. In late October 1942, the British stopped the Germans at **El Alamein**—200 miles from the Suez Canal. Label El Alamein ①.

   b. By early November, the British finally broke through German lines at El Alamein. They pursued the Germans to **Tobruk** along the Libyan coast. The British captured Tobruk. Label it ②.

   c. The Germans retreated toward Tunisia. Trace the arrow from Egypt to Tunisia.

2. Meanwhile, the Americans launched a campaign in Africa.

   a. Some American troops landed in **Morocco**. On Morocco's Atlantic coast, put an **X**.

   b. British and American troops landed in **Algeria**. In northwest Algeria, put another **X**.

   c. The Allies fought briefly with **Vichy French** troops. (Vichy France cooperated with the Germans.) The French then joined the Allies. The Allies headed for Tunisia. From both Xs to Tunisia, draw arrows.

3. The Allies hoped to catch the Germans between their troops from Morocco and Algeria and troops from Egypt. But the Germans reached Tunisia first.

   a. The Germans won the battle at **Kasserine Pass**. Label it ③.

   b. However, in May 1943, the Allies forced the Germans out of North Africa. From Kasserine Pass to the Mediterranean Sea, trace the arrow.

4. The Allies now had bases on the Mediterranean from which they could launch a campaign against southern Europe. In July they landed on **Sicily** by sea and by air. This was the first time amphibious ducks (vehicles that could be driven on land and water) were used. Thirty-nine days later, the island was theirs. Label Sicily ④.

5. **Mussolini**, the premier of Italy, was forced from power on July 25, 1943. Italy secretly surrendered on September 3. East of Italy, write **ITALY SURRENDERS**.

6. However, German troops stayed on in Italy. In September Allies fought them in **Salerno**. Label it ⑤.

7. In January 1944, Allied troops tried to capture **Anzio**. They were pinned down on the beaches for four months. Thousands died on both sides. Label Anzio ⑥.

8. The Allies slowly battled their way up the Italian peninsula. Fighting was brutal. However, Germans managed to hold northern Italy through the fall and winter of 1944.

   a. From Sicily to northern Italy, trace the arrow.

   b. In spring, the Allies swept into the Alps. German troops in Italy surrendered on May 2, 1945—just days before the end of the war in all of Europe. East of Italy, add **GERMANY SURRENDERS**.

 For further discussion:
- Why do you think the Americans launched their first campaign in Africa rather than Europe?
- Why do you think the Germans fought so hard for Italy?

 Ask the class to make a raised relief model of Italy. Have them see why terrain played such a big part in the Italian campaign.

Correlates with:
- *The Nystrom Atlas of United States History,* pages 96–97
- *Mapping United States History* To the Present, Lesson 34

The D-Day Invasion

Objective: To provide an overview of the battle.

Teaching Notes and Mapping Activity

You or your students can mark the following on the *D-Day* map.

1. D-Day was the **largest invasion by sea** in history. The British and Americans had been planning it for over a year. They called it **Operation Overlord**.

   a. Draw a box around the *D-Day* map.

   b. Use the *World War II in Europe* map to make a locator map for the battle.
      - In the United Kingdom, underline the word KINGDOM.
      - Also underline the word FRANCE.
      - Finish the box by connecting the ends of each line.

2. The Germans expected the Allies to invade France. So they built a long line of fortifications along the French coast. They called it the **Atlantic Wall**.

   a. On land they buried mines on the beaches. They strung barbed wire and added huge steel spikes and concrete barriers. They also built protective bunkers for their troops. On the *D-Day Map*, along the Atlantic Wall, trace some of the fortification symbols.

   b. In the English Channel, they also laid mines. In the minefields, draw a row of dots.

3. The Germans thought the Allies would invade at **Calais**. However, the Allies chose **Normandy** instead. With your finger, from the United Kingdom to Calais, draw the shortest route. Then draw the shortest route to Normandy.

4. The invasion was scheduled to begin June 5, 1944. However, it was delayed a day because of foul weather. At night, the Allies dropped **paratroopers** behind enemy lines. They captured or destroyed bridges. In Normandy, draw a few paratrooper symbols ⊖.

5. Meanwhile 6,000 **vessels**—battle ships, transport ships, landing craft, and hospital ships—began crossing the English Channel. In the channel, draw a few ships.

6. Normandy has about 60 miles of coastline. Each beach along the coast was given a code name and Allied divisions were assigned specific beaches to land on.

   a. The British division leaving from Newhaven was assigned **Sword** beach. Label their landing site **S** for Sword.

   b. The Canadians, leaving from Portsmouth, were assigned **Juno** beach. Label their landing site **J** for Juno.

   c. The British division leaving from Southampton was assigned **Gold** beach. Label their landing site **G** for Gold.

   d. The American division leaving from Portland was assigned **Omaha** beach. Label their landing site **O** for Omaha.

   e. The American division leaving from Plymouth was assigned **Utah** beach. Label their landing site **U** for Utah.

7. Allied troops began landing at 6:30 a.m.

   a. Those on Sword, Juno, Gold, and Utah beaches met some resistance, but quickly secured their beaches. Near these four beaches, draw troop symbols ⚲.

   b. Omaha beach was more difficult to secure. Because of strong winds, no unit landed where they had planned. About 90 percent of their tanks sank. Their bombs missed the German bunkers. Germans fired relentlessly on the invading Americans. The water and beach were littered with bodies. Amazingly, by nightfall the Allies had secured the beach. Near Omaha beach, add a troop symbol ⚲.

   ☆ Have students watch a movie about D-Day, such as *The Longest Day*. Discuss.

Correlates with:
- *The Nystrom Atlas of United States History,* pages 96–97
- *Mapping United States History To the Present,* Lesson 34

Battles in Northern Europe

Objective: *To trace Allied advances through eastern and western Europe.*

Teaching Notes and Mapping Activity

You or your students can mark the following on
the *World War II in Europe* map.

1. By 1942 the **Soviet Union** was anxious for the Allies to open a western front—to draw German troops away from the Soviet front.

   a. **Stalingrad** had been under attack for months. Thousands on both sides froze or starved. Label Stalingrad **S** for its 1943 Soviet victory.

   b. Germans attacked **Kursk** in one of the greatest **tank battles** in history. Soviet mines and tanks blew apart hundreds of German tanks. Label Kursk with **S** for the Soviet victory and draw a tank.

   c. **Leningrad** had been under attack since 1941. People had no electricity, no heat, no food. The water was contaminated. Over a million people died, but the city never surrendered. Label Leningrad **S** for its 1944 Soviet victory.

2. In 1943, the Soviets began forcing the Germans back. By March of 1944, Soviet troops entered **Poland**. Poland had been occupied by the Germans since 1939.

   a. From Kursk to Poland, trace the arrow.

   b. From Stalingrad to Poland, trace the arrow.

3. In July of 1944, Soviet troops reached the outskirts of **Warsaw**.

   a. At that same time, Poland's Home Army rebelled. They fought the Germans for two months before surrendering. The Soviets refused to help. Label the 1944 Warsaw victory **G** for German.

   b. In early 1945, the Soviets captured Warsaw. Label the victory **S**.

4. The Soviets also advanced though Romania, Bulgaria, and Hungary.

   a. From Stalingrad to Budapest, trace the arrow.

   b. The Soviets captured **Budapest** in February 1945. They now occupied most of eastern Europe. Label Budapest **S**.

   c. The Soviets also captured **Vienna** in April. Label Vienna **S**.

5. Meanwhile, in June of 1944, the Allies opened up a western front with the **D-Day** invasion. Label D-Day **ABC** for the American, British, and Canadian victory.

6. The Germans soon were forced out of northwest France.

   a. The people of **Paris** rose up against the German forces who had occupied their city since 1940. Label Paris **AF** for the Americans and French who liberated the city.

   b. Germans retreated toward their border. From D-Day to the German border, trace the arrow.

7. In December 1944, Germans overwhelmed American troops in Belgium and Luxembourg. However, there was no clear victor in the **Battle of the Bulge**. Label the battle **A/G**.

8. In early 1945, the Soviets reached Germany's eastern borders; the Allies had reached its western borders.

   a. Trace the arrow from Warsaw to Berlin. Also trace the arrow from the Battle of the Bulge to Berlin.

   b. In April, the Soviets surrounded Germany's capital, **Berlin**. Hitler committed suicide. Label Berlin **S**.

   c. On May 7, 1945, **Germany surrendered**. Draw a box around the call-out about the surrender.

 Millions were killed in World War II. The Soviets were the hardest hit. About 56 percent of all civilian deaths and 44 percent of all military deaths were theirs. Have students redraw the *Lives Lost to Total War* graph to reflect those losses.

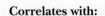

Correlates with:

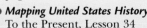

- *The Nystrom Atlas of United States History,* pages 96–97
- *Mapping United States History* To the Present, Lesson 34

Key Elements

★ *World War II in the Pacific* map

★ *Atomic Bombing of Hiroshima, Japan* map

★ Locator map

Getting Started

To give students an overview of *World War II in the Pacific,* ask them:

• What is the title of the main map?

• What part of the world is shown on this map?

• What does the color orange represent on this map?

• What does the color purple represent on this map?

• What does the inset map show?

• Where is Hiroshima on the main map?

• What do the symbols on Hiroshima represent?

Teaching Notes and Mapping Activities

~ Japanese Expansion

~ Battles in the Pacific 1941–1942

~ Battles in the Pacific 1943–1945

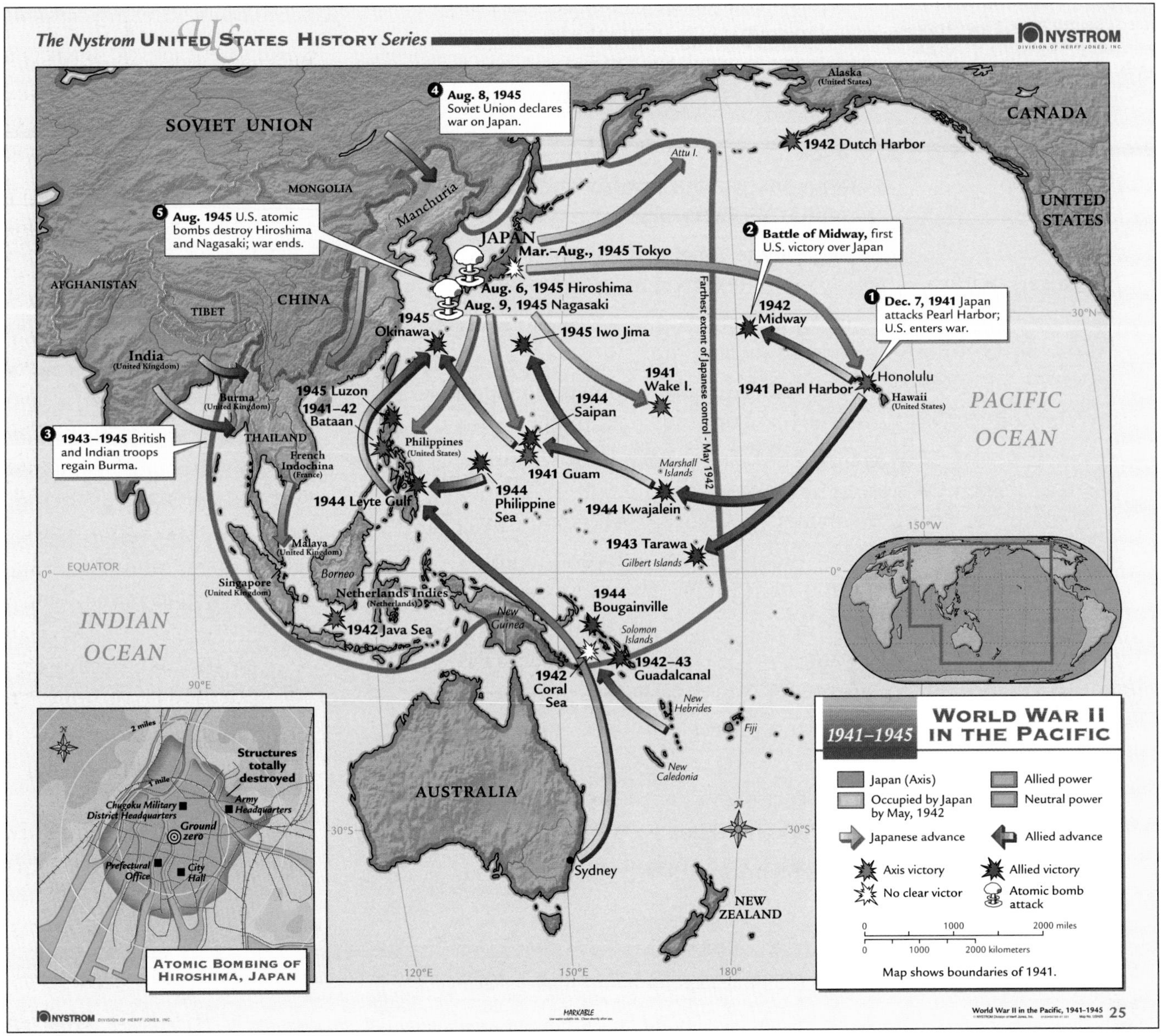

The Nystrom **UNITED STATES HISTORY** *Series* ■■■■ NYSTROM
DIVISION OF HERFF JONES, INC.

4 Aug. 8, 1945 Soviet Union declares war on Japan.

Alaska (United States)

CANADA

1942 Dutch Harbor

SOVIET UNION

MONGOLIA

Manchuria

5 Aug. 1945 U.S. atomic bombs destroy Hiroshima and Nagasaki; war ends.

JAPAN

Mar.–Aug., 1945 Tokyo

2 Battle of Midway, first U.S. victory over Japan

UNITED STATES

AFGHANISTAN

CHINA

TIBET

Aug. 6, 1945 Hiroshima
Aug. 9, 1945 Nagasaki

1942 Midway

1 Dec. 7, 1941 Japan attacks Pearl Harbor; U.S. enters war.

30°N

India (United Kingdom)

1945 Okinawa

1945 Iwo Jima

1941 Wake I.

1941 Pearl Harbor

Honolulu

Hawaii (United States)

PACIFIC OCEAN

Burma (United Kingdom)

1945 Luzon

1941–42 Bataan

1944 Saipan

3 1943–1945 British and Indian troops regain Burma.

THAILAND

French Indochina (France)

Philippines (United States)

1941 Guam

Marshall Islands

1944 Kwajalein

1944 Leyte Gulf

1944 Philippine Sea

1943 Tarawa

Gilbert Islands

150°W

Malaya (United Kingdom)

Borneo

0° EQUATOR

Singapore (United Kingdom)

Netherlands Indies (Netherlands)

New Guinea

1944 Bougainville

Solomon Islands

0°

INDIAN OCEAN

1942 Java Sea

New Hebrides

Fiji

1942–43 Guadalcanal

1942 Coral Sea

New Caledonia

90°E

AUSTRALIA

Sydney

30°S

2 miles

Structures totally destroyed

1 mile

Chugoku Military District Headquarters

Army Headquarters

Ground zero

Prefectural Office

City Hall

ATOMIC BOMBING OF HIROSHIMA, JAPAN

120°E

150°E

NEW ZEALAND

180°

1941–1945 WORLD WAR II IN THE PACIFIC

Japan (Axis)	Allied power
Occupied by Japan by May, 1942	Neutral power
Japanese advance	Allied advance
Axis victory	Allied victory
No clear victor	Atomic bomb attack

0 — 1000 — 2000 miles
0 — 1000 — 2000 kilometers

Map shows boundaries of 1941.

Farthest extent of Japanese control · May 1942

NYSTROM DIVISION OF HERFF JONES, INC.

HARKABLE

World War II in the Pacific, 1941–1945 **25**

Japanese Expansion

Objective: *To show the expansion of Japanese control up to 1942.*

Teaching Notes and Mapping Activity

You or your students can mark the following on the *World War II in the Pacific* map. Note that the map shows 1941 boundaries.

1. **Japan** is a small, mountainous island country with limited natural resources. Outline Japan.

2. Japanese expansion began in 1895. As a result of the Chinese-Japanese War, the Russo-Japanese War, and World War I, Japan's empire grew on both the Asian mainland and on islands in the Pacific.

   a. In 1895, Japan seized **Formosa** (Taiwan). Formosa is the large island north of Luzon. Label it **J** for Japanese control.

   b. In 1910, Japan seized **Korea**. Korea is on the peninsula west of Japan. Label Korea **J**.

   c. During World War I, Japan seized the **Marshall**, **Mariana**, and **Caroline Islands**. Label the Marshall Islands and the islands north of Guam **J**.

   d. By the end of World War I, Japan controlled the areas labeled with **J**. With your finger, on the main map, trace the extent of Japan's empire in 1918.

   e. With a marker, on the locator map, outline the same area.

3. While Germany and Italy were expanding in Europe and Africa, Japan began a program of aggressive expansion in Asia. Japan's military leaders began calling their empire the Greater East Asia Co-Prosperity Sphere.

   a. In 1931, Japan invaded and occupied **Manchuria**. On the main map, label Manchuria **J**.

   b. Japanese troops continued to move south. By 1938, they occupied many of **China's key ports**. Label several occupied areas of China's coast **J**.

4. To cut off China's supply route (and keep the supplies for itself), Japan invaded southeast Asia in 1940.

   a. By 1941 Japan had occupied all of **French Indochina**. Label it **J**.

   b. Now, with your finger, trace Japan's empire up to 1941.

   c. With a marker, on the locator map, outline the same area.

5. To protest Japan's invasion of Indochina, the United States refused to export oil and other raw materials to Japan. Realizing that the United States stood in the way of its expansion, Japan decided to capture or cripple U.S. military bases in the Pacific.

   a. In December 1941, Japan captured U.S. bases on both **Guam** and **Wake Island**. Label them both **J**.

   b. By April 1942, Japan had captured the **Philippines**, a U.S. territory. Label the Philippines **J**.

6. By May of 1942, Japan's empire extended from the Aleutian Islands in the north to the Solomon Islands in the south. The empire extended from 90° E to 180°.

   a. In southeast Asia, Japan captured **Burma**, **Thailand**, the **Netherlands Indies**, northern **New Guinea**, and the **Solomon Islands**. Label each of them with a **J**.

   b. In the Aleutians, label **Attu Island J**.

   c. Now trace the line that marks the farthest extent of Japanese control.

   d. On the locator map, outline this area.

 Have students compare the size of Japan's empire in 1920 and in 1942. They might make a list Japan's possessions. Or they could use the map scale to calculate area in square miles.

Correlates with:
● *The Nystrom Atlas of United States History,* pages 92–93

Teaching Notes and Mapping Activity

You or your students can mark the following on the *World War II in the Pacific* map.

1. On December 7, 1941, Japanese troops attacked U.S. military bases at **Pearl Harbor** in Hawaii. Hours later, the Japanese also attacked U.S. bases on **Wake Island** and **Guam**, the British colony of **Hong Kong**, and **Thailand**. The United States and Great Britain immediately declared war on Japan.

   a. Trace the arrow from Japan to Hawaii. Below the victory symbol, write ①.

   b. Also trace the arrow from Japan to Guam. Below the victory symbol, write ②.

   c. Next, trace the arrow from Japan to Wake Island. Below the victory symbol, write ③.

   d. On Hong Kong (above the word *Luzon*) and Thailand, draw victory symbols ✹ and label them **AXIS**.

2. Two days later, Japanese troops landed in the **Philippines**. The U.S. and Philippine troops on the **Bataan Peninsula** battled the Japanese until April 9, 1942, when the Allies surrendered. Roughly 75,000 exhausted Allied troops were forced to walk 65 miles in what became known as the Bataan Death March.

   a. Trace the arrow from Japan to the Philippines.

   b. Below Bataan, write ④.

3. Meanwhile, the Japanese gained control of British-held Burma and Singapore. In spring, the Netherlands Indies also fell after the Battle of the **Java Sea**. Below the battle, write ⑤.

4. In May, the Japanese navy sailed toward an Allied base in New Guinea—close to Australia. In the **Coral Sea**, Allied and Japanese planes launched from aircraft carriers fought the battle. Neither side could be called the victor. However, the Allies were successful in stopping Japanese advances toward Australia. In the Coral Sea, write ⑥.

5. In June, Japan launched a two-prong attack on U.S. military bases. In the **Aleutians** (off the coast of Alaska), the Japanese were able to occupy the islands of Attu, Agattu, and Kiska. However, further south, they were unable to take **Midway Island**. Midway was the first clear Allied victory in the Pacific.

   a. Trace the arrow from Japan to Attu Island. Below Dutch Harbor, write ⑦.

   b. The Allies won their first victory in the Pacific at the Battle of Midway. Below Midway, write ⑧.

☆ Have students use the information on the *World War II in the Pacific* map to make a timeline of battles in the War in the Pacific. Ask them to list Japanese victories on one side of the timeline and Allied victories on the other.

☆ Because islands in the Pacific are so far apart, the Allies used a strategy called *island-hopping* in the War in the Pacific. Have students use the map scale to measure distances between islands in the Pacific.

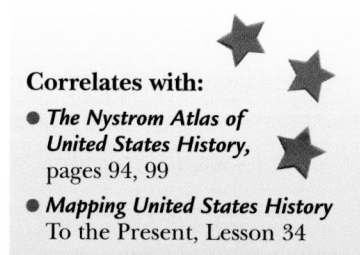

Correlates with:

● *The Nystrom Atlas of United States History,* pages 94, 99

● *Mapping United States History* To the Present, Lesson 34

Battles in the Pacific 1943–1945

Objective: *To sequence events in World War II in the Pacific from 1943 to 1945.*

Teaching Notes and Mapping Activity

You or your students can mark the following on the *World War II in the Pacific* map.

1. After the Battle of Midway, the Allies launched two major campaigns against the Japanese—one in the southeast Pacific, the other in the central Pacific.

   In the southeast, the Allies fought for six months to capture the island of **Guadalcanal**.

   In the central Pacific, one goal of the campaign was to cut off Japanese supply routes. First, the Allies captured **Tarawa** in the Gilbert Islands and then **Kwajalein** in the Marshall Islands.

   a. In the southeast Pacific, trace the arrows from Australia and from New Hebrides to Guadalcanal. Below the battle, write ①.

   b. In the central Pacific, trace the arrow from Hawaii to Tarawa. Below the battle, write ②.

   c. Also trace the arrow from Hawaii to Kwajalein. Label it ③.

2. Both campaigns continued to work their way west and northwest. After Guadalcanal, in their southeast campaign, the Allies worked their way along the Solomon Islands until they defeated the Japanese at **Bougainville**. In the central campaign, the Allies island-hopped until they regained Guam and captured **Saipan**. This put the Allies within bombing distance of Japan.

   a. Continue the arrow from Guadalcanal to Bougainville. Label Bougainville ④.

   b. In the central Pacific, continue the arrow from Kwajalein to Guam. Below Saipan, write ⑤.

3. The two campaigns then joined forces to liberate the Philippines. The Battle of **Leyte Gulf** damaged the Japanese fleet badly. However, fighting continued on the Philippine island of **Luzon** until the end of the war.

   a. Trace the arrows from Bougainville and from Guam to the Philippines.

   b. Then label Leyte Gulf ⑥ and Luzon ⑦.

4. From the Philippines, the Allies headed for two key islands under Japanese control—**Iwo Jima** and **Okinawa**. Both of these Allied victories were bloody battles with enormous casualties on both sides.

   a. Trace arrows heading toward Iwo Jima and Okinawa.

   b. Label Iwo Jima ⑧ and Okinawa ⑨.

5. Despite this long series of defeats, Japan refused to surrender. To avoid a costly invasion of Japan, the Allies dropped atomic bombs on the Japanese cities of **Hiroshima** and **Nagasaki**. On August 14, 1945, Japan agreed to surrender—ending World War II.

   a. Near Hiroshima and Nagasaki, circle the two symbols marking atomic bomb attacks.

   b. Also circle the inset map of Hiroshima. Draw a line from the inset map to Hiroshima on the main map.

   c. Label the call-out marking the end of the war ⑩. Above it, write **JAPAN SURRENDERS**.

 Have students make a timeline of battles in the War in the Pacific from 1943 to 1945. (See page 102 for more information on the timeline.) Then have them compare this timeline with a similar timeline from 1941 to 1942.

Correlates with:
- *The Nystrom Atlas of United States History,* pages 98–99
- *Mapping United States History To the Present,* Lesson 34

26

THE GREAT MIGRATION
1940–1970

Key Elements

★ *The Great Migration* map
★ *Jim Crow Laws* map
★ *A Changing Nation* graphs

Getting Started

To give students an overview of
The Great Migration, ask them:

- What is the title of the main map?
- What years does the map cover?
- What do the colors of the
  states show?
- What do the red arrows represent?
- What is the title of the small map?
- What is the subtitle of this map?
- On the graphs, what do the colors
  of the bars represent?

Teaching Notes and
Mapping Activities

~ Moving North and West
~ Moving to Cities
~ Moving Toward Desegregation

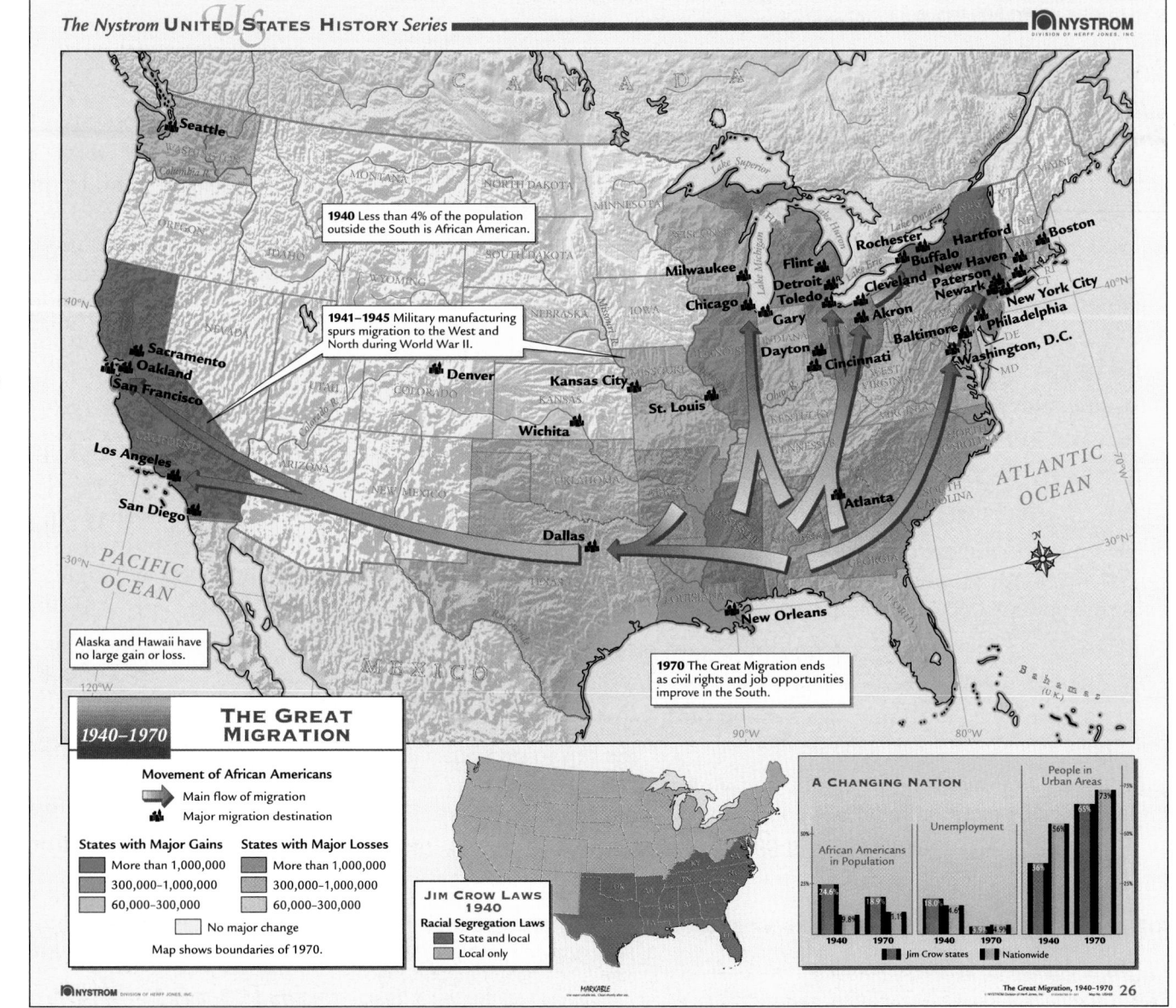

The Nystrom UNITED STATES HISTORY *Series* — NYSTROM DIVISION OF HERFF JONES, INC.

1940 Less than 4% of the population outside the South is African American.

1941–1945 Military manufacturing spurs migration to the West and North during World War II.

1970 The Great Migration ends as civil rights and job opportunities improve in the South.

Alaska and Hawaii have no large gain or loss.

THE GREAT MIGRATION
1940–1970

Movement of African Americans
➡ Main flow of migration
🏭 Major migration destination

States with Major Gains
- More than 1,000,000
- 300,000–1,000,000
- 60,000–300,000

States with Major Losses
- More than 1,000,000
- 300,000–1,000,000
- 60,000–300,000

☐ No major change

Map shows boundaries of 1970.

JIM CROW LAWS 1940
Racial Segregation Laws
- State and local
- Local only

A CHANGING NATION

African Americans in Population

Unemployment

People in Urban Areas

| | 1940 | 1970 | 1940 | 1970 | 1940 | 1970 |
Jim Crow states | Nationwide

The Great Migration, 1940–1970 26

Moving North and West

Objective: *To explain how the migration of African Americans affected population in the South, North, and West.*

Teaching Notes and Mapping Activity

You or your students can mark the following on *The Great Migration* map. Begin the lesson by reading the call-out for 1940.

1. Between 1940 and 1970, more than 5 million African Americans migrated from the South.

   a. Point to states that lost 60,000–300,000 blacks.

   b. Draw a minus sign **–** on states that lost 300,000–1,000,000 blacks.

   c. Draw two minus signs **– –** on the state that lost more than 1,000,000 blacks.

2. Some blacks left the South to escape **racial discrimination**. Three states had particularly large losses.

   a. Between 1940 and 1970, the population of **Mississippi** stayed roughly the same. Its white population grew while its black population dropped 24 percent. On Mississippi, write **–24%**.
      - In 1940, almost half of the population of Mississippi was black. Across Mississippi, write ◑ **1940**.
      - By 1970, Mississippi's population was only one-third black. Across Mississippi, add ◔ **1970**.

   b. **Arkansas'** population also was the same in 1940 and 1970. Its white population grew while its black population dropped. On Arkansas, write **–27%**.

   c. The population of **Georgia** grew 50 percent in 30 years, but its black population dropped. On Georgia, write **–30%**.
      - In 1940, almost half of the population of Georgia was black. Across Georgia, write ◑ **1940**.
      - By 1970, Georgia's population was only a quarter black. Across Georgia, add ◔ **1970**.

3. During World War II, **jobs** in military manufacturing plants attracted blacks to the North and West.

   a. Trace all the arrows heading away from the south.

   b. Point to states that gained 60,000–300,000 blacks.

   c. Draw a plus sign **+** on states that gained 300,000–1,000,000 blacks.

   d. Draw two plus signs **++** on states that gained more than 1,000,000 blacks.

4. This migration had a major impact on the total population of some areas, and very little impact on others.

   a. The black population of the **District of Columbia** almost tripled between 1940 and 1970. Near Washington, D.C., write **+288%**.
      - In 1940, about one-quarter of its population was black. East of Washington, D.C., write ◔ **1940**.
      - By 1970, its population was almost three-quarters black. East of Washington, D.C., add ◕ **1970**.

   b. The black population of **California** increased significantly, but blacks remained a minority. On California, write **+1,129%**.
      - In 1940, 2% of its population was black. Across California, write ○ **1940**.
      - By 1970, its population was still only 7% black. Across California, write ○ **1970**.
      - California's overall population also increased. Whites migrated to California too. Draw arrows from Michigan, Nebraska, and Louisiana to California.

 For further discussion:
   - Between 1940 and 1970, how did the African American population change in the South? in the nation? (Refer students to the *A Changing Nation* graphs.)
   - What cities were migration destinations in the North?

Correlates with:
- *The Nystrom Atlas of United States History,* pages 106–107

Objective: *To compare urban populations in the South before and after the use of the mechanical cotton picker.*

Teaching Notes and Mapping Activity

You or your students can mark the following on *The Great Migration* map.

1. In the 1940's, many states in the south produced **cotton**. Mark the following states with cotton symbols 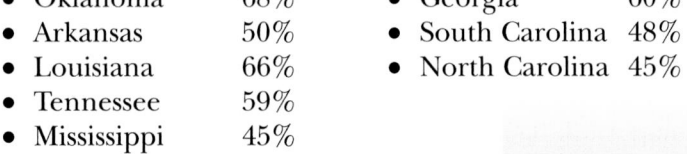.

   - Texas
   - Oklahoma
   - Arkansas
   - Louisiana
   - Tennessee
   - Mississippi
   - Alabama
   - Georgia
   - South Carolina
   - North Carolina

2. In the early 1940s, many southern landowners rented their land to **sharecroppers**. Sharecroppers would plant, raise, and pick cotton. Cotton was **picked by hand**. It took a fast worker roughly a hour to pick 20 pounds of cotton or 25 hours for a bale (500 pounds). One farmer paid his workers $39.41 per bale. In the lower right corner of the map, write ▯ **25 HOURS, $39/BALE**.

3. In the early 1940s, the population of the South was primarily **rural**.

   a. On the *A Changing Nation* graph, have students compare the urban population in Jim Crow states (most were also cotton-producing states) in 1940 with the urban population nationwide.

   b. Now, on *The Great Migration Map*, write the following urban population percentages on the appropriate states. Also draw a line below each figure.

•Texas	45%	• Mississippi	20%
•Oklahoma	38%	• Alabama	30%
•Arkansas	22%	• Georgia	34%
•Louisiana	41%	• South Carolina	25%
•Tennessee	35%	• North Carolina	27%

4. On October 2, 1944, the **mechanical cotton picker** was introduced in Clarksdale, Mississippi. These machines could pick 1,000 pounds or two bales of cotton in an hour. The machine could pick a bale of cotton for just $5.26. In the lower right corner of the map, add ▯ **½ HOUR, $5/BALE**.

5. With the mechanical cotton picker, landowners no longer needed sharecroppers. Black and white sharecroppers were literally driven off their land. In Mississippi, some communities gave sharecroppers free bus tickets to Chicago, to encourage them to leave their farms.

   a. Trace the arrow from Mississippi to Chicago.

   b. Trace other arrows to urban centers in the North.

6. While some sharecroppers moved to urban centers in the North, others moved to large **cities** in their own states.

   a. Draw an arrow from eastern Georgia to Atlanta.

   b. Draw an arrow from northern Louisiana to New Orleans.

   c. Draw an arrow from northwest Texas to Dallas.

7. By 1970 roughly 75 percent of all African Americans lived in cities.

   a. On the *A Changing Nation* graph, have students compare the urban population in Jim Crow states in 1940 and 1970.

   b. Now, on *The Great Migration Map*, write the following 1970 urban population percentages below the 1940 figures.

• Texas	80%	• Alabama	58%
• Oklahoma	68%	• Georgia	60%
• Arkansas	50%	• South Carolina	48%
• Louisiana	66%	• North Carolina	45%
• Tennessee	59%		
• Mississippi	45%		

☆ Have students use the population information on the map to make bar graphs or urban/rural circle graphs.

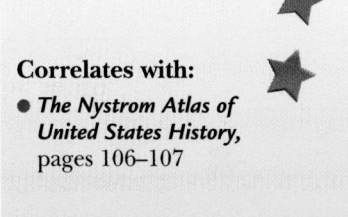

Correlates with:

- *The Nystrom Atlas of United States History,* pages 106–107

Moving Toward Desegregation

Objective: *To identify key events in the overturning of Jim Crow segregation laws.*

Teaching Notes and Mapping Activity

You or your students can mark the following on
The Great Migration map.

1. In 1940 the south was **segregated**. Laws restricted the rights of African Americans. These laws were referred to as **Jim Crow laws**.

   a. On the *Jim Crow Laws* map, draw a line between states that have state and local Jim Crow laws and those that only have local laws.

   b. On *The Great Migration* map, draw that same line.

2. In the south, under Jim Crow laws, black students were not allowed to attend the same schools white students attended. These **segregated schools** were supposed to be equal—but rarely were.

   a. In 1954, the Supreme Court ruled in the *Brown v. the Board of Education of Topeka* that separate schools for blacks and whites were unequal. Public schools were ordered to desegregate "with all deliberate speed." Across the top of the map, write **DESEGREGATION**. Below that, write and underline **SCHOOLS** 🏫. Below that, write **1954–COURT RULING**.

   b. In 1957, nine black students enrolled in the all-white **Little Rock Central High School**. The Arkansas National Guard blocked their entrance to the school. The President sent federal troops to escort the students into school. In Arkansas, draw a school desegregation symbol 🏫.

   c. The **Prince Edward County schools** closed from 1959 to 1964, rather than desegregate. In Virginia, draw a school desegregation symbol 🏫 with a slash through it.

   d. By 1963, only .5 percent of all school systems in the south were desegregated. Six years later, the Supreme Court ruled that schools systems must end segregation "at once." Below 1954–COURT RULING, add **1969–ANOTHER COURT RULING**.

3. In the south, under Jim Crow laws, restaurants, bus stations, movie theaters, hotels, and other public buildings had separate facilities or areas for blacks. Trains and buses were also segregated.

   a. In 1946, the Supreme Court ruled that segregated seating on interstate transportation was unconstitutional. Below DESEGREGATION, write and underline **BUSES** 🚌. Below that, write **1946–COURT RULING**.

   b. In 1955 **Rosa Parks** was arrested for refusing to give up her seat on a bus to a white man. For 13 months, blacks in Montgomery, Alabama, boycotted the city buses.
   - In 1956 the Supreme Court ruled that buses in Alabama must be desegregated. Below BUSES, add **1956–COURT RULING**.
   - In Alabama, draw a bus desegregation symbol 🚌.

   c. In 1961 **Freedom Riders** integrated buses traveling from Washington, D.C., to New Orleans. One bus was stoned, fire-bombed, and its tires were slashed. The passengers on another bus were severely beaten. But more Freedom Riders continued to ride the buses all summer.
   - Between Washington, D.C. and New Orleans, draw several bus desegregation symbols 🚌.
   - In September, the Interstate Commerce Commission outlawed segregation on buses. Below BUSES, add **1961–ICC RULING**.

   d. Segregation continued. But in 1964, Congress passed the Civil Rights Act. It banned discrimination in jobs and public facilities, businesses, and schools. Below BUSES, write **1964–CIVIL RIGHTS ACT**.

 Have students prepare a timeline of events in the overturning of Jim Crow laws.

Correlates with:
- *The Nystrom Atlas of United States History,* pages 106–107
- *Mapping United States History* To the Present, Lesson 37

27

KOREAN WAR
1950–1953

Key Elements

★ *June–Oct. 1950 Korean War* map
★ *Oct. 1950–July 1953 Korean War* map
★ *Locator* map

Getting Started

To give students an overview of *Korean War*, ask them:

- What are the titles of these maps?
- What part of the world is shown on these maps?
- What do the different colors on these maps represent?
- What do the symbols on these maps represent?
- What do the solid and dashed lines on these maps represent?
- What do the solid arrows on these maps represent?
- What do the dashed arrows on these maps represent?

Teaching Notes and Mapping Activities

~ Opening Stages
~ Closing Stages
~ A War of Firsts

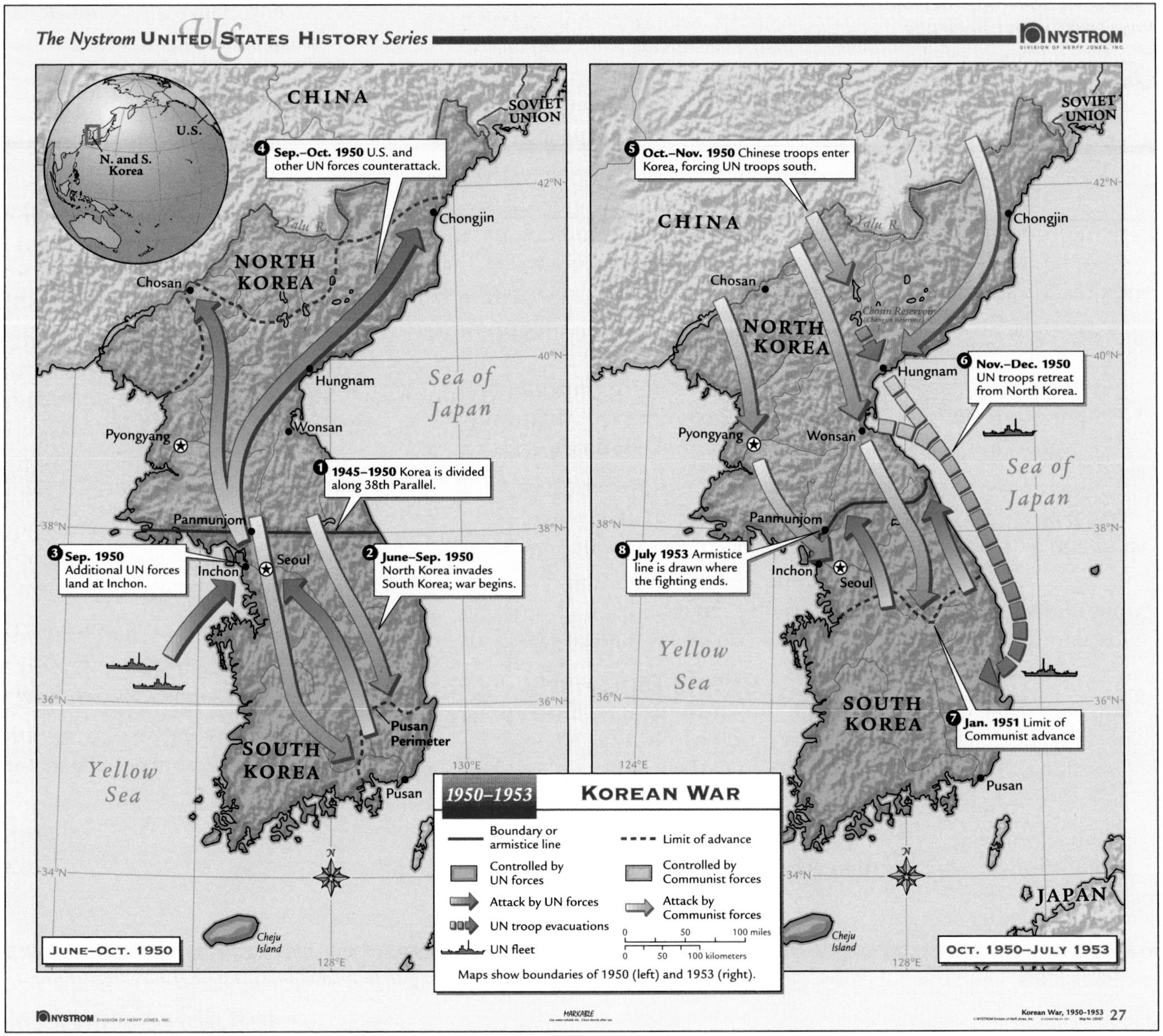

The Nystrom UNITED STATES HISTORY *Series*

NYSTROM
DIVISION OF HERFF JONES, INC.

CHINA

SOVIET UNION

U.S.

N. and S. Korea

4 **Sep.–Oct. 1950** U.S. and other UN forces counterattack.

Chongjin

Yalu R.

NORTH KOREA

Chosan

Hungnam

Sea of Japan

Pyongyang

Wonsan

1 **1945–1950** Korea is divided along 38th Parallel.

Panmunjom

3 **Sep. 1950** Additional UN forces land at Inchon.

Inchon

Seoul

2 **June–Sep. 1950** North Korea invades South Korea; war begins.

Pusan Perimeter

SOUTH KOREA

Yellow Sea

Pusan

Cheju Island

JUNE–OCT. 1950

CHINA

SOVIET UNION

5 **Oct.–Nov. 1950** Chinese troops enter Korea, forcing UN troops south.

Chongjin

Yalu R.

Chosan

Chosin Reservoir

NORTH KOREA

Hungnam

6 **Nov.–Dec. 1950** UN troops retreat from North Korea.

Pyongyang

Wonsan

Sea of Japan

Panmunjom

8 **July 1953** Armistice line is drawn where the fighting ends.

Inchon

Seoul

Yellow Sea

SOUTH KOREA

7 **Jan. 1951** Limit of Communist advance

Pusan

Cheju Island

JAPAN

OCT. 1950–JULY 1953

1950–1953 **KOREAN WAR**

— Boundary or armistice line
- - - Limit of advance

Controlled by UN forces
Controlled by Communist forces

➤ Attack by UN forces
➤ Attack by Communist forces

▶▶▶ UN troop evacuations

UN fleet

0   50   100 miles
0   50   100 kilometers

Maps show boundaries of 1950 (left) and 1953 (right).

NYSTROM DIVISION OF HERFF JONES, INC.

MARKABLE

Opening Stages

Objective: *To map the chronology of events during the first and second stages of the Korean War.*

Teaching Notes and Mapping Activity

You or your students can mark the following on the *June–Oct. 1950* map.

1. **Korea** had been controlled by Japan since 1895. After World War II, the Allies divided Korea at the 38th parallel. The **Soviet Union** occupied the northern part of the country, and the **United States** occupied the southern part.

   a. Find and read Call-out ❶.

   b. In May 1948, the people of South Korea elected a national government. In the Sea of Japan, south of 38°N, write **DEMOCRATIC GOVT**.

   c. In September 1948, the Soviets helped set up a Communist government in North Korea. In the Sea of Japan, north of 38°N, write **COMMUNIST GOVT**.

2. Both North and South Korea claimed the entire country, and there were many clashes along the 38th parallel from 1948 to 1950.

   a. In June 1950, North Korea invaded South Korea in an attempt to unite the two countries under Communist rule. This was the first stage of the Korean War. Read Call-out ❷. Above the call-out, write **STAGE 1A**.

   b. Label each of the orange arrows **NK INVASION**.

3. In July 1950 the United States sent troops to support South Korea, and other UN forces soon followed. UN and South Korean troops managed to hold a small area in the southeastern part of the peninsula. In the small area bordered by the **Pusan Perimeter**, write **STAGE 1B - UN FORCES**.

4. The second stage of the Korean War began with a UN counterattack. While forces behind the Pusan Perimeter pushed their way north, UN forces launched a surprise attack, landing at **Inchon**—*behind* the invading North Korean army.

   a. Read Call-out ❸. Above the call-out, write **STAGE 2A**.

   b. General Walton Walker and the U.S. 8th Army led the push north from Pusan. Label the arrow from Pusan to Seoul **STAGE 2B - 8TH ARMY**.

   c. U.S. General Douglas MacArthur, the commander of all UN forces, and the U.S. 10th Corps led the invasion of Inchon. Label the arrow pointing to Inchon **10TH CORPS - MACARTHUR**.

5. The Inchon landing trapped the invading North Korean army between the 8th Army and the 10th Corps. North Korean forces retreated, and UN forces pursued them.

   a. UN forces continued their counterattack with a two-pronged drive into North Korea. Read Call-out ❹. Above the call-out, write **STAGE 2C**.

   b. The 8th Army led the drive toward Chosan. Label the arrow pointing toward Chosan **8TH ARMY**.

   c. The 10th Corps led the northeastern attack. Label the arrow pointing toward Chongjin **10TH CORPS**.

6. The UN decision to invade North Korea was controversial. Its detractors argued that in doing so, the United Nations was behaving no better than North Korea. They believed that UN forces should have stopped their counterattack at the 38th parallel. Below Call-out ❹, write **CONTROVERSIAL**.

 Have your students use the Korean War map call-outs as a starting point for creating a detailed timeline of the events of the Korean War.

Correlates with:

- *The Nystrom Atlas of United States History,* pages 100–101
- *Mapping United States History,* To the Present, Lesson 38

Closing Stages

Objective: *To map the chronology of events during the third and fourth stages of the Korean War.*

Teaching Notes and Mapping Activity

You or your students can mark the following on the *June–Oct. 1950* map and the *Oct. 1950–July 1953* map.

1. By October 1950, the UN counterattack against North Korea was nearing the Chinese border. **China**, a Communist nation, saw UN forces as a threat to its security. The Chinese government warned against further advances toward its border.

   a. As a Communist country, China was an ally of North Korea, but it did not participate in the invasion of South Korea. On both maps, write **COMMUNIST** across China.

   b. On the *June–Oct. 1950* map, above Call-out ❹, write **CHINA THREATENED**.

   c. **General MacArthur** ignored Chinese warnings and ordered UN troops to press on. Along the battlefront in North Korea, write **UN CONTINUES ATTACK**.

   d. The continued UN advance led China to enter the war. Read Call-out ❺ on the *Oct. 1950–July 1953* map. Then draw an arrow from UN CONTINUES ATTACK to the call-out.

   e. You may want to inform your students that President Truman eventually fired General MacArthur in April 1951.

2. After several small battles failed to halt the UN advance, China launched a massive assault in late November of 1950. This marked the third stage of the Korean War.

   a. Above Call-out ❺, write **STAGE 3A**.

   b. Pitted against an army with superior numbers, UN forces retreated. Read Call-out ❻. Above the call-out, write **STAGE 3B**.

   c. In January 1951, UN forces regrouped and halted the Communist armies. Read Call-out ❼. Above the call-out, write **STAGE 3C**.

3. During the final stage of the war, UN forces again fought their way north. In June of 1951, the two armies came to a **standstill** along a battlefront north of the 38th parallel.

   a. The second UN advance began the final stage of the war. Label the two green arrows pointing north **STAGE 4A**.

   b. It soon became clear that neither side could push the other back, and peace talks began in July 1951. The peace talks and the fighting went on for two more years. Above the Armistice Line, write **STAGE 4B - PEACE TALKS, 1951–1953**.

4. Finally, after two years of peace talks and fighting, both sides agreed to an armistice which would end the fighting. The **Armistice Line** was drawn along the existing battlefront.

   a. To show that the Armistice Line was the final battlefront, draw a dashed line along it.

   b. Above Call-out ❽, write **STAGE 4C**.

   c. An armistice and a peace treaty are not the same thing. The armistice officially ended the fighting. But because no peace treaty was signed, the two Koreas are technically still at war today. In the Yellow Sea, write **ARMISTICE ≠ PEACE TREATY**.

5. Today there is still a 2¹/₂ mile wide buffer area between North and South Korea. It is known as the **Demilitarized Zone**. In the Sea of Japan, write **DMZ** and then draw an arrow from it to the Armistice Line.

☆ Ask your students to research the differences and/or similarities between North Korean and South Korean:
   - lifestyle
   - economy
   - culture

Correlates with:
- ● **The Nystrom Atlas of United States History,** pages 100–101
- ● **Mapping United States History,** To the Present, Lesson 38

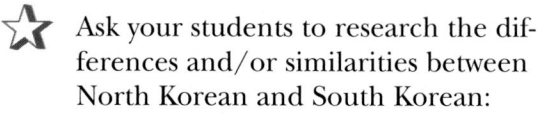

A War of Firsts

Objective: *To map some of the "firsts" that occurred as a result of the Korean War.*

Teaching Notes and Mapping Activity

You or your students can mark the following on the *June–Oct. 1950* map and the *Oct. 1950–July 1953* map.

1. The Korean War was the first war in which a world organization—the **United Nations**—played a military role.

   a. Though the United States supplied most of the soldiers and weapons, 15 other UN members sent armed forces to Korea. On the *June–Oct. 1950* map, draw a line along the 38th parallel.

   b. In the Yellow Sea, below the line you drew, write and underline **MILITARY**. Then write the names of the countries that sent military units to Korea.

   - Australia
   - Belgium
   - Canada
   - Colombia
   - Ethiopia
   - France
   - Greece
   - Luxembourg
   - Netherlands
   - New Zealand
   - Philippines
   - South Africa
   - Thailand
   - Turkey
   - United Kingdom
   - United States

   c. Some countries chose to offer medical assistance instead. Below the 38th parallel in the Sea of Japan, write and underline **MEDICAL**. Then write the names of the countries that sent medical units to Korea.

   - Denmark
   - India
   - Italy (not a UN member)
   - Norway
   - Sweden

2. The Korean War was the first war in which **jet airplanes** were used for battles.

   a. Early in the war, Allied planes bombed North Korea with little or no opposition. Across North Korea, write ✈ **ALLIED BOMBERS**.

   b. As the war progressed, the Soviet Union provided North Korea with fighter jets called MIG-15s. On the *Oct. 1950–July 1953* map, circle the label for the Soviet Union and draw an arrow from it toward North Korea.

   c. Label the arrow ✈ **MIG-15s**.

   d. North Korea used MIGs to shoot down Allied bombers. The Allies used fighter jets to protect their bombers. "Dogfights" between jets became so common that the area between the Yalu River and the city of Pyongyang was called "MIG Alley." Write ✈ **MIG ALLEY** across North Korea north of Pyongyang.

3. The Korean War was the first war in which **helicopters** were widely used.

   a. Helicopters transported wounded from the battlefront to medical units. South of the Armistice Line, draw a helicopter and below it write **TRANSPORT WOUNDED**.

   b. Helicopters were also used to transport troops and supplies to and from combat zones. Below TRANSPORT WOUNDED, write **TRANSPORT TROOPS & SUPPLIES**.

   c. Helicopters also enabled UN armies to find the enemy's position and strength. Below TRANSPORT TROOPS & SUPPLIES, write **ENEMY OBSERVATION**.

 Have your students use a world map to locate the countries that offered military and medical assistance during the Korean War.

- How many countries are in North America? Europe? Asia? Australia/Oceania?
- Which country/countries are farthest from South Korea?
- Which are closest?

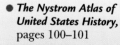

Correlates with:

- *The Nystrom Atlas of United States History,* pages 100–101
- *Mapping United States History,* To the Present, Lesson 38

28

COLD WAR
1945–1991

Key Elements

★ *Cold War* map
★ *Threat of the Atomic Bomb* map
★ Locator map
★ *Nuclear Firepower* graph

Getting Started

To give students an overview of *Cold War*, ask them:

- What is the title of the main map?
- What part of the world is shown on this map?
- What do the colors on this map represent?
- What symbols are shown on this map? What do they represent?
- What does the secondary map show?
- What do the symbols on this map represent?
- What do the arrows on this map indicate?
- What does the *Nuclear Firepower* graph show?
- What do the colors on the graph represent?

Teaching Notes and Mapping Activities

~ Cold War Chronology
~ Nuclear Arms Race
~ Cold War Perspectives

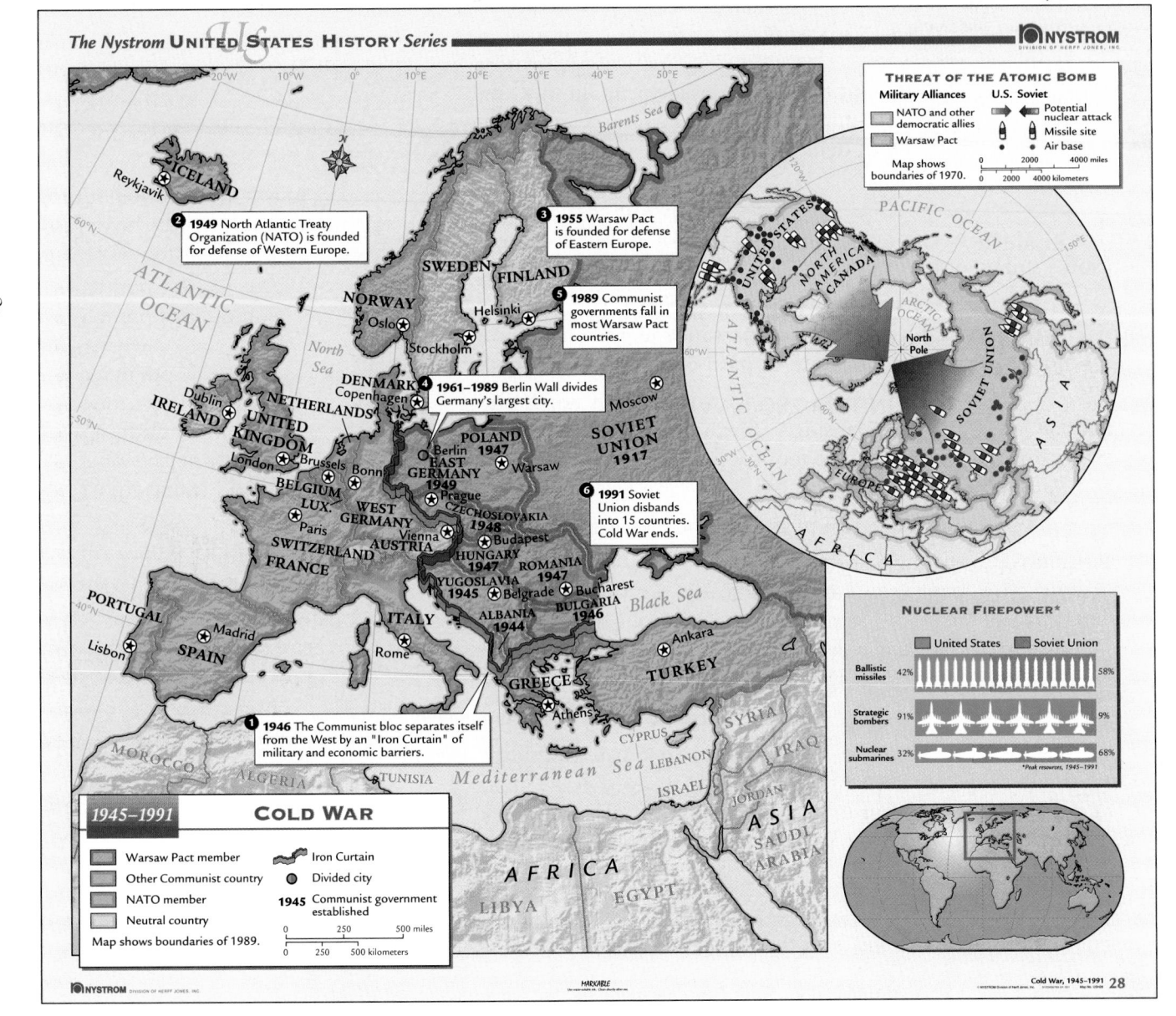

The Nystrom UNITED STATES HISTORY *Series*

NYSTROM
DIVISION OF HERFF JONES, INC.

2 **1949** North Atlantic Treaty Organization (NATO) is founded for defense of Western Europe.

3 **1955** Warsaw Pact is founded for defense of Eastern Europe.

5 **1989** Communist governments fall in most Warsaw Pact countries.

4 **1961–1989** Berlin Wall divides Germany's largest city.

6 **1991** Soviet Union disbands into 15 countries. Cold War ends.

1 **1946** The Communist bloc separates itself from the West by an "Iron Curtain" of military and economic barriers.

THREAT OF THE ATOMIC BOMB

Military Alliances
- NATO and other democratic allies
- Warsaw Pact

U.S. Soviet
- Potential nuclear attack
- Missile site
- Air base

Map shows boundaries of 1970.

0 2000 4000 miles
0 2000 4000 kilometers

NUCLEAR FIREPOWER*

United States | Soviet Union

Ballistic missiles 42% — 58%
Strategic bombers 91% — 9%
Nuclear submarines 32% — 68%

*Peak resources, 1945–1991

1945–1991 COLD WAR

- Warsaw Pact member
- Other Communist country
- NATO member
- Neutral country

- Iron Curtain
- Divided city
- **1945** Communist government established

Map shows boundaries of 1989.

0 250 500 miles
0 250 500 kilometers

NYSTROM DIVISION OF HERFF JONES, INC.

Cold War, 1945–1991 28

Cold War Chronology

Objective: *To put events of the Cold War in chronological order.*

Teaching Notes and Mapping Activity

You or your students can mark the following on the *Cold War* and the *Threat of the Atomic Bomb* maps.

1. The **Cold War** officially began after World War II, but the two main adversaries of the Cold War—the **United States** and the **Soviet Union**—had distrusted each other long before the war.

   a. Read the call-outs on the *Cold War* map in chronological order.

   b. U.S.-Soviet relations had been tense since the Communists came to power in Russia. On the *Cold War* map, circle the label "SOVIET UNION 1917." Next to it write ①.

   c. Soviet leaders believed in the worldwide destruction of **capitalism**, the economic system of the United States. Therefore, many Americans saw **Communism** as a threat. On the *Threat of the Atomic Bomb* map, write ② **FEAR OF COMMUNISM** across the United States.

2. Despite their differences, the two countries were allies against Germany during World War II. From 1943 to 1944, the Soviet Army advanced on Germany from the east, and by 1945, the Soviets controlled most of Eastern Europe.

   a. Draw three or four arrows from the circled "SOVIET UNION" label to different points along the Iron Curtain.

   b. Label each arrow ③ **WWII -1945**.

3. Once the war was over, the alliance between the United States and the Soviet Union quickly faded. The Soviet Union had been invaded in both World War I and World War II. The Soviets wanted to protect their country from possible future attacks, so after the war, they refused to remove their army from **Eastern Europe**. Countries had been liberated from the German Army only to be occupied by the Soviet Army.

   a. On the *Threat of the Atomic Bomb* map, write ④ **FEAR OF INVASION** across the Soviet Union.

   b. On the *Cold War* map, write ⑤ next to the call-out describing the **Iron Curtain**.

   c. To create a buffer against possible invasion, the Soviets set up **Communist governments** in the occupied countries. Underline the year that each country east of the Iron Curtain established a Communist government.

4. The United States and many of the countries of Western Europe saw the Soviet actions as a threat to the rest of Europe. In 1949, **NATO** was created as a response to this perceived threat. Read Call-out ❷. Then cross out the ❷ and write ⑥.

5. The Soviets, in turn, viewed NATO as a sign of aggression against Communism. In 1955, they responded by creating the **Warsaw Pact** with other Communist countries in Europe. Read Call-out ❸. Then cross out the ❸ and write ⑦.

6. For the next 34 years, NATO and Warsaw Pact countries, eyed each other with suspicion. But in the late 1980s, the Communist governments of Europe began to fall apart. Read Call-out ❺. Then cross out the ❺ and write ⑧.

7. Eventually, the Communist government of the Soviet Union **was overthrown** as well. Read Call-out ❻. Then cross out the ❻ and write ⑨.

 Have your students answer the questions below.
- How many European countries were members of NATO?
- How many were members of the Warsaw Pact?
- How many were neutral?
- Which Communist countries were not members of the Warsaw Pact?

Correlates with:
- *The Nystrom Atlas of United States History,* pages 102–103
- *Mapping United States History,* To the Present, Lesson 36

Nuclear Arms Race

Objective: *To map the development and deployment of nuclear weapons during the Cold War.*

Teaching Notes and Mapping Activity

You or your students can mark the following on the *Cold War* and the *Threat of the Atomic Bomb* maps.

1. One of the reasons the Cold War created so much international tension was because both the United States and the Soviet Union had **nuclear weapons**.

   a. In 1945, the United States was the first country to create an atomic bomb. On the *Threat of the Atomic Bomb* map, write **1945 A-BOMB** across the United States.

   b. The Soviet Union tested its first atomic bomb only four years later. Across the Soviet Union, write **1949 A-BOMB**.

   c. Neither country developed a *thermonuclear* weapon, such as those that are built today, until the early 1950s. Below 1945 write **(1952) THERMO**, and below 1949 write **(1953) THERMO**.

2. Soon, **other countries** began to develop nuclear weapons. They believed that having these weapons put their country in a more powerful position when dealing with other countries.

   a. The **United Kingdom** was the third country to develop nuclear weapons. It tested its first atomic bomb in 1952. On the *Cold War* map, write **1952 A-BOMB** across the United Kingdom.

   b. The United Kingdom created its first thermonuclear device in 1957. Below 1952, write **(1957) THERMO**.

   c. **France** tested its first atomic bomb in 1960 and created a thermonuclear weapon in 1968. Across France, write **1960 A-BOMB**, and below that write **(1968) THERMO**.

3. **China** became the second Communist country to develop nuclear weapons, testing its first atomic bomb in 1964.

   a. On the *Threat of the Atomic Bomb* map, across China, write **1964 A-BOMB**.

   b. China detonated its first thermonuclear weapon between 1967 and 1968. Below 1964, write **(1968) THERMO**.

4. While the Soviet Union had more ballistic missiles and nuclear submarines, the United States had far more **strategic bombers**.

   a. Airplanes designed to drop nuclear warheads were stationed at strategic locations, such as Alaska and Greenland. Draw bomber planes ✈ in Alaska and Greenland.

   b. The United States also had warheads and bombers at military bases in many NATO countries. On the *Cold War* map, draw a plane and write **US** in each of the countries listed below.

   - Belgium
   - France
   - Greece
   - Italy
   - Netherlands
   - Spain
   - Turkey
   - United Kingdom
   - West Germany

   c. Have students look at the *Threat of the Atomic Bomb* map to get an idea of the proximity of these locations to the Soviet Union.

5. The buildup of nuclear weapons was known as **brinksmanship**. To dissuade the other side from acts of aggression, each side showed that it was willing go to the "brink" of nuclear war. Each reasoned that fear of a retaliatory strike would keep the other from firing its weapons first. This policy was known as **Mutual Assured Destruction** (MAD). On the *Threat of the Atomic Bomb* map, write **MAD** where the arrows come together.

☆ Ask your students to look at the *Nuclear Firepower* graph and then answer the questions below.
   - In which area did the Soviet Union have nuclear superiority?
   - In which area did the United States have nuclear superiority?
   - In which area was the nuclear firepower of the two countries roughly equal?

Correlates with:
- *The Nystrom Atlas of United States History,* pages 102–103
- *Mapping United States History,* To the Present, Lesson 36

Cold War Perspectives

Objective: *To match quotations about the Cold War with the country of the speaker.*

Teaching Notes and Mapping Activity

Below are quotations revealing different perspectives on the Cold War. Write selected quotations on the board and then write the number of each quotation in the country of the speaker on the appropriate map.

1. [After Communism succeeds]...then, there will come a peace across the earth.
   –Joseph Stalin, Soviet dictator

2. ...the actions resulting from the Communist philosophy are a threat to the efforts of free nations to bring about world recovery and lasting peace.
   –Harry S Truman, U.S. President, 1949

3. I worked at a factory owned by Germans, at coal pits owned by Frenchmen, and at a chemical plant owned by Belgians. There I discovered something about capitalists...All they wanted from me was the most work for the least money that kept me alive. So I became a Communist.
   –Nikita Khrushchev, Soviet First Secretary

4. Today we are engaged in a final, all-out battle between communistic atheism and Christianity.
   –U.S. Senator Joseph McCarthy, 1950

5. The release of atom power has changed everything except our way of thinking, and thus we are being driven...towards a catastrophe...
   –Albert Einstein, German-born U.S. scientist, 1946

6. ...[T]he defense of the United States and the defense of other freedom-loving nations are indivisible.
   –Harry S Truman, U.S. President, 1949

7. ...the Soviet Union couldn't really afford to let the country go its own way. That road would have definitely led to some sort of a collapse of Communism.
   –Vaclav Havel, Czech president/playwright, on the Soviet invasion of Czechoslovakia during the *Prague Spring* of 1968

8. About the capitalist states, it doesn't depend on you whether or not we exist...Whether you like it or not, history is on our side. We will bury you.
   –Nikita Khrushchev, 1956

9. Our capacity to retaliate must be, and is, massive in order to deter all forms of aggression.
   –John Foster Dulles, describing U.S. nuclear strategy, 1955

10. Our country..is the point of tension between two world blocs...Isolation would mean that the U.S. would withdraw its troops from Europe...[T]he moment that happens, Germany will become a satellite.
    –Konrad Adenauer, Chancellor of West Germany, 1953

11. ...today it is Hungary and tomorrow, or the day after tomorrow, it will be the turn of other countries, because the imperialism of Moscow does not know borders...
    –Imre Nagy, Prime Minister of Hungary, last message before Soviet invasion of 1956

12. Ours is a world of nuclear giants and ethical infants. If we continue to develop our technology without wisdom or prudence, our servant may prove to be our executioner.
    –U.S. General Omar Bradley, 1948

 Have your students evaluate one or two of the quotations listed above.
- Is the speaker from a Communist or non-Communist country?
- Does the quote reveal the speaker's opinion of Communism? If so, what is it?
- Does the quote reveal the speaker's opinion of nuclear weapons? If so, what is it?

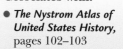

Correlates with:
- ***The Nystrom Atlas of United States History,*** pages 102–103
- ***Mapping United States History,*** To the Present, Lesson 36

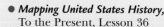

29

VIETNAM WAR
1957–1975

Key Elements

★ *1957–1968 Vietnam War* map

★ *1969–1975 Vietnam War* map

★ Locator map

Getting Started

To give students an overview of *Vietnam War*, ask them:

• What are the titles of these maps?

• What do the different colors on the maps represent?

• What do the different battle symbols on these maps represent?

• What do the other symbols on the maps represent?

• What do the thin green arrows on these maps represent?

• What do the wide arrows on these maps represent?

Teaching Notes and Mapping Activities

~ The Road to U.S. Involvement

~ A Different Kind of War

~ U.S. Withdrawal, South Vietnamese Defeat

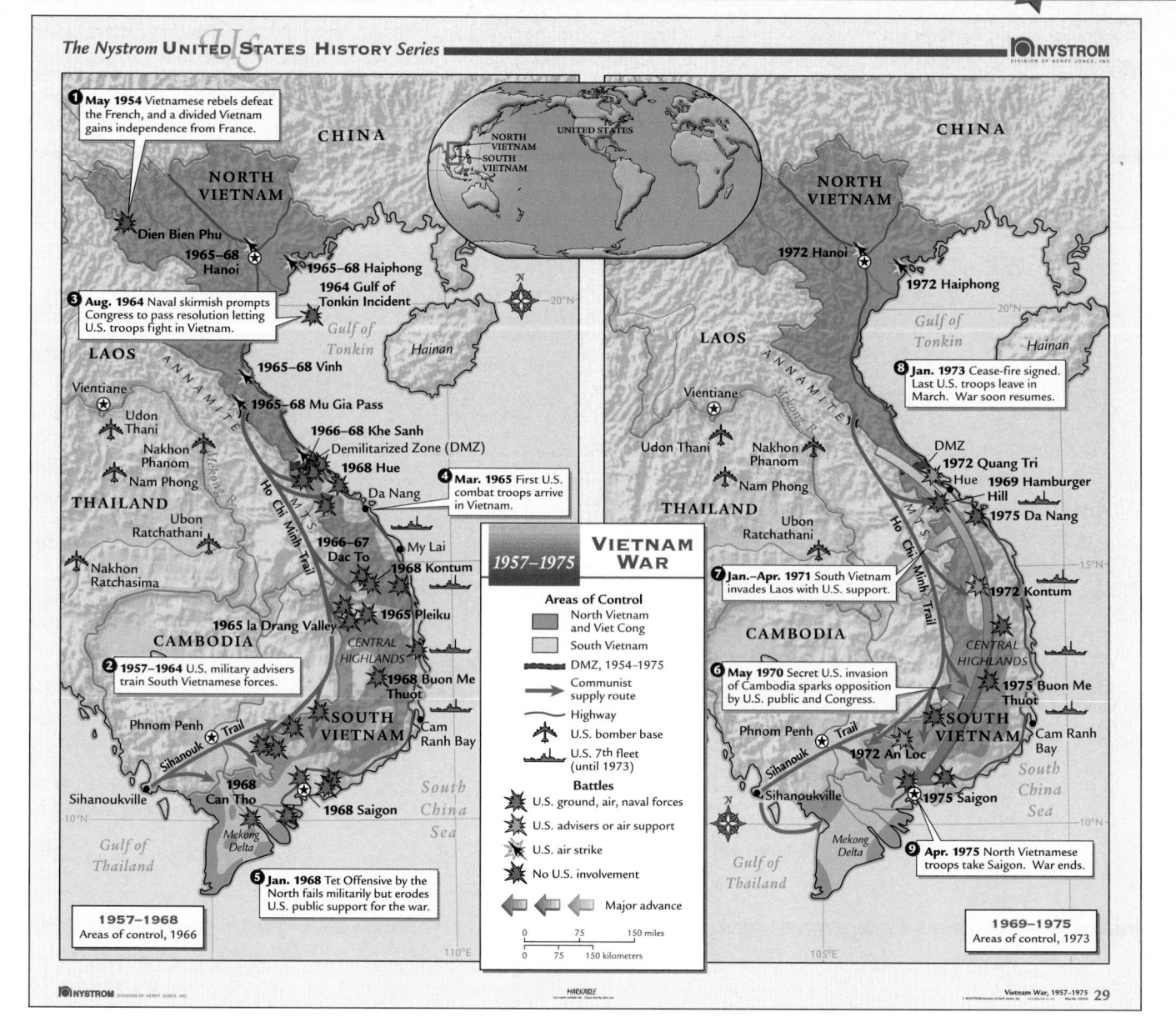

The Nystrom UNITED STATES HISTORY Series

1 May 1954 Vietnamese rebels defeat the French, and a divided Vietnam gains independence from France.

3 Aug. 1964 Naval skirmish prompts Congress to pass resolution letting U.S. troops fight in Vietnam.

2 1957–1964 U.S. military advisers train South Vietnamese forces.

4 Mar. 1965 First U.S. combat troops arrive in Vietnam.

5 Jan. 1968 Tet Offensive by the North fails militarily but erodes U.S. public support for the war.

6 May 1970 Secret U.S. invasion of Cambodia sparks opposition by U.S. public and Congress.

7 Jan.–Apr. 1971 South Vietnam invades Laos with U.S. support.

8 Jan. 1973 Cease-fire signed. Last U.S. troops leave in March. War soon resumes.

9 Apr. 1975 North Vietnamese troops take Saigon. War ends.

VIETNAM WAR
1957–1975

Areas of Control
- North Vietnam and Viet Cong
- South Vietnam
- DMZ, 1954–1975
- Communist supply route
- Highway
- U.S. bomber base
- U.S. 7th fleet (until 1973)

Battles
- U.S. ground, air, naval forces
- U.S. advisers or air support
- U.S. air strike
- No U.S. involvement

Major advance

1957–1968 Areas of control, 1966

1969–1975 Areas of control, 1973

The Road to U.S. Involvement

Objective: *To show the chronology of events that led to the start of the Vietnam War.*

Teaching Notes and Mapping Activity

You or your students can mark the following on the *1957–1968 Vietnam War* map and the locator map.

1. In 1883, France gained control over a region in **Southeast Asia**. The region, then known as French Indochina, consisted of what are today the countries of Laos, Cambodia, and Vietnam.

   a. On the 1957–1968 map, draw a line along the northern boundary of North Vietnam.

   b. Draw a line along the parts of the western boundaries of Cambodia and Laos that appear on the map.

   c. In the Gulf of Thailand, write ① **FRENCH INDOCHINA, 1883**.

2. During World War II, the Japanese captured France's colonies in Asia. Japan controlled French Indochina from 1940–1945.

   a. On the locator map, circle Japan and draw an arrow from it to the box showing the location of North and South Vietnam.

   b. Label the arrow ② **JAPAN, 1940–1945**.

3. After World War II, **Vietnamese Communists** took control of many areas of the country and declared Vietnam's independence. France attempted to reestablish control over its former colony, which led to nearly eight years of war.

   a. The Vietnamese Communists, or **Vietminh**, were led by Ho Chi Minh. Below the label for North Vietnam, write **HO CHI MINH - LEADER**.

   b Above Call-out ❶ on the 1957–1968 map, write ③ **VIETMINH VS. FRANCE, 1946–1954**.

   c. The Vietminh defeated French forces in 1954. Read Call-out ❶. Then cross out the ❶ to the left of the call-out and replace it with a ④.

4. Because there were many **non-Communists in the south**, the Vietminh agreed to divide the country at 17°N. The peace agreement stated that in 1956 free elections would be held to reunite North Vietnam and South Vietnam.

   a. Draw a line along the DMZ and label it ⑤ **PEACE TREATY, 1954**.

   b. Next to the label for North Vietnam, write ⑤ **COMMUNIST, 1954**. Then next to the label for South Vietnam, write ⑤ **NON-COMMUNIST, 1954**.

5. In 1956 the leader of South Vietnam, **Ngo Dinh Diem**, refused to allow free elections. He feared that the Communists would not permit fair elections. The United States, which also feared Communism, supported Diem's decision. Below NON-COMMUNIST, write ⑥ **NO ELECTIONS, 1956**.

6. In 1957 South Vietnamese Communists, known as **Viet Cong**, began to rebel against Diem's government. North Vietnam publicly supported the revolt and supplied the rebels with weapons.

   a. Next to "North Vietnam and Viet Cong" on the legend *Vietnam War*, write ⑦ **ATTACKS BEGIN, 1957**.

   b. In 1957 the United States began sending military advisors to help South Vietnam to fight Communist attacks. On the 1957–1968 map, find and read Call-out ❷. Then cross out the ❷ and replace it with an ⑧.

 Have students look at the distance between the United States and Vietnam on the locator map. Discuss with students why the United States might have involved itself in the affairs of a country so far away.

Correlates with:
- *The Nystrom Atlas of United States History,* pages 108–109
- *Mapping United States History,* To the Present, Lesson 38

A Different Kind of War

Objective: *To describe the escalation of U.S. involvement in the Vietnam War.*

Teaching Notes and Mapping Activity

You or your students can mark the following on the *1957–1968 Vietnam War* map.

1. U.S. involvement in the Vietnam War escalated gradually. Before 1965, **U.S. military advisers** trained South Vietnamese forces to fight the Viet Cong and cut their supply lines.

    a. Find and read Call-out ❷ on the 1957–1968 map. Cross out the ❷ and replace it with a ①.

    b. North Vietnam, in turn, began supplying the Viet Cong rebels with weapons. Next to the label for the Ho Chi Minh Trail, write ② **ESTABLISHED 1959**.

2. Distrustful of Communist North Vietnam, U.S. warships patrolled the **Gulf of Tonkin**. An altercation between U.S. and North Vietnamese ships in 1964 led to the deployment of U.S. troops in Vietnam.

    a. Point out the symbol that marks the Gulf of Tonkin incident. Then find and read Call-out ❸.

    b. Point out the symbol that marks the city of Da Nang. Then find and read Call-out ❹.

3. The first goal of U.S. forces was to cut off the supplies of the Viet Cong. To accomplish this, U.S. planes **bombed targets** in North Vietnam in the hopes of destroying resources.

    a. Circle two or three of the symbols that represent U.S. air strikes.

    b. Below the label for Laos, write ⑤ **DESTROY RESOURCES**.

    c. Draw lines from the ⑤ to each of the symbols you circled.

4. In many ways, the Vietnam War was different from other wars fought by the United States. U.S. ground troops found combat difficult, because there was no established battlefront.

    a. Outline two or three of the yellow areas that mark territory controlled by South Vietnam.

    b. Below ⑤, write ⑥ **NO EST. BATTLEFRONT**.

    c. Draw lines from ⑥ to each of the areas you outlined.

5. Because the United States had superior weapons and technology, the Viet Cong used *guerrilla tactics*, such as booby traps, ambushes, and bombs, against U.S. forces.

    a. Circle two or three of the symbols that designate battles involving U.S. forces.

    b. Below ⑥, write ⑦ **GUERRILLA TACTICS**.

    c. Draw lines from ⑦ to each of the symbols you circled.

6. The constantly changing battlefront and Viet Cong guerrilla tactics caused an enormous number of civilian casualties. Civilians were killed and wounded in Viet Cong attacks, and also by U.S. troops, who were often unable to tell friends from enemies. Below ⑦, write ⑧ **CIVILIAN CASUALTIES**.

7. In 1968, the Viet Cong attacked major cities in South Vietnam during **Tet**, the **Vietnamese New Year**. The surprise attacks, vicious fighting, and enormous number of casualties stunned the American public.

    a. Find and read Call-out ❺.

    b. Cross out the ❺ and replace it with a ⑨.

☆ Have your students discuss the characteristics of the conflict in Vietnam and their effect on the country.
- How was the Vietnam War different from other wars in which the United States participated?
- What aspects of the Vietnam War might have eroded U.S. public support?

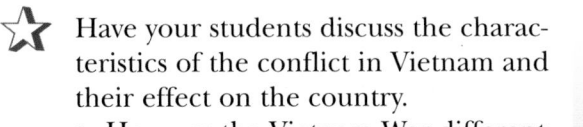

Correlates with:
- *The Nystrom Atlas of United States History,* pages 108–109
- *Mapping United States History,* To the Present, Lesson 38

U.S. Withdrawal, South Vietnamese Defeat

Objective: *To illustrate the gradual American withdrawal from Vietnam and its consequences.*

Teaching Notes and Mapping Activity

You or your students can mark the following on the *1969–1975* map.

1. The **Tet Offensive** led the United States to change its policy in Vietnam. Gradually the United States began to scale back its involvement in the war.

   a. In 1968, President Johnson cut back the bombing of North Vietnam. On the *1969–1975* map, circle the two U.S. air strike symbols.

   b. Above the symbols, write ① **CUT BACK BOMBING, 1968**.

   c. The following year, President Nixon, who succeeded President Johnson, began withdrawing U.S. troops. To the left of the air strike symbols, write ② **U.S. TROOP WITHDRAWAL BEGINS, 1969**.

2. Despite the gradual withdrawal, U.S. troops in Vietnam continued to battle Communist forces. They also continued to train South Vietnamese troops to do the same.

   a. In 1970, the United States **invaded Cambodia** in the hope of destroying Communist supply lines. Write ③ over the red arrow marking this invasion.

   b. In 1971, the United States helped South Vietnam conduct a similar invasion of Laos. Write ④ over the orange arrow marking this invasion.

3. Encouraged by the U.S. withdrawal, North Vietnam invaded South Vietnam in March 1972. U.S. forces managed to stop the invasion in August.

   a. The wide green arrow indicates a major advance by North Vietnamese forces. Where it begins in North Vietnam, write ⑤ **NV INVASION, MARCH 1972** along the arrow.

   b. Below NV INVASION, write ⑥ **STOPPED, AUG. 1972**.

   c. Both sides suffered many casualties from the invasion. The losses led to peace talks. Above Call-out ❽, write ⑦ **PEACE TALKS BEGIN, 1972**.

4. In January 1973, a **cease-fire** was signed. The last U.S. troops left Vietnam two months later.

   a. From each of the symbols for the U.S. 7th fleet, draw arrows pointing away from Vietnam.

   b. Over each symbol, write an ⑧.

5. The war resumed soon after U.S. troops left the area. South Vietnamese troops fought the North Vietnamese and Viet Cong forces alone.

   a. Circle two or three of the battle symbols that indicate no U.S. involvement.

   b. In the South China Sea, write ⑨ **SV FIGHTS ALONE**.

   c. Draw lines from the ⑨ to the symbols you circled.

6. A little over two years after U.S. forces left the country, North Vietnam **captured Saigon**, the capital of South Vietnam. This ended the war and unified Vietnam under Communist rule.

   a. Find Call-out ❾. Cross out the ❾ and replace it with a ❿.

   b. Below the call-out box, write **UNIFIED VIETNAM - COMMUNIST**.

 Have your students compare the Vietnam War to the U.S. wars below:
- Revolutionary War (USH8)
- War with Mexico (USH12)
- Civil War (USH16)
- Indian Wars (USH17)
- World War I (USH21)
- World War II (USH23, USH24)
- Korean War (USH27)

Correlates with:
- *The Nystrom Atlas of United States History,* pages 108–109
- *Mapping United States History,* To the Present, Lesson 38

30

PERSIAN GULF WAR
1990–1991

Key Elements

★ *Persian Gulf War* map
★ Locator map
★ *U.S. Oil Imports in 1989* graph
★ *Operation Desert Storm* graph

Getting Started

To give students an overview of *Persian Gulf War*, ask them:

- What part of the world is shown on the map?

- What do the different country colors indicate?

- What do areas of gray represent?

- What does the ship symbol represent? The airplane symbol? The barracks symbol?

- What other symbols can be found on the map? What does each symbol represent?

- What data does the *U.S. Oil Imports in 1989* graph show?

- What four military statistics are compared on the *Operation Desert Storm* graph?

Teaching Notes and Mapping Activities

~ The Middle East Before the War

~ The United Nations Coalition

~ War Strategy and Its Consequences

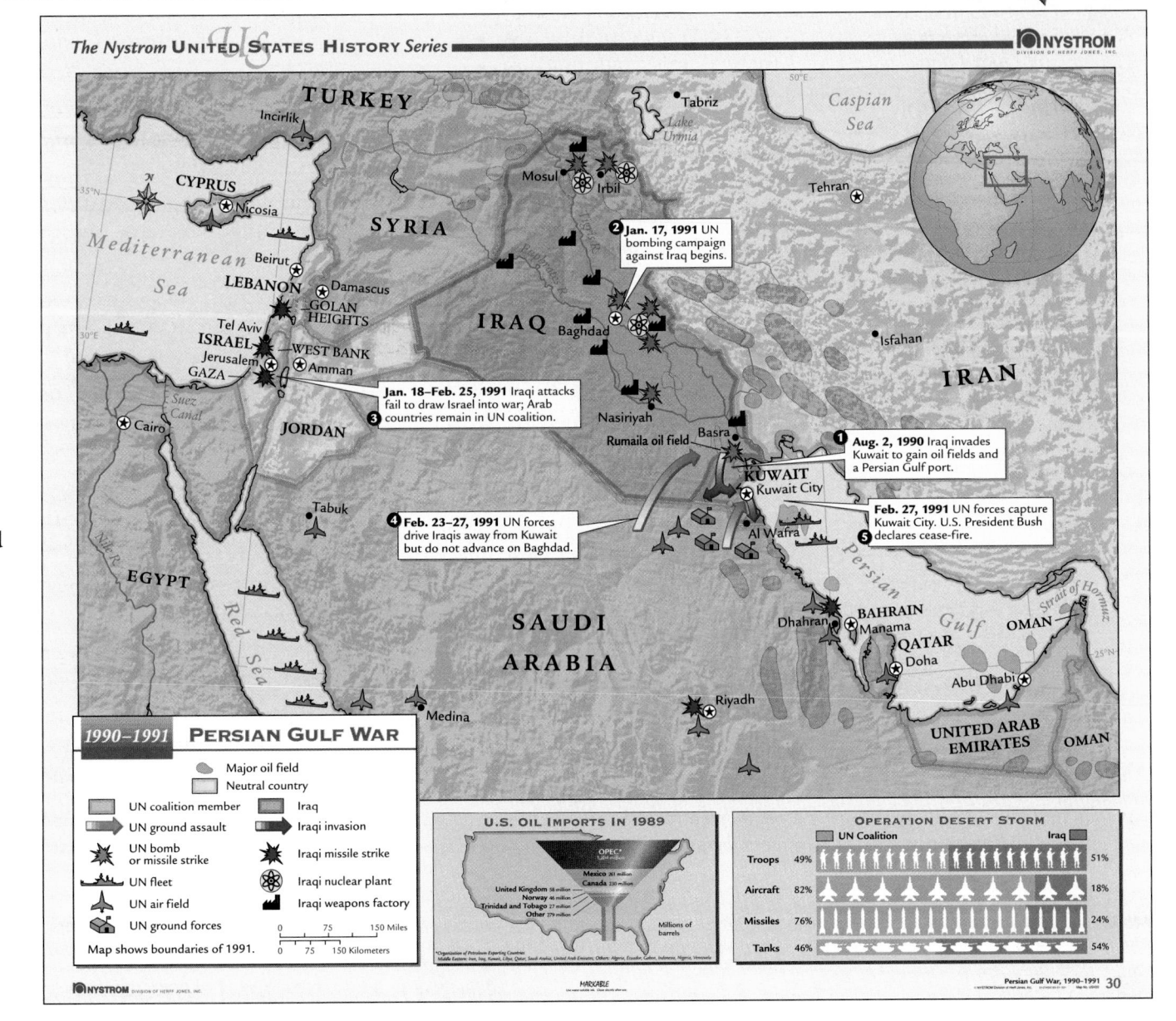

The Nystrom UNITED STATES HISTORY Series

NYSTROM
DIVISION OF HERFF JONES, INC.

Jan. 17, 1991 UN bombing campaign against Iraq begins. ②

Jan. 18–Feb. 25, 1991 Iraqi attacks fail to draw Israel into war; Arab countries remain in UN coalition. ③

Aug. 2, 1990 Iraq invades Kuwait to gain oil fields and a Persian Gulf port. ①

Feb. 27, 1991 UN forces capture Kuwait City. U.S. President Bush declares cease-fire. ⑤

Feb. 23–27, 1991 UN forces drive Iraqis away from Kuwait but do not advance on Baghdad. ④

1990–1991 PERSIAN GULF WAR

- Major oil field
- Neutral country
- UN coalition member
- Iraq
- UN ground assault
- Iraqi invasion
- UN bomb or missile strike
- Iraqi missile strike
- UN fleet
- Iraqi nuclear plant
- UN air field
- Iraqi weapons factory
- UN ground forces

Map shows boundaries of 1991.

0   75   150 Miles
0   75   150 Kilometers

U.S. OIL IMPORTS IN 1989

OPEC
Mexico
Canada
United Kingdom
Norway
Trinidad and Tobago
Other

Millions of barrels

OPERATION DESERT STORM

	UN Coalition	Iraq
Troops	49%	51%
Aircraft	82%	18%
Missiles	76%	24%
Tanks	46%	54%

Persian Gulf War, 1990–1991   30

The Middle East Before the War

Objective: *To show the economic, political, and military situation in the Persian Gulf region prior to the war.*

Teaching Notes and Mapping Activity

You or your students can mark the following on the *Persian Gulf War* map, the *U.S. Oil Imports in 1989* graph, and the locator map.

1. The **Middle East** is one of the most economically important regions of the world, because it contains huge deposits of oil. Countries throughout the world depend on oil from the Middle East.

   a. In the red box on the locator map, write **OIL**.

   b. The United States is particularly dependent on oil from the Middle East. On the *U.S. Oil Imports in 1989* graph, outline the amount of oil imports that come from **OPEC**.

   c. Read the footnote at the bottom of the graph to find how many OPEC countries are located in the Middle East.

2. Before the Persian Gulf War, **Iraq** fought a war against **Iran** that lasted for eight years.

   a. Circle the labels for Iraq and Iran, and draw a line connecting the two labels.

   b. Above the line, write **WAR: 1980–1988**.

3. **New leaders** had come to power in both Iraq and Iran the year before the two countries went to war.

   a. In 1979, Saddam Hussein took control of the Iraqi government. In Iraq, write **1979 SADDAM HUSSEIN**.

   b. In Iran a religious leader, the Ayatollah Khomeini, came to power. In Iran, write **1979 AYATOLLAH KHOMEINI**.

4. The main religion of the Middle East is **Islam**, the religion of Muslims. Most Iranians are Shiite Muslims, whose beliefs are very conservative. Most Muslims in Iraq are Sunnis, who often regard Shiites with suspicion.

   a In Iran, write **SHIITE**.

   b. In Iraq, write **SUNNI**.

5. Because most people in **Kuwait** and **Saudi Arabia** are also Sunni Muslims, these countries supported Iraq over Iran. Neither entered the war, but both loaned large amounts of money to Iraq to aid its war efforts.

   a. Circle the labels for Kuwait and Saudi Arabia.

   b. Draw arrows from each label to Iraq, and label them **LOANS**.

6. Although Kuwait and Saudi Arabia lent money to Iraq, neither country entirely trusted Saddam Hussein. Iraq was building up its military, and the two countries feared that Iraq might decide to attack its southern neighbors. So Kuwait and Saudi Arabia turned to the **United States** for help.

   a. To deter attacks on Kuwaiti and Saudi oil tankers, U.S. ships patrolled the Persian Gulf. In the Persian Gulf, write **US NAVY**.

   b. Saudi Arabia would not allow U.S. troops in its country, but it did accept U.S. help in building military bases of its own. Circle three or four air field symbols in Saudi Arabia.

7. Iraq and Iran finally declared a **truce** in 1988. After eight years of fighting, Iraq had the strongest armed forces in the Middle East. But it also had the largest debt. Iraq owed nearly $70 *billion* dollars, most of it to Kuwait and Saudi Arabia.

   a. In Iraq, write **MILITARY POWER**.

   b. Below MILITARY POWER, write **DEBT = $70 BILLION**.

 Ask your students:
   - Why do you think Kuwait and Saudi Arabia asked the United States for support?
   - Why do you think the United States agreed to help these two countries?

Correlates with:
- ***The Nystrom Atlas of United States History,*** pages 110, 112

Objective: *To provide an overview of the UN coalition and how it was affected by the politics of the Middle East.*

Teaching Notes and Mapping Activity

You or your students can mark the following on the *Persian Gulf War* map and the locator map.

1. On August 2, 1990, Iraq invaded **Kuwait**. Six days later, it annexed Kuwait, claiming that the country was a province of Iraq. With Kuwait as one of its provinces, Iraq no longer had to pay its debts to Kuwait. In addition, Iraq also gained control of Kuwait's rich oil fields.

   a. Read and circle Call-out ❶ on the *Persian Gulf War* map.

   b. Saddam Hussein then stationed thousands of troops along Kuwait's southern border, causing fears that Iraq would invade Saudi Arabia as well. Trace the arrows that show Iraqi troop movements.

2. The **United Nations** condemned the invasion and quickly formed an **anti-Iraq coalition**. Many countries in the coalition were neither Middle Eastern nor Arab countries. Non-Arab members of the coalition included Afghanistan, Argentina, Australia, Bangladesh, Belgium, Canada, Czechoslovakia, Denmark, France, Germany, Greece, Honduras, Hungary, Italy, Netherlands, New Zealand, Niger, Norway, Pakistan, Poland, Portugal, Senegal, Sierra Leone, Singapore, South Korea, Spain, Sweden, Turkey, United Kingdom, and United States.

   a. You may want to have your students locate the different countries that were non-Arab members of the UN coalition on a world map.

   b. Coalition forces began their campaign against Iraq by **bombing** the country. Read and circle Call-out ❷.

   c. After over a month of bombing, coalition forces launched a **ground attack**. Read and circle Call-out ❹.

   d. Trace the arrows that show UN troop movements.

3. Hussein attempted to sway **Arab countries** to Iraq's cause, but most Arab countries joined the UN coalition. Those that did not join the coalition remained neutral. The names of the Arab coalition members are listed below. Point out these coalition members on the map.

   - Bahrain
   - Egypt
   - Kuwait
   - Morocco (not on the map)
   - Oman
   - Qatar
   - Saudi Arabia
   - Syria
   - United Arab Emirates

4. Hussein attempted to gain Arab support by attacking **Israel**. Many Muslims felt hostility toward Israel, and several Arab countries had fought wars against Israel in the past.

   a. UN officials asked Israel not to join the coalition. They worried that Arab countries would refuse to support an alliance if Israel were a part of it. Outline Israel.

   b. Hussein tried to draw Israel into the war by firing missiles at the neutral country. Draw arrows from the label for Iraq to the missile strike symbols in Israel.

   c. Hussein's efforts to break up the coalition failed. Read and circle Call-out ❸.

   d. Coalition forces quickly defeated Iraq. Read and circle Call-out ❺.

5. The Persian Gulf War was not without critics. Some argue that, had it not been for oil, the United Nations would never have intervened. In the red box on the locator map, write **OIL**.

☆ Using the list of Arab and non-Arab coalition countries, have your students identify the only coalition country shown on the map that is not an Arab country.

Correlates with:
- ***The Nystrom Atlas of United States History,*** pages 110, 112

War Strategy and Its Consequences

Objective: *To show some of the effects of the Persian Gulf War on Iraq and the rest of the Middle East.*

Teaching Notes and Mapping Activity

You or your students can mark the following on the *Persian Gulf War* map, the locator map, and the *Operation Desert Storm* graph.

1. **UN coalition forces** had an extreme numerical advantage over Iraq in aircraft and missiles, while Iraq had only a slight advantage in its number of soldiers and tanks.

   a. The UN coalition opened the war with a bombing campaign of Iraq. On the *Operation Desert Storm* graph, write **BOMBING CAM-PAIGN** across the UN portions of the aircraft and missiles bars.

   b. Read and circle Call-out ❷.

   c. After bombing Iraq for more than a month, UN forces launched a **ground campaign**. Read and circle Call-out ❹.

   d. Within four days, UN forces had **captured Kuwait** and **defeated the Iraqi army**. Read and circle Call-out ❺.

2. Although the Persian Gulf War lasted only a few months, it caused **severe environmental damage** to the Middle East.

   a. Before Iraqi forces fled Kuwait, they dumped large amounts of oil into the Persian Gulf. In the Persian Gulf off the coast of Kuwait, write **OIL SPILLS**.

   b. Fleeing Iraqi soldiers also set fire to many Kuwaiti oil wells. Along the Iraq-Kuwait boundary, write **OIL FIRES**.

   c. The smoke from these oil fires caused air pollution throughout southwest Asia. In the red box on the locator map, write **AIR POLLUTION**.

3. **Iraq** itself suffered a great deal as a result of the war. Coalition bombing severely damaged Iraq's transportation system, communications, electricity, and industry.

   a. Just above the label for Iraq, write **POST-WAR**.

   b. Underline the label for Iraq and below it write **BOMB DESTRUCTION**.

   c. Damage to the country's electrical system wiped out much of Iraq's ability to provide clean water. As a result, disease ran rampant after the war. Below BOMB DESTRUCTION, write **DISEASE**.

   d. Damage to the country's transportation and industry harmed Iraq's economy. Below DISEASE, write **POOR ECONOMY**.

4. In addition to the problems caused by the bombings, the United Nations imposed **economic sanctions** against Iraq until it complied with the cease-fire agreement that ended the war. Iraq would face a trade embargo until it destroyed nuclear and other weapons facilities. Below POOR ECONOMY, write **UN TRADE EMBARGO**.

5. Although **Iraqi citizens** have suffered from the economic sanctions, the United Nations has yet to entirely lift the trade embargo. UN officials believe that Iraq still has nuclear plants and chemical weapons factories, in violation of the cease-fire agreement.

   a. Draw a **?** over each the symbols for Iraqi nuclear plants.

   b. Also draw a **?** over two or three of the symbols for Iraqi weapons plants.

 Have your students answer the questions below.
   - Which countries were probably affected by the oil spills?
   - Which Middle Eastern countries were probably affected by the air pollution from the oil fires?
   - What countries outside the Middle East might have been affected by the pollution?

Correlates with:
- ***The Nystrom Atlas of United States History,*** pages 110, 112

A SHIFTING POPULATION
1990–1995

Key Elements

★ *A Shifting Population* map
★ *Center of Population* map
★ *Large Population Changes* graph

Getting Started

To give students an overview of
A Shifting Population, ask them:

• What is the title of the main map?

• What do the green areas
represent? The purple areas?
The yellow areas?

• What do the symbols shown on
the map represent?

• What does the *Center of Population*
map show?

• What is the title of the graph?

• What do the green bars on the
graph represent?

• What do the purple bars on the
graph represent?

Teaching Notes and Mapping Activities

~ Regions of Loss
~ Growth in the Sun Belt
~ Other Growing Regions

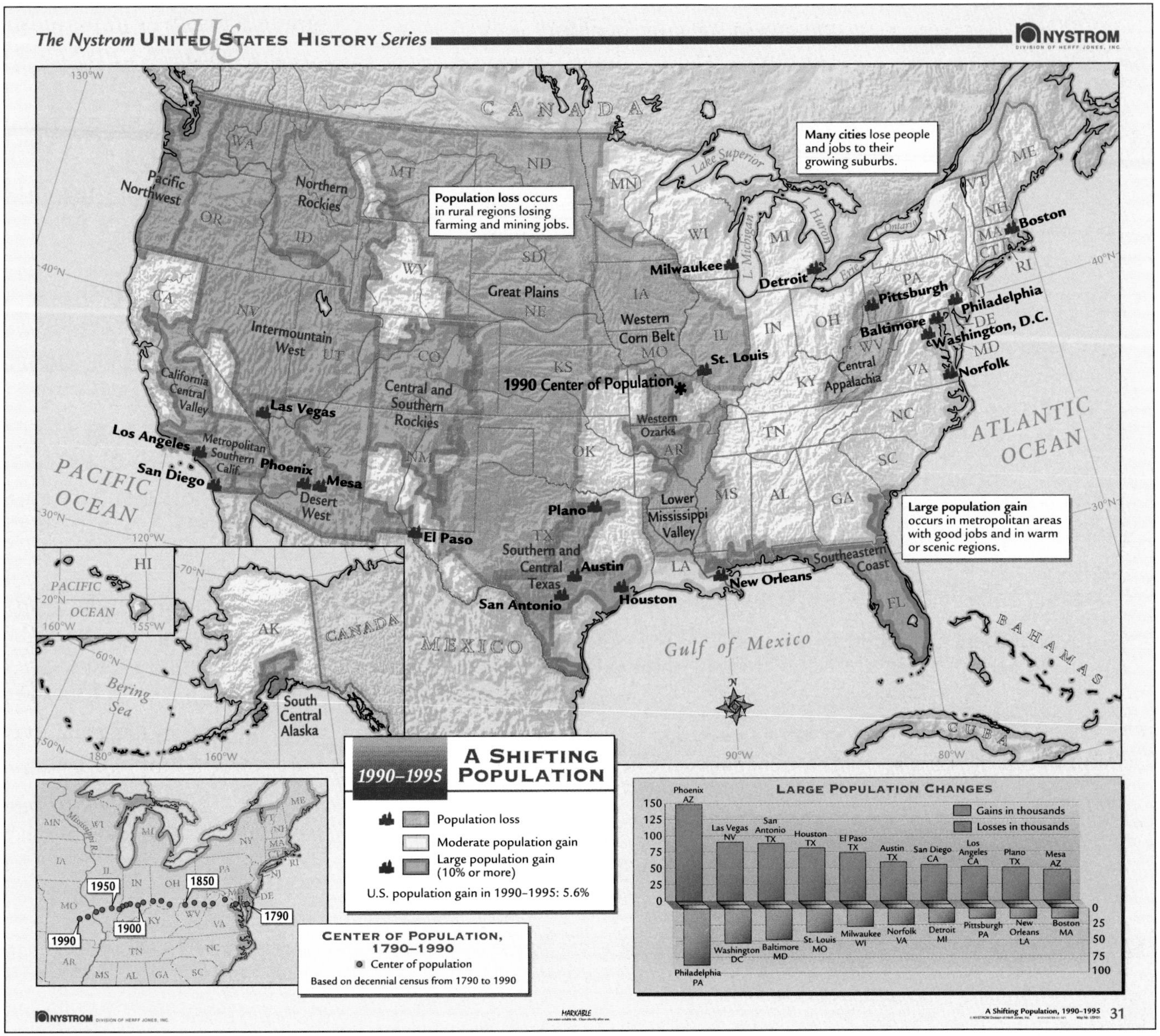

The Nystrom UNITED STATES HISTORY Series

Many cities lose people and jobs to their growing suburbs.

Population loss occurs in rural regions losing farming and mining jobs.

Large population gain occurs in metropolitan areas with good jobs and in warm or scenic regions.

A SHIFTING POPULATION
1990–1995

- Population loss
- Moderate population gain
- Large population gain (10% or more)

U.S. population gain in 1990–1995: 5.6%

CENTER OF POPULATION, 1790–1990
- Center of population
Based on decennial census from 1790 to 1990

LARGE POPULATION CHANGES
Gains in thousands
Losses in thousands

Regions of Loss

Objective: *To identify U.S. regions that experienced a loss in population and to provide some reasons for that loss.*

Teaching Notes and Mapping Activity

You or your students can mark the following on the *Shifting Population* map and the *Large Population Changes* graph.

1. From 1990 to 1995, four large rural areas in the United States experienced **population losses**. The region that suffered the largest loss was the **Great Plains**, where the economy relies heavily on agriculture. Technological advances replaced farm workers with machines, and a decline in the farming industry resulted in even more lost jobs. Many residents of the Great Plains were forced to seek employment elsewhere.

   a. Read the call-out describing population loss in rural areas.

   b. On the *Shifting Population* map, in the Great Plains region, write **FARMING TECHNOLOGY** ⇑.

   c. Below FARMING TECHNOLOGY, write **AGRICULTURE** ⇓.

   d. Below AGRICULTURE, write **NOT ENOUGH JOBS**.

2. Other agricultural areas faced the same fate as the Great Plains. In the **Western Corn Belt** and the **Lower Mississippi Valley**, advanced technology and a decline in agriculture cost many farm workers their jobs. Like the residents of the Great Plains, people left these regions to find new jobs.

   a. Across the Western Corn Belt and the Lower Mississippi Valley, write **FARMING TECHNOLOGY** ⇑.

   b. In each region, below FARMING TECHNOLOGY, write **AGRICULTURE** ⇓.

   c. In each region, below AGRICULTURE, write **NOT ENOUGH JOBS**.

3. **Central Appalachia** also saw a decline in their farming industry, but more important to the region's economy were the coal mines and the steel industry those mines supported. When the coal and steel industries declined, many workers in Central Appalachia lost their jobs. Like farm workers, these people moved away to find new jobs.

   a. Across Central Appalachia write **STEEL & COAL INDUSTRIES** ⇓.

   b. Below STEEL & COAL INDUSTRIES, write **NOT ENOUGH JOBS**.

4. Many **cities**—most in the Midwest and Northeast—also suffered population losses in the 1990s. In some cases, industries shut down, depriving residents of jobs. In other cases, overcrowding in the cities drove residents to move to more spacious suburbs.

   a. Read the call-out describing population loss in cities.

   b. Point out Milwaukee, Detroit, and Pittsburgh as examples of **Rust Belt** cities where a decline in industry and manufacturing played a major role in population loss.

   c. On the *Large Population Changes* graph, write **RB** for Rust Belt on the bars that show the population losses of these three cities.

   d. Point out Philadelphia, Washington, D.C., Norfolk, and Boston as examples of cities where **urban flight** to the suburbs played a major role in population losses.

   e. On the graph, write **UF** for urban flight on the bars that show the population losses of these four cities.

 When the economy of a region is dependent on a single industry, that region is vulnerable to economic hardship if the industry fails. Detroit was dependent on the auto manufacturing industry. Pittsburgh was dependent on the steel industry. Norfolk, Virginia, is a city dependent on military bases for business and jobs. Have your students write a paragraph explaining what they think would happen if military bases at Norfolk closed.

Correlates with:
● *The Nystrom Atlas of United States History,* pages 116–117

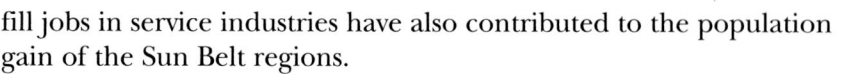

Teaching Notes and Mapping Activity

You or your students can mark the following on the *Shifting Population* map and the *Large Population Changes* graph.

1. Major **Sun Belt growth** began when industries moved south and west to take advantage of the warm climate, cheaper land, and lower operation costs. The warm climate also made Sun Belt regions popular with tourists and retirees.

   a. On the *Center of Population* map, show your students how the U.S. population has gradually shifted west and south. Point out the cluster of symbols that mark the years 1900–1950, when the Northeast and Midwest dominated manufacturing and industry.

   b. **Metropolitan Southern California** is one of the regions of the Sun Belt where many industries relocated. On the *Shifting Population* map, write **INDUSTRY** ⇑ in this region.

2. Large amounts of cheap land made the **Desert West** another popular place for industries to relocate.

   a. On the map, write **INDUSTRY** ⇑ in this region.

   b. The Desert West is also one of the Sun Belt regions that is a popular retirement location. Below INDUSTRY, write **RETIREES** ⇑.

3. **Southern and Central Texas** gained population for many of the same reasons as the Desert West—cheap land and lots of it! However, the region is not as popular with retirees. On the map, write **INDUSTRY** ⇑ in this region.

4. The **Southeastern Coast** not only gained population as a result of industry, but it has also become one of the nation's most popular retirement destinations.

   a. On the map, write **INDUSTRY** ⇑ in this region.

   b. Below INDUSTRY, write **RETIREES** ⇑.

5. Regions with large populations require many **services** for the people who live there. Services include grocery stores, malls, restaurants, cleaners, schools, hospitals, and so forth. People who have moved to fill jobs in service industries have also contributed to the population gain of the Sun Belt regions.

   a. In each of the Sun Belt regions, write **SERVICE JOBS** ⇑.

   b. Tourism also increases the number of jobs in a region's service industries. Southern California and the Southeastern Coast are both popular tourist spots. Their tourist industries created many jobs in hotels, theme parks, and so forth. Write **(TOURISM)** after SERVICE JOBS in each of these regions.

6. Most of the population gain in Sun Belt regions took place in **urban or suburban areas**.

   a. On the map, point out cities in the Sun Belt that experienced large population gains.

   b. Then, have your students identify Sun Belt cities on the *Large Population Changes* graph.

   c. For each Sun Belt city on the graph, write **SB** on the bar that shows the population gain.

   d. Point out to your students that all the cities shown on the graph that had large population changes between 1990 and 1995 are located in the Sun Belt.

☆ Have your students analyze the economy of their own community by answering the questions below.
   - What kind of jobs do your parents and/or other members of your family have?
   - Which types of businesses in your community have a large number of employees?
   - Are there many different kinds of businesses and/or companies in your community?
   - If a large company closed down, could people find other jobs?

Correlates with:
- *The Nystrom Atlas of United States History,* pages 116–117

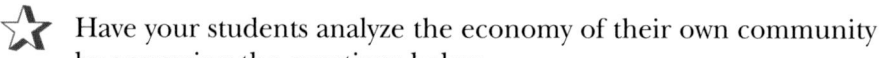

Other Growing Regions

Objective: *To identify other regions that experienced population gains and to provide some reasons for those gains.*

Teaching Notes and Mapping Activity

You or your students can mark the following on the *Shifting Population* map.

1. Regions outside the Sun Belt also experienced large population gains. The **Western Ozarks** experienced a gain in population for many of the same reasons as the Southeastern Coast. It is popular as a tourist spot and a place for retirees to settle. This popularity led to many jobs in the service industries.

   a. On the *Shifting Population* map, across the Western Ozarks, write **TOURISM + RETIREES = SERVICE JOBS.**

   b. The Western Ozarks offer the isolation and scenery of a rural life, but are located within a day's drive of many major cities. Point out cities located near the region. You may want to include/add cities not shown on the map.

2. Growth in the **California Central Valley** was tied to growth in other parts of California. Metropolitan Southern California and the San Francisco Bay Area are crowded and have a high cost of living. The Central Valley is less crowded and more affordable.

   a. Across the Central Valley region, write **LESS CROWDED.**

   b. Below LESS CROWDED, write **MORE AFFORDABLE.**

3. The **Pacific Northwest** has seen a large influx of people due to its expanding technology industry—computers, software, programming, the Internet, and so forth. On the map, across the Pacific Northwest, write **HI TECH IND.** ⇑.

4. Some regions that were once among the most sparsely populated in the United States experienced high population growth due to a combination of urban flight and improved technology. Faxes, cellular phones, Internet connections, and e-mail have enabled many city dwellers to move to more isolated, scenic regions without having to give up their jobs. This type of arrangement is often referred to as *telecommuting*.

   a. In the regions listed below, write **URBAN FLIGHT.**
      - Intermountain West
      - Northern Rockies
      - Central and Southern Rockies
      - South Central Alaska

   b. Below URBAN FLIGHT in each of these regions, write **TELECOMMUTING.**

5. Because most newcomers to the Intermountain West, the Northern Rockies, the Central and Southern Rockies, and South Central Alaska moved to escape city life, big cities in these regions had a smaller population gain than the cities of the Sun Belt.

   a. Point out to your students that there are no symbols designating cities with a large population gain in any of the regions mentioned above.

   b. Also point out to your students that a region's population gain is relative. The actual *numbers* of the population increase in these four regions was much lower than that of the Sun Belt regions, but because these regions were so sparsely populated to begin with, the *percentage* of the population gain is very sizeable.

 Have your students answer the questions below.
   - In which region do you live?
   - Do you live in a region that has gained or lost population?
   - Do you live in a city experiencing large population gains? If so, what do you think the reasons are for these gains?
   - Where do you live with respect to the Center of Population?

Correlates with:
- *The Nystrom Atlas of United States History,* pages 116–117

32

IMMIGRANTS SINCE 1970

Key Elements

★ *Immigrants* map
★ *Our Immigrant Origins* graph

Getting Started

To give students an overview of *Immigrants*, ask them:

- What is the title of this map?
- What years does it cover?
- What do the arrows represent?
- Why are the arrows different colors?
- Why are the arrows different widths?
- Why are the names of some ethnic groups in all capital letters and others are not?
- Look at the graph. Why are the bars different sizes?
- From which region have the greatest number of immigrants come? the fewest?
- Why are the bars on the graph different colors? How do the colors relate to the main map?

Teaching Notes and Mapping Activities

~ Why Immigrants Come
~ Today's Top Immigrant Groups
~ Immigrants and Aliens

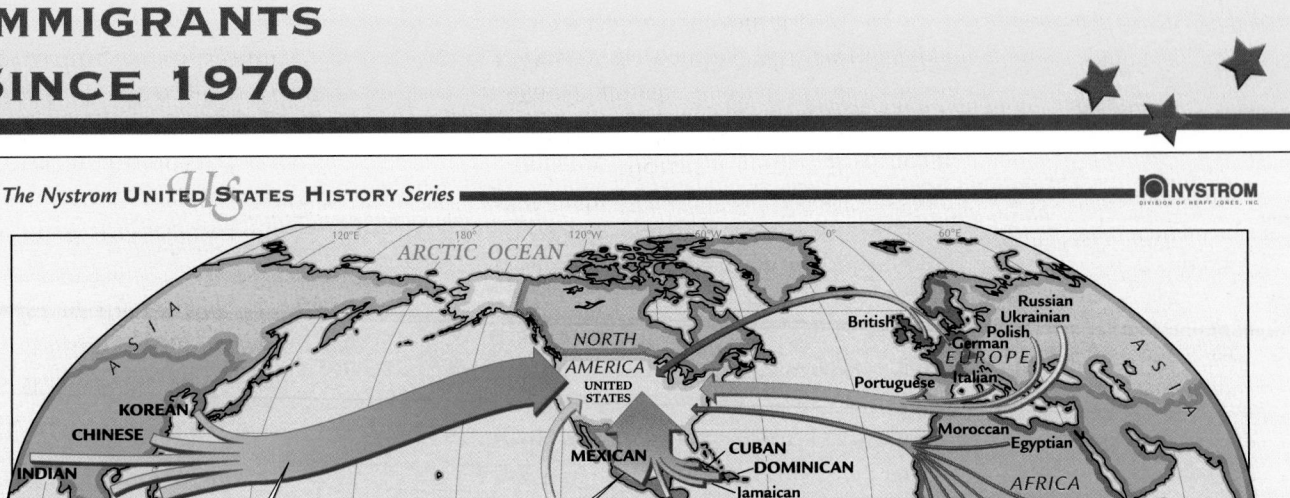

The Nystrom UNITED STATES HISTORY Series

Immigration from Korea and Vietnam grows after the Korean and Vietnam Wars.

After 1970, more immigrants come from Mexico than from any other country.

Since 1970 — IMMIGRANTS

MEXICAN 500,000 or more immigrants

Nigerian Less than 500,000 immigrants

AFRICA Continent

Width of arrow shows relative number of immigrants from its continental region.

Regions

- Northern & Western Europe
- North America
- Africa
- Australia & Oceania
- Southern & Eastern Europe*
- South America
- Asia*

*Southern & Eastern Europe includes the European and Asian portions of Russia.

Equatorial scale
0 1000 2000 3000 miles
0 1000 2000 3000 kilometers

OUR IMMIGRANT ORIGINS

AFRICA 544,601
- Egypt 89,912
- Nigeria 89,070
- Ethiopia 67,852
- South Africa 43,527
- Ghana 43,193
- Morocco 22,358
- Liberia 21,912
- Others 166,977

NORTHERN & WESTERN EUROPE 841,039
United Kingdom 371,413
- Germany 185,376
- Others 284,250

SOUTH AMERICA 1,137,203
Colombia 296,686
- Guyana 200,749
- Peru 170,998
- Ecuador 159,159
- Others 309,611

SOUTHERN & EASTERN EUROPE 1,661,344
Former Soviet Union 516,220
- Poland 283,207
- Italy 179,743
- Portugal 163,300
- Others 518,874

ASIA 6,658,896

| Philippines 1,253,074 | China 984,543 | Vietnam 937,439 | Korea 739,213 | India 713,138 | Others 2,031,489 |

NORTH AMERICA 7,818,139

| Mexico 4,088,710 | Dominican Republic 684,971 | Cuba 564,598 | Others 2,479,860 |

Immigrants Since 1970 32

Why Immigrants Come

Objective: *To identify major reasons for immigration to the United States.*

Teaching Notes and Mapping Activity

You or your students can mark the following on the *Immigrants* map.

1. In the last two centuries, immigrants have come to the United States for a variety of reasons. One common reason is to escape **poverty**. Many recent immigrants left **Mexico** because of its poor economic conditions. The proximity of the United States and the availability of jobs for unskilled workers makes the U.S. an attractive destination.

   a. On Mexico draw a poverty symbol ¢.

   b. Now draw an arrow from Mexico to the United States.

2. Some immigrants have come to the Unites States to escape **hunger**. **Ethiopia** in Africa has experienced several droughts in the last three decades. Without enough rain, crops fail and millions of people go hungry.

   a. On Ethiopia, draw an empty bowl.

   b. Draw an arrow from Ethiopia to the United States.

3. People also move to the United States to escape **overcrowding**. **India** in Asia is a crowded country. India is about one-third the size of the United States, but it has over three times as many people.

   a. On India, draw several stick figures 웃 웃 웃.

   b. Draw an arrow from India to the United States.

4. Some people have come to the United States to escape **war**. For 12 years, **El Salvador** in North America was involved in a civil war. Thousands died. While the war was going on, immigration to the United States increased. When the war ended, immigration from El Salvador dropped.

   a. On El Salvador, draw a war symbol .

   b. Draw an arrow from El Salvador to the United States.

5. People have also immigrated to the United States because of **political change**. For example, in 1959 Fidel Castro seized control of **Cuba**, an island country in North America. Many of his opponents were imprisoned or executed. In the 1960s, there was a flood of Cuban immigrants to nearby United States. Many settled in Florida, only 90 miles away. Each year, thousands of Cubans still immigrate to the United States.

   a. On Cuba, write **POLITICAL CHANGE**.

   b. Then draw an arrow from Cuba to the United States.

6. **Vietnam** in Asia also underwent **political change**. Like El Salvador, Vietnam was involved in a lengthy civil war. When the war ended in 1975, the victors, the Communist North Vietnamese, united the country. Many South Vietnamese fled.

   a. On Vietnam, write **POLITICAL CHANGE**.

   b. Then draw an arrow from Vietnam to the United States.

7. In Europe, **Russia** also underwent **political change**. With the breakup of the Soviet Union in 1991, many restrictions were lifted. More Russians are now able to leave their country.

   a. On Russia, write **POLITICAL CHANGE**.

   b. Then draw an arrow from Russia to the United States.

 Ask students to interview someone who has immigrated to the United States. Have them try to determine why the immigrant left his or her homeland. Ask if they still have family there and how conditions have changed. Find out what traditions from their homelands they still follow.

Correlates with:

- *The Nystrom Atlas of United States History,* pages 118–119
- *Mapping United States History To the Present,* Lesson 42

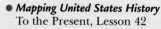

Today's Top Immigrant Groups
Objective: *To identify the top eight immigrant groups to the United States since 1970.*

page 130

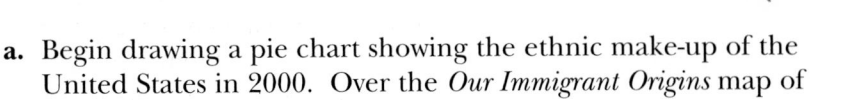

Teaching Notes and Mapping Activity

You or your students can mark the following on the *Our Immigrant Origins* graph and the *Immigrants* map.

1. In the last 30 years, over half of all immigrants to the United States came from just eight countries.

   a. Direct students to the *Our Immigrant Origins* graph. Ask them to identify the one country from which most U.S. immigrants have come since 1970.

   b. On the bar graph, label **Mexico** ①.

   c. In the same way, have students identify and number the other top countries.
   ② Philippines
   ③ China
   ④ Vietnam
   ⑤ Korea
   ⑥ India
   ⑦ Dominican Republic
   ⑧ Cuba

2. These countries are concentrated in two areas of the world.

   a. Transfer the numbers from the bar graph to the *Immigrants* map. For example, next to Mexico, write ①.

   b. Countries ①, ⑦, ⑧ and are all in North America—more specifically, in Middle America. Draw a box around this area. Below the box, write **MIDDLE AMERICA**.

   c. Countries ②, ③, ④, ⑤, and ⑥ are all in Asia. They are concentrated in south and southeast Asia. Draw a box around this area. Above the box, write **S AND SE ASIA**.

3. In contrast to the last three decades of immigration to the United States, the majority of immigrants from 1840 to 1960 were from Europe. This pattern had a lasting affect on the ethnic make-up of our country.

a. Begin drawing a pie chart showing the ethnic make-up of the United States in 2000. Over the *Our Immigrant Origins* map of the United States, draw a large circle.

b. Roughly 72 percent of our population descended from or are European immigrants. In the circle, draw a wedge that size. Label it **EUROPEAN**.

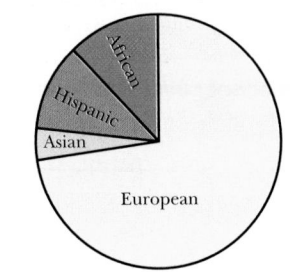

c. Roughly 12 percent of our population descended from or are African immigrants. Draw a wedge that size. Label it **AFRICAN**.

d. Another 11 percent of our population descended from or are Hispanic immigrants. Draw a wedge that size. Label it **HISPANIC**.

e. Just 4 percent of our population descended from or are Asian immigrants. Label the remaining wedge **ASIAN**.

 For further discussion:
- Do you know any Mexican Americans? Filipino Americans? Chinese Americans? How long have their families lived in the United States?
- How did immigration from 1895 to 1929 differ from immigration since 1970?
- How do you think the current trend in immigration will affect the ethnic makeup of our country in the future?
- How has immigration affected your community? the area as a whole?

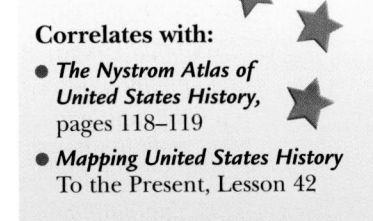

Correlates with:
- ***The Nystrom Atlas of United States History,*** pages 118–119
- ***Mapping United States History*** To the Present, Lesson 42

Immigrants and Aliens

Objective: *To explain the difference between temporary visitors, immigrants, and illegal aliens.*

Teaching Notes and Mapping Activity

You or your students can mark the following on the *Immigrants* map.

1. **Aliens** are citizens of one country living in or visiting another country. Some aliens do not plan to stay in the United States permanently. These **temporary visitors** often need a **visa** or permit to come to the United States.

   a. Millions of people come to the United States each year as tourists. Tourists from some countries are required to have **tourist visas.**

      • As is the case with many countries, tourists from Poland need visas. Draw an arrow from Poland to the United States and label it **TOURISTS**.

      • Tourist visas are only valid for 90 days. Then the tourist has to leave the United States. Draw an arrow back to Poland.

   b. Over 400,000 people come to the United States each year as students. They study at high schools, colleges, and trade schools in the United States. Many of these students are required to have **student visas.**

      • A large number of students come from Korea. Draw an arrow from Korea to the United States and label it **STUDENTS**.

      • Student visas are valid until the student finishes his or her studies. Then the student has to leave the United States. Draw an arrow back to Korea.

   c. Over 200,000 people come to the United States each year to work. They are required to have **work visas**.

      • A large number of workers come from India. Draw an arrow from India to the United States and label it **WORKERS**.

      • Work visas are valid for one to three years, depending on the job. Then the worker has to leave the United States. Draw an arrow back to India.

2. Other aliens *do* plan on staying in the United States permanently. They are **immigrants**. Before immigrants can come to the United States, they need **immigration visas**. Some people wait years for a visa.

   a. In recent years, the largest number of immigrants have come from Mexico. Draw an arrow from Mexico to the United States and label it **IMMIGRANTS**.

   b. Label seven other arrows to the United States **IMMIGRANTS**.

   c. About 15 percent of all immigrants eventually return to their homeland. Trace one of your arrows back home.

3. An estimated 5 million people enter the United States each year without visas. They are illegal aliens. Over 80 percent of them come from the Western Hemisphere. Draw several dotted lines from Central or South America to the United States and label them **ILLEGAL ALIENS**.

4. Legal immigrants to the United States are entitled to many of the same rights as citizens. However, they do not have the right to vote or hold public office unless they become **naturalized citizens**. Each year, about 125,000 immigrants pass an examination and legal hearing and become naturalized U.S. citizens. On the United States, write **CITIZENS**.

 To become a citizen, immigrants take a test on U.S. history and government. Ask students the following sample questions from the test:
   • Who makes the laws in the U.S.?
   • For how long do we elect each senator?
   • Who is the Chief Justice of the Supreme Court?
   • Can you name the 13 original states?

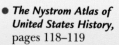

Correlates with:
● *The Nystrom Atlas of United States History,* pages 118–119
● *Mapping United States History* To the Present, Lesson 42